"There is a country, Crete, in the midst of the wine-dark
sea, a fair land and a rich, begirt with water.
The people there are many, innumerable indeed,
and they have ninety cities.
Their speech is mixed; one language joins another.
Here are Achaeans, here brave native Cretans,
here Cydonians, crested Dorians, and noble Pelasgians.
Of all their towns, the capital is Knossos,
where Minos became king
when nine years old -
Minos the friend
of mighty Zeus."

Homer, The Odyssey, Book XIX

Foreword

Crete: where should one begin the story of this island, an island which encapsulates within itself a complete and individual history? Words nearly fail one. This island has centuries of glory behind it; as a centre and beacon of Greek and European civilisation, its roots are lost in the mists of history. It was here that Zeus, father of gods and men, chose to be born and grow to manhood. It was here that Minoan civilisation developed and shone, and that Minos created his thalassocracy. Myth and history, grandeur and heroism, have been interwoven here since time began. The earth of Crete is soaked in blood and raki; its people, the Cretans, are untamed, proud and tough, but at the same time hospitable lovers of honour. A visit to Crete is a pilgrimage to freedom, a greeting to bravery and pride.

This island was richly endowed by nature and blessed by the gods. It is so crammed with contradictions that each bend in the road has a surprise for the visitor. The soil is rich and fertile and has the islanders have never had to abandon their homes because of starvation. As a result, the history of Crete contains no interruptions.

The landscape is constantly changing, with warm and gently tropical areas close to wild, inaccessible, rocky places which gave birth to the figures we can recognise in Kazantzakis and El Greco. The coastline is sometimes calm, with deep, clear water, and sometimes steep cliffs plunge into the roaring waves. There are peaceful green plains, but there are also mountains as impregnable as castles, with famous gorges which have hidden freedom in all its forms and still do today. The mountains of Crete have been the lair of rebels and resistance fighters as well as a refuge for those fleeing from justice. Here lives the Cretan wild goat, the 'agrimi', and among the rocks grows dittany, the herb which was believed to have miraculous powers.

The superb delicacy and labyrinthine layout of the Minoan palaces, the fortifications and aqueducts, the fortresses, the churches, the works of art and the customs of the people, their songs running down the centuries: all these are testimony to the turbulent history of this island. For many centuries now, the strong of the earth have wanted Crete to be their own. Yet each prospective conqueror has been brought to his knees by the strength of this island. None of the invaders managed to break the spirit, the passion and the belief in liberty of the Cretans; all they succeeded in doing was to nurture a proud, free people. In Crete, manly bravery and pride are a tradition.

That is the very least one can say about Crete: this is an island which is generous not just in size, but in its soul. Book upon book has been written about it, and the limited size of this volume cannot encompass it all. Our aim is that what we have said here should be a guide to that which visitors can discover for themselves. As they travel, they will visit the archaeological sites or enjoy the sun and the sea on the island's superb beaches, finding out all the things which we had no space for here. They will talk to the locals, drink raki (or tsikoudia) with them and, if they are lucky, they will be invited to local feastswhere the brave Cretan dances are performed.

A knowledge of Crete comes slowly - but as it grows, so does the visitor's love of this island and its people.

CRETE

today and yesterday

**A complete guide for travellers
with tours of the cities,
archaeological sites and museums,
with 19 routes, with a detailed map of the island
and with 302 colour illustrations**

MICHALIS TOUMBIS EDITIONS SA - ATHENS

Texts: G. DESIPRIS, HANS LANGENFASS (archaeologist), K. SANTORINAIOU
Trips - Maps: NORA DRAMITINOU-ANASTASOGLOU
Photographs: V. DROSOS, N. KONTOS, EVT. KROKIDAKIS, G. YIANNELOS
M. TOYMPIS, G. VOYIATZIS

Artwork: NORA DRAMITINOU-ANASTASOGLOU
Four-colour editing: YIANNIS KOLLAROS
Photosetting: KIKI SANTORINAIOU
Montage: NIKOS PRASIANAKIS
Printed by: M. TOUMBIS GRAPHIC ARTS SA, Athens - Tel. no. 9923874

Contents

Geographical Presentation

Crete lies at the centre of the Eastern Mediterranean basin, where the continents of Europe, Asia and Africa meet. It is the largest Greek island (and the fifth largest in the Mediterranean), and for that reason the Greeks often call it 'Megalonisos' ('the big island'). It has an area of 8,335.9 square km and is long and narrow in shape, stretching for 257 km along an east-west axis. It was this shape which gave the island its ancient name: Doliche, which means precisely 'long and narrow'.

This geographical position, in conjunction with the terrain and the island's natural wealth, created a world with a personality of its own, full of variety and contradictions. In western Crete, the orange groves give way to deserted mountain plateaus, while in the east palm trees interchange with slopes where olives and vines are grown.

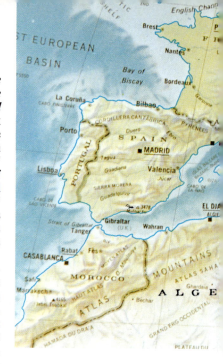

Of the 1,046.4 km of coastline, 155 km. consists of sandy beaches — most of them on the north coast, which is washed by the restless Cretan Sea. On the south coast, the land plunges steeply into the deep Libyan Sea, and the beaches lie in little coves. Here, too, is the wide Bay of Messara. The main bays on the north coast are those of Kisamos, Souda, Almyros, Herakleio, Mallia, Merabello and Siteia. Souda Bay forms an enormous natural harbour (the largest in the Mediterranean). Since it has bays, the north coast also has capes; here, too, are the capitals of the island's four prefectures: Chania, Rethymno, Herakleio and Ayios Nikolaos.

Among the numerous uninhabited islets around the coastline are Ayii Theodori, Ayii Pantes, Dia (which

are refuges and breeding grounds for the Cretan wild goat, a species unique in the world), Gramvousa, Spinalonga, Pseira, Koufonisi and Chrysi. Off the southern coast is the larger, inhabited, island of Gavdos, which is one of the candidates for the role of Calypso's island in the *Odyssey*.

The terrain of the island is generally mountainous, with 1/3 of its total area lying above 500 m. and only 1/4 capable of being described as low-lying. The geophysical layout is determined by the three important mountain ranges which cross the spine of the island and rear up to heights of 2,500 m.: the White Mountains, Mt Ida (or Psiloritis) and Dikte. Together with the Siteia Mountains, these ranges form a continuation of the mountains of Greece as they swing east in the direction of Carpathos and Rhodes before ending in Asia Minor.

The greater part of the mountains of Crete consists of limestone deposits whose principal component is calcium carbonate ($CaCO_3$), which is insoluble in water.

However, the rainwater picks up carbon dioxide ($CO2$) from the air and the surface of the ground to reach the rock in the form of a weak acid (H_2CO_3), which dissolves the calcium carbonate and erodes it. In this way, the cracks in the limestone are widened and a complex network of underground passages through the mass of the mountains is formed. Most commonly, the chambers formed are roughly circular: caves, in other words.

On the flat surfaces in the White Mountains there is constant subsidence and hollows of various sizes (locally called 'gourgouthia') and pits ('dafki') are formed.

Another important feature in the geological behaviour of the island is the fact that a branch of the Greek seismic arc passes to the south of Crete.

Along this arc, the African plate and the European plate collide, with the former being driven under the latter.

As a result, the European plate is rising, and Crete with it. According to the experts, the south coast of the island is rising at a rate of 2-2.5 cm per year.

The famous Samaria gorge came about in the Tertiary period. The dolomitic limestone plates of which the rock formations of the area are composed have been cracked by the action of various agents —frost, Karstic phenomena, etc.— and this can be seen most clearly in areas such as Gigilos and Portes.

Of the dense forests for which Crete was famous in antiquity and which covered the higher mountains, only that of Rouva (on the southern slopes of Dikte) and Vai (the famous forest of palm trees on the eastern extremity of the island) have survived. The gradual stripping of the island's forests —by overintensive woodcutting— caused the rivers to dry up; now there are seasonal torrents which are also fed by numerous springs. These torrents, when filled with rainwater, easily form the island's many wild gorges (of which that of Samaria is the best-known for its unique beauty; others include the Imvros, Kotsyfos and Kourtalioti gorges) and more than 1,000 caves (of which the best-known are the Idaean Cave, the Diktaean Cave, the cave of Eileithyia and the cave of Melidoni) of great historical and archaeological interest.

A typical example of a Karst phenom

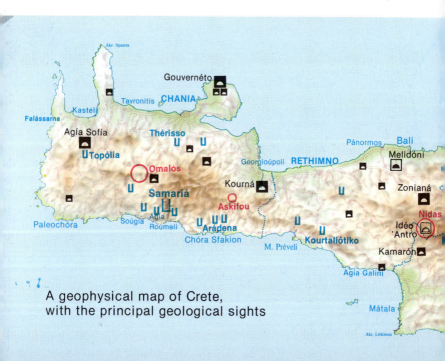

A geophysical map of Crete, with the principal geological sights

...n (erosion) in the White Mountains

A stalactite in the Diktaean Cave

∐ Ravines

◯ Plateaus

⌂ Caves
with archaeological interest

⌂ Caves
with historical interest

⌂ Caves
with natural beauty

Agia Pelagia

IRAKLIO

Akr. Hersoniaos

Akr. Ag. Ioannis

Siderns

Ilithiías

Skotinó

Málla

Mílatos

Váï

Sitia

Akr. Vamvakia

AGIOS NIKOLAOS

Móchlos

Diktéo 'Antro

Lassithi

Lavirinthos

Nekrón

Katharó

Axio Théas

Ierápetra

Akr. Goudoura

Perivolákia

...ntas

The only lake on the island is that called Kourna, in the Prefecture of Chania, in an idyllic setting. It has an area of 150 acres.

The fertile plateaus of Crete lie in between —and protected by— the high mountain ranges. The richest and most beautiful of these plateaus is that of Lasithi, followed by the Omalos, Askyfou and Nida plateaus. The plains, too, are fertile, particularly those on the south coast, the largest of which is the plain of Messara, 50 km. in length and 7 km. in breadth.

The climate changes sharply from the mountains, whose peaks are almost always snow-capped, to the interior of the island, the plateaus and the coastal plains. Spring and summer come early to Messara and along the Libyan Sea coast, while winter is slow in receding from the plateaus and mountain-sides. Crete has been described as one of the few places in the world where one can ski on water and snow in the same day.

In general, the climate of Crete is Mediterranean, and it is the mildest in Europe. The climate was responsible for one of the names the island bore in antiquity; Aeria. Early travellers always comment on the healthy climate, and Hippocrates, the father of medicine, recommended Crete to those recuperating from illness. Even in the hottest months, there is always a breeze in Crete, and the winters are very mild. January is the coldest month and June and July the hottest, though even they are cooler than mainland Greece. Autumn is the mildest period of all; it extends into mid-December and temperatures are higher than in spring. At this time of the year, too, clouds are rare and there are long spells of sunshine. The rainfall varies from place to place, and is three times as high in western Crete than it is in the east.

These marked climatic and geophysical differences assure Crete of an unusual range of products all the year round. *The soil is very fertile and Cretan produce has been famous for its quality and taste since ancient times.* Approximately 1/3 of the surface area of the island is under cultivation, and the crops include olives, citrus fruit, grapes (from which superb wine is made), chestnuts, cherries, almonds and early vegetables. Cheese and aromatic honey is also produced. In relation to Greece as a whole, Crete produces almost half the country's olive oil, most of its sultanas and large quantities of wine, fruit and vegetables.

The grape harvest in the Messara plain

A typically Cretan landscape, with verdant hills and naked mountain-tops

The traditional manner of winnowing, rarely seen today.

The unique Cretan ibex

The peculiar geographical position of Crete and the variety of its terrain have assured the island of a vast range of flowers and plants. Apart from the generally familiar Mediterranean *flora*, there are 130 species of wild flower and herb which are unique to Crete. One of these is dittany, a herb known for its medicinal properties since ancient times. Aristotle wrote that the Cretan wild goats, when injured, would eat dittany to heal their wounds. Even today, women take it during pregnancy to ease labour. All the herbs which were known to the ancient physicians can still be found today, growing on the same hills, on the same slopes, in the same ravines.

There is also variety in the *fauna* of the island. ***Here, once more, Crete***

has a unique feature: the ibex or wild goat, known on the island as the 'agrimi'. Today the population is preserved. There are also deer of various sizes (the hunting of which is strictly prohibited), hares, partridges, wild pigeons, snipe and other game. The seas around the island are a marvellous playground for divers and also contain substantial populations of many types of fish. At Zaro in the Prefecture of Herakleio there is a fish-farm producing trout and salmon.

Administratively, Crete constitutes one of the ten geographical departments into which Greece is divided. It itself is divided into four Prefectures which in turn consist of Eparchies. According to the 1981 census, the total population of the island is in excess of 500,000. The four Prefectures of Crete are as follows:

The Prefecture of Chania, with Chania as its capital; it consists of the Eparchies of Kydonia, Apokoronou, Kissamos, Selinou and Sfakia.

The Prefecture of Rethymno, with Rethymno as its capital; it consists of the Eparchies of Rethymno, Ayios Vasileios, Amari and Mylopotamos.

The Prefecture of Herakleio, with Herakleio as its capital; it consists of the Eparchies of Temenos, Viannos, Kenourgio, Malevizi, Monofatsiou, Pediada and Pyrgiotissa.

The Prefecture of Lasithi, with Ayios Nikolaos as its capital; it consists of the Eparchies of Merabelo, Ierapetra, Lasithi and Siteia.

Ecclesiastically, Crete belongs to the Patriarchate of Constantinople. The Church of Crete is autocephalous and the Archbishopric is based in Herakleio, to which it was moved after the destruction of Gortyn.

Plants indigenous in Crete:
1. *Dittany* **2.** *Iris* **3.** *Lily*
4. *'Aristolochia Cretica'* **5.** *Cyclamen*

MYTHOLOGY

The Greek myths have guarded Greek history and proved to be a key in the great archaeological discoveries of the 19th century: after the discoveries at Troy and Mycenae came the turn of Knossos.

The Minoan civilisation may have come to light relatively recently and have become known to the world in general with the excavations of Arthur Evans (1900), but it was always alive in the Greek myths: Crete was an important place, a place famed for the first civilisation in Greece and Europe, which flourished here.

The mythology of Crete is associated with the birth of Zeus, the first of the Olympian gods, who was called 'the Cretan-born', and also with Europa, daughter of an Asian king, who gave her name to our continent.

Far back in the infancy of the world, the universe was ruled by Uranus; his wife was called Gaea and his son Kronos. Kronos overthrew his father and, in order to defeat a prophecy in which he had been told that he, in turn, would be displaced by his son, he swallowed his children immediately after birth. But when Rhea, his wife, was pregnant with her last child, Zeus, she called on Uranus and Gaea for help. They decided together that Zeus should be born in Crete and that they would hide the child there. So Zeus came into the world in the Diktaean Cave and was brought up by the Nymphs and by Adrasteia and Melissa, the daughters of King Melissos of Crete. To trick Kronos, Rhea gave him a swaddled stone to swallow.

The Rape of Europa
(mural from Pompeii)

Zeus was nourished on the milk of the goat Amaltheia, whom he later rewarded by making her horn a symbol of plenty (the cornucopia) and by transforming her into a constellation of stars. The baby was protected by brave warriors, the Kouretes, who beat their spears upon their shields so as to cover up the cries of the infant and prevent Kronos from hearing them. When Kronos learned of this deception, he punished the Kouretes by turning them into lions, a punishment which Zeus later alleviated by making the lion king of the animals.

When Zeus eventually managed to wrest power from his father —after a frightful struggle— he embarked on a series of eventful love affairs. One of these began when his attention was drawn by the innocence and grace of Europa, daughter of King Agenoras or Phoenix of Syria. In order to approach the girl without being found out by Hera, his wife, Zeus transformed himself into a bull and made his appearance close to Europa and her maidens. Europa was the first of the group to pluck up the courage to approach the handsome bull; while her friends decked the animal with garlands, she mounted on its back. Zeus then set off at full tilt, crossed the sea and arrived in Crete. While living with Europa there, he gave her three sons: Minos, Rhadamanthys and Sarpedon. This myth is closely interwoven with the history of Crete, since the historians now believe that the Minoans came from somewhere in the Middle East and had the bull as their sacred animal.

Zeus gave Europa three marvellous gifts: a golden dog which was an incomparable hunter, a quiver of arrows which never missed their mark, and Talos, a copper giant forged by Hephaistus, who kept the law on the island and guarded it. Three times a year (or according to other sources

sources three times a day), Talos ran all round the island and drove out any enemies who might have appeared. Talos was eventually defeated by Medea: when the Argonauts approached Crete in the *Argo*, the giant began to throw boulders at them. Medea immobilised him by magic and went up to him: she knew he was invulnerable, but he did have one single vein in his body, which ran from his neck to his heel. Medea pulled out the pin which sealed this vein, and that was the end of Talos.

Zeus married Europa off to Asterios, King of Crete, who may have been another manifestation of Zeus himself, since we know that there was a cult of 'Zeus Asterios', and he brought up her three sons. Of Zeus's three sons by Europa, Minos became king of Crete after Asterios while Sarpedon left the island and went to distant Lycia, which he ruled according to the laws of Crete. Rhadamanthus was known as the most just man in the world. He helped Minos run the island and also administered justice. But Minos was afraid of the reputation his brother was gaining for his wise judgements, and diverted his attention elsewhere. Homer says that Rhadamanthus became king at the ends of the earth, in the Isles of the Blessed.

Minos married Pasiphae, daughter of Helios and the nymph Crete, who gave her name to the island. Minos —a semi-historical figure as well as part of the myth— was a wise legislator who organised his state and was chief priest of the Minoan religion. He managed to unite at least one hundred different cities on on the island, and governed them —and areas outside Crete— from his capital Knossos. Minos divided his state into three administrative districts: the first centred on Knossos, the second on Phaistos and the third on Kydonia. Every nine years he ascended to the Idaean Cave (or according to others the Diktaean Cave) and communed with his father Zeus, receiving a mandate to govern for a further nine years. He also received the new laws of state, in writing. Minos founded the Cretan thalassocracy, which made Crete the greatest naval power in the area and expunged the scourge of piracy from the seas.

In order to win the throne of Crete, Minos asked Poseidon to lend him a bull to prove to the Cretans —and to his brothers— that he was the man chosen by the gods to succeed their king. He promised that afterwards he would sacrifice the bull to Poseidon. However, Minos broke his promise and kept the handsome bull (which he put out into his meadows to graze), sacrificing an ordinary bull in its place. To punish him, Poseidon caused Minos's wife Pasiphae to become infatuated with the bull. In order to satisfy her passion, Pasiphae managed with the help of Daedalus, the greatest inventor of antiquity, to hide herself inside an artificial cow and thus have intercouse with the animal. Of their union was born the Minotaur, a monster with a bull's head and the body of a man.

The myth of Daedalus reflects the technological and cultural development of Minoan Crete. The famous craftsman and inventor was credited with most of the tools invented at this time and with giving architecture and sculpture a new look. Until his time, statues had shown the human figure standing, legs together and arms by

*A red-figure
cylex of the 5th century BC. The central theme is the death of the Minotaur*

the sides. Daedalus, say the myths, was the first artist to make his sculptures look life-like, showing them in positions of movement and adding eyes which resembled human eyes. Daedalus was credited with carving all the statues in Crete and also with building the huge palaces with their luxurious apartments.

On Minos's orders, Daedalus built the Labyrinth to house the Minotaur. Every year, the Athenians sent seven youths and seven maidens to be sacrificed to the Minotaur and its lust for human flesh in this complex building.

Minos had laid siege to Athens to avenge the death of his son Androgeos, who had been victorious at the Panathenaic Games and had then been killed either by those with whom he was travelling or by the wild bull of Marathon. Zeus aided Minos by sending down a plague on the city. In their desperation and to put an end to hostilities, the Athenians agreed to send the human tribute to the Minotaur each year.

It was Theseus, son of King Aegeus of Athens, who rid the Athenians of the tribute to the Minotaur, with the help of Ariadne, one of Minos's daughters, who had fallen in love with him. Ariadne gave Theseus a ball of wool —'Ariadne's thread'— one end of which he tied to the entrance of the Labyrinth. Thus no matter how far he penetrated into its depths, he would always be able to find his way out again. The Athenian hero fought the Minotaur and killed it. Then he secretly sailed away, taking Ariadne with him as he had promised. On the way back to Athens, they stopped at Naxos, and Theseus left Ariadne there on the instructions of the goddess Athena. According to another version of the story, the god Dionysus fell in love with her and stole her from Theseus.

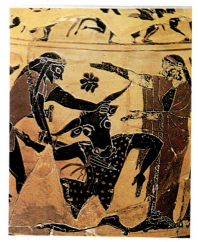

Theseus, the Minotaur and Ariadne (a 4th century amphora)

The point of the Minotaur story is that it demonstrates the power of Minoan Crete and the subjugation of Athens to it.

To punish Daedalus for helping Queen Pasiphae, Zeus locked him and his son Icarus up in the Labyrinth. Daedalus was unable to bear the imprisonment and made wax wings for himself and his son so that they could fly out. But the attempt had a tragic end for one of these first airmen: Icarus disobeyed his father's orders and flew too close to the sun, where his wings melted. Icarus fell into the sea and was drowned; the area into which he plunged has since been called the Icarian Sea.

Daedalus himself sought refuge at the court of King Cocalus, in Sicily. Minos hunted him down, despite the distance, but met his own end in Sicily, and according to the myths Daedalus had a hand in his death.

Zeus made Minos and his brothers Rhadamanthus and Sarpedon immortal, but there were protests from the other gods, who saw this as a bad precedent. Zeus was thus obliged to make them judges in the Underworld.

After the death of Minos, his son Deucalion was defeated in Crete by Theseus, who sailed back to the island with his fleet.

Deucalion's descendants Idomeneas and Meriones are known because they headed the Cretan contingent to the Trojan War.

At this time, the subjugation of mainland Greece to Crete ended, and the spark of the Minoan civilisation was transferred to Mycenae.

The fall of Icarus: from a Roman mural

HISTORY

The Prehistoric Period (6000 BC - 2600 BC)

The earliest traces of human habitation in Crete go back to the Neolithic age. The first inhabitants of the island lived in caves, which later became places of worship, and in houses with stone foundations and brick walls.

These people were farmers and shepherds. They used simple tools and utensils made of animal bones and stone, many of which have been turned up during archaeological excavations.

We know very little about their religious beliefs. It is hypothesised that they worshipped the fertility goddess Gaea, the Mother, and many figurines showing this female form have been found in Crete and throughout the eastern Mediterranean basin.

For many centuries afterwards the Mother was the most important deity for the cultures of the Mediterranean lands.

The Minoan Period

The century between 2700 BC and 2600 BC was of decisive importance for the development of Crete. Many historians think that at this time a new wave of peoples came to Crete and interbred with the local population. The new arrivals may have come from Asia Minor, but we have no proof of this so far. Even their

A map of the island
with its principal archaeological sites

language is still a matter for speculation. However, we can be sure that the culture they brought to Crete was an advanced one.

Even though we cannot be sure that these colonists introduced metalworking into Crete, there is no doubt that the Bronze Age in Crete began around the year 2600 BC. This was the beginning of the culture which has come to be called 'Minoan civilisation'.

The name, from Minos, the mythical king of Crete, was first used by the archaeologist Arthur Evans.

The Minoan epoch is broken down into three periods: Early Minoan, Middle Minoan and Late Minoan, each of which is in turn subdivided into three stages designated with the Roman numerals I, II and III.

The Greek archaeologist Nikolaos Platon used the historical facts as a basis for a different division of the Minoan epoch into periods which he called Protoplatial, Neopalatial, Late Palace and Final-Palace.

These divisions of the Minoan civilisation were made on the basis of objects found in Crete but originating in Egypt and the Middle East — from countries, that is, whose historical chronology has been fixed and agreed upon.

The chronological division which most scholars now accept is as follows:

Early Minoan period:
2600 BC-2000 BC

Middle Minoan period:
2000 BC-1580 BC

Late Minoan period:
1580-1100BC

The first palaces were built in Crete around the start of the Middle Minoan period, that is, around 2000 BC. Economic and political power seems to have centred on the palaces at Knossos, Phaistos, Mallia, Archanes, Zakros and Kydonia.

An earthquake which shook the whole island and was followed by extensive fires seems to have destroyed the palaces around 1700 BC.

However, we do not know whether the destruction of the palaces was the work of nature alone, or whether there was also an invasion of the island. Immediately after the disaster the palaces were rebuilt even larger and more magnificent than before, and the period from 1700 BC to 1400 BC is often called the Final Palace period.

Mallia, Zakros, Phaistos and above all Knossos were at the height of their power during this period.

At about this time, the ruler of Knossos seems to have expanded his kingdom to include control of Phaistos. Knossos, with its favourable geographical situation in the centre of the island, was able to unite the entire island, building a network of good roads and controlling economic and political life. The size and the refined luxury of the Knossos palace are indications that this was the seat of power. Minoan Crete may have been organised along bureaucratic lines similar to those of the kingdoms of the East.

Excavations have revealed that more than one script was in use in Crete at this time: a hierographic script (of which the Phaistos Disc in Herakleio Archaeological Museum is an example) and a syllabic script, that known as Linear A. Linear A has not yet been deciphered.

Excavations in the islands and along the coasts of the Aegean show that the Minoans of Crete built trading posts in these places.

The economy of the island flourished. Farming and stock-breeding produced large yields, and the workshops of the palaces and the villages turned out goods for export to the other islands and to mainland Greece. Works of art made in Crete found byers in Egypt, Phoenicia and Syria, and Minoan pottery has been discovered throughout the eastern Mediterranean.

Around 1400 BC there was a tremendous natural disaster which heralded the end of the Minoan culture. Earthquakes and fires destroyed Knossos and the other palaces, and the towns were deserted. The catastrophe may have been caused by the eruption of the Santorini volcano, although it is possible that this may have coincided with a foreign invasion. At Knossos, part of the archives have been found to include tablets in Linear B script, which is identical to the writing found in Mycenean palaces.

However, the disaster in 1400 BC was not the absolute end of Minoan culture in Crete. For some centuries —down to 1100 BC— it struggled on even though the island was under the domination of the Achaeans.

Nonetheless, it was unable to regain the brilliance or prosperity of the past.

The snake goddess of Knossos (1600 BC)

Religion in Minoan Crete

The Minoan religion strongly influenced that of the Greeks who followed, and in whose mythology Crete plays an important part (such as being the place where Zeus was born). Figurines of the Great Goddess have survived from the crowning period of Minoan art, together with pictorial representations of religious ceremonies, utensils used during these ceremonies and depictions of the sacred symbols: the pair of horns, the double axe, the sacred knot, the octagonal shield, and sacred tree and so on. The female figure occupies a central position, and we can be certain that the divinity of fertility and eternal life was worshipped.

A rhyton from Knossos (1500 BC)

From the very inception of their culture the Cretans believed in some sort of life after death. The dead were accompanied with pots of foodstuffs and the utensils of daily life, for use not only on the journey to the next world but until the body had disintegrated entirely. The deities of Minoan Crete were worshipped not only in parts of the palaces but also out of doors, in natural sanctuaries, in caves and on mountain peaks. The cult of the bull and the festivals held in its honour —attended by thousands of spectators— were the nucleus of the Minoan religion. Bull-fighting, or rather bull-leaping, was the most important of these ceremonies and was held in the spring, when nature and man are reborn. It relied on the sanctity of the bull (an animal into which Zeus frequently transformed himself, as we have seen in the myth of Europa) and on its relationship with fertility.

The bull-dancing or bull-leaping seems to have been the Minoans' favourite sport, too.

The event was held in an arena in the palace and attracted enthusiastic crowds. The bull was sacrificed later, but was never killed during the leaping itself.

The bull would rush snorting into the enclosed area; young boys and girls, nearly naked, would skip out of his way, grasp his horns and vault neatly upwards, their bodies reaching high into the air.

As they flew through the air, they would twist so as to land gracefully on the back of the enraged animal; and from there it was easy to somersault off into the arms of a waiting companion.

Bullfighting (bull-leaping) in a mural from Knossos (1500 BC)

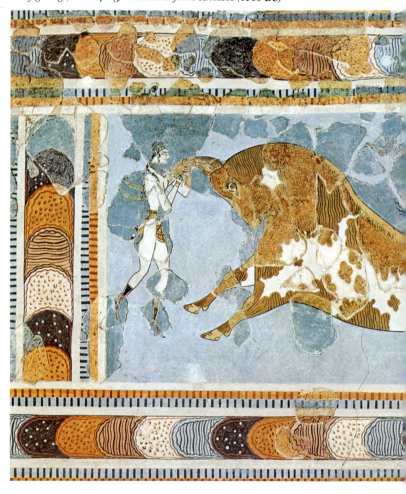

Minoan Art

To judge by their art, the Minoans must have loved nature, elegance and beauty. The works of art they produced are generally on a small scale. Painting seems to have been their chief affection, and all their murals are dominated by the element of movement, which is rendered with delicacy and vitality. The spiral was the central decorative motif.

Minoan art, too, is divided into three periods: Early Minoan (3600-2100 BC), Middle Minoan (2100-1600 BC) and Late Minoan (1600-1200 BC). Each period is further subdivided into three. The Late Minoan period contained the golden age of Minoan art, which lasted approximately one hundred years.

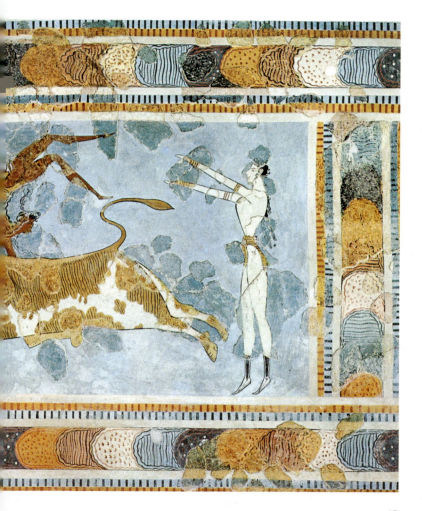

Depictions in painting and sculpture give us some idea of what the Minoans must have looked like. It would seem that the men dressed in very light clothing: they wore only a piece of multi-coloured cloth round the waist. However, we also have pictures of officials wearing rich cloaks and head-dresses. Tight belts accentuated the narrow waists of men and women alike. The women of Crete, delicate and light-footed as we can see in the murals, took great care over dressing their hair, which they then adorned with jewels and multi-coloured ribbons. Their dresses were very low-cut (in effect, they went topless) and their dresses, pulled tight at the waist, hung down low.

The women of Minoan Crete would seem to have been emancipated: the murals show them attending religious ceremonies, dancing and sporting events in complete equality with the men.

The murals and the skeletons which have been found in caves show the Minoans to have been short, slim and quick-footed. They were certainly fond of a good time and had very little interest in the art of war. In fact, war and hunting scenes are completely absent from Minoan art, and with the exception of stoats, wild cats, polecats and ibexes (which have survived to the present day) there do not seem to have been wild animals on the island.

Minoan decorative motifs

Of the greatest interest are the small plaques which have been found and which must have decorated a wooden chest: they show the houses of a typical Minoan city and tell us that the Minoans lived in multi-storey buildings whose tall windows were flanked with geometrical designs.

The **Minoan palaces:** In the memories of the Greeks thousands of years afterwards, the Minoan palaces assumed mythical dimensions; they were constructed with outstanding artistic skill and arranged in a labyrinthine manner.

The excavations at Phaistos, Mallia and Zakros —but above all at Knossos— have shown us now exactly what those palaces looked like. The first thing that strikes one is the complete absence of walls or fortifications of any kind. Along general lines, the palaces rather resemble each other, the main features being their inner courtyards around which were the rooms for rituals and official ceremonies. At Knossos, the main courtyard was surrounded by the public rooms, including the throne room with the king's throne and the benches for his councillors. This was followed immediately by the sacred area and the treasury, opposite which were the apartments of the king and queen. Behind the throne room were the storehouses for the harvest. The walls throughout the building are of stone and the flat roofs were supported by pillars or brackets. The inner rooms were lit by numerous windows, balconies and light-shafts. There were broad staircases and landings on various levels to give an air of luxury and magnificence.

Care had been taken to ensure that all those who lived in the palace did so in comfort. Even the drainage system was cunningly constructed and there were pipes to ensure the palace of a constant supply of running drinking water.

A reconstruction of the palace of Knossos

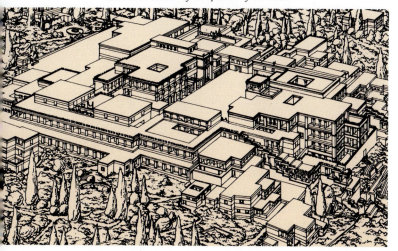

Painting

The interior decoration of the palaces was particularly impressive, with outstanding wall-paintings. These murals were painted straight on to wet plaster (the fresco technique), presumably after a preliminary design had been made, and the artist had to work fast and accurately. Perhaps this accounts for the vividness of the figures.

The most complex of the frescoes are from the palace of Knossos. The human figure was the basic component in the subject-matter of these paintings. However, there was no shortage of other motifs, notably from the plant and animal kingdom. Today, we are impressed by the vitality of the figures and the refinement of the use of bright colour. The depiction of animals and plants, too, strikes us for its vigour and realism. Another admirable element is the ease with which the Minoan painters dealt with themes showing large numbers of people. We are often shown a whole crowd of people, each

figure being rendered in a very few lines. Sometimes the groups of human figures are on small surfaces, and sometimes the frescoes are life-size: one example here would be the frescoes from the Corridor of the Procession at Knossos.

These **Minoan frescoes** are a wonderful and brightly-coloured chronicle of life especially as it was lived in the palace: religious ceremonies, bull-leaping, scenes from everyday life, acrobats, bulls and wrestlers. Sometimes we are shown people seated in tiers to watch the events in a stadium, and we can see the women chatting together.

Apart from the scenes of everyday life, many of the frescoes from Minoan Crete show landscapes and activities at sea, such as the famous dolphin fresco. However, the most famous frescoes are undoubtedly the 'Prince of the Lilies', a portion of an exceptional fresco from the Knossos palace, and 'La Parisienne', a section of a fresco showing a beautiful priestess taking part in a religious ceremony.

The sacrificing of an ox - a detail from the Ayia Triada sarcophagus

*La Parisienne,
Knossos, 1500 BC*

The rhyton-bearer, Knossos, 1500 BC

The limestone sarcophagus from Ayia Triada, 1400 BC

Pottery

The love of the Cretan artists for colour can also be seen in their pottery. The types of pottery which are most common in Early Minoan Crete are the rhyton, the hydria and the long-stemmed goblet. Many of these works take their names from the places where they were found. Most of them are painted in red against a background of a light shade of clay, while others have linear designs in light colours against a dark background.

Kamares ware pottery (dating from around 1900 BC, Middle Minoan), which takes its name from the first finds in the Kamares cave, is richly coloured: the dominant colours are red, orange, yellow and white. In the pottery, as in the frescoes, themes are taken from nature: in other words, we are shown plants and sea creatures. The purpose of this type of painting was to decorate the vase while at the same time being faithful to its harmony and form. Here, inspiration is entirely free and each figure helps to make up a most elegant whole.

A flask from Palaikastro, 1500 BC

In this way, we can see painted octopuses whose tentacles give the impression of holding the vase together. Even in later years of the so-called 'Palace Style' (16th century BC), when the themes from nature have declined to spiral motifs, plants and sea-creatures continue to serve as models for the decoration of vases. Elements of Minoan vase-painting continued to be used by Mycenean artists for centruries afterwards.

The delicate Kamares ware pottery was so popular in its time that the Minoans exported it to the rest of the Mediterranean. The superb crystal vases are of a later date.

The figurines of deities, such as the goddess with the snakes, and the vases with decoration in relief showing scenes from daily life, such as that called the 'report goblet', the Harvester vase and the rhyton with representations of athletes in four bands, are all of a later date.

A Kamares ware vessel with a spout, Phaistos, 1800 BC

A terracotta Kamares ware krater (Old Palace, Phaistos, 1800 BC)

Stone carving, seal-making, gold:
Apart from the frescoes, we can also see wonderful work with a marked tendency towards the faithful depiction of reality in the Minoan carvings on stone, ivory and precious stones. In many cases, we have copies in more everyday materials of authentic pieces which have been lost and which would presumably have been on metal. The symbol of the double axe dominates sculpture on stone and other materials as it did in the frescoes.

The work of the Minoan artists in miniatures reached very advanced levels, as can be seen in the jewellery and other products turned out by the island's craftsmen. Thoughout the centuries of the Minoan culture, these artists were great masters in working stone. Countless seal-stones which served perfectly practical purposes when they were made have survived to be admired today. Their microscopic motifs are drawn, as always, from the plant and animal kingdoms. The gold jewellery, such as the pendant with the two bees found at Mallia, or that with the duck from Knossos, or the one with the lion from Ayia Triada are testimony to the level reached by miniaturists and goldsmiths in Minoan Crete.

Numerous smaller but no less admirable pieces of jewellery have been found in tombs in Crete: bracelets, pendants, ear-rings and jewels to be worn in the hair, all in gold or precious stones of many colours, they display very advanced techniques. The finest gold jewellery (diadems, pendants, etc.) consists of work in leaves or showing the figures of animals.

Gold jewellery from Mallia, 2000 BC

Seal-stones of semi-precious stone

A gold seal-stone from Mycenae with Minoan symbols

The Sub-Minoan, Geometric and Archaic Periods (1100-900 BC)

After the destruction of the palaces and the collapse of the Minoan culture, Crete was conquered by the Dorians, who sailed across from mainland Greece. These invaders founded a number of city-states, each independent of the others in accordance with the Dorian model, and they dominated the island both socially and polically. The Minoan Cretans fought hard to resist the invaders, but in the end they had to give in and accept subjection. Those who wished to remain free sought refuge in the high mountains.

The Doric cities of Crete had the same system of government as Sparta, that is, they a senate consisting of the nobility of the city. The towns were protected by walls and each had its acropolis. Although all these cities shared the same customs and even the same language and religion, there was no shortage of conflict between them.

The cities could be kept united under the leadership of Knossos, but only when this was necessary for the purposes of repelling some new invader. Quite a number of traces of these Doric cities have survived down to the present day: at Prinia, some 40 km from Herakleio, traces have been found on a low hill of one of the most important Archaic sanctuaries of the 7th century BC. The architectural decoration from this site is in Herakleio Archaeological Museum.

The ancient city of Lato stood on a hill commanding the bay of Merabelo, some 15 km from Ayios Nikolaos. Its ruins are scattered throughout the surrounding area.

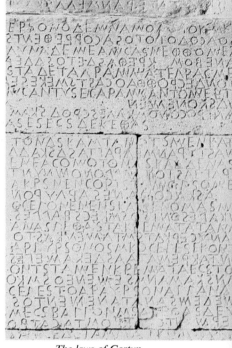

The laws of Gortyn

Lato is a well-preserved Archaic city, with its agora, numerous public buildings and temples.

Gortyn, approximately 45 km from Herakleio and 17 km to the east of Phaistos, was from time to time the most important and powerful city in Crete. Traces of all the periods in the history of the island have been found here. Of particular interest are the inscriptions giving the Laws of Gortyn, which include legislation in family law and the law of inheritance (see p. 215).

The fine shields from the Idaean Cave and the copper figurines from Driros show that valuable artistic work continued to be done in Crete during this period.

The Classical, Hellenistic and Roman Periods

During the Classical period (500-323 BC), Crete did not play a particularly important part in the political and cultural spheres. This situation did not change during the Hellenistic and Roman periods which followed. Throughout this time, Crete remained on the sidelines of the political and artistic activities of the Greeks. The disputes and clashes between the city-states continued, and in the end the island became a particularly vicious nest of pirates.

The campaign which Rome undertook to overcome the corsairs of the eastern Mediterranean was an excellent opportunity to annexe Crete to the Roman Empire.

After many years of fighting, Crete became a Roman province. Under the Romans, Gortyn became the island's capital, and the living conditions of the islanders began slowly to improve. The population increased, and densely-populatied towns grew up in the plains and along the coasts.

*A Roman statue
from Herakleio Museum*

The Byzantine chapel of St Paul, to the east of Ayia Roumeli

Byzantium (330-1204/10 AD)

Crete experienced Byzantine rule in two periods: the first of these (330-826 AD) was interrupted by occupation by the Arabs (826-961), and was followed by the second Byzantine period (961-1204/10).

In 395 AD, the Roman Empire was divided into the Eastern and Western Empires. Later, Crete became a Theme (administrative province) of the Byzantine state, a situation which lasted from the 5th to the 9th centuries. It was during the first Byzantine period that Christianity spread to the island and established itself. During the Early Christian period (5th-6th centuries), fine churches were built, of which that of St Titus, at Gortyn, is of particular interest from the architectural point of view. Remains of Early Christian basilicas have also survived at Knossos, Chersonisos and Vizari (in the Amari valley).

Crete frequently suffered from Arab raids. In 823, the Saracens conquered the island and laid siege to Herakleio, digging a moat all the way round the town. It was from this moat that town got the name by which it was known throughout the Middle Ages: Handak (meaning 'moat'). In 826, the Byzantine general Karteros landed at Amnisos with a large fleet and an enormous army, but his forces were annihilated. Under the rule of the Arabs, there was much persecution of Christianity and the religion's hold over the island slackened. In was not until 961 that the Byzantine general Nicephorus Phocas was able to liberate Crete and bring it back into the Byzantine Empire.

The outcome of this campaign was also judged at Herakleio, which fell into the hands of the Byzantines after a four-month siege. In the massacre which followed, it has been estimated that as many as 200,000 Arabs lost their lives. Crete returned to Byzantium (second Byzantine period) and Christianity gained in strength. It was at this time that Herakleio became the seat of the Archbishop, and churches and monasteries sprang up everywhere.

Venetian Rule (1204-1669)

When the Crusaders took Constantinople in 1204 and dismembered the Byzantine Empire, Crete passed into the hands of Boniface of Monferrat, who then sold it to the Venetians. For some years, the Genoese, who were the Venetians' principal opponents in the markets of the eastern Mediterranean, attempted to keep a foothold on Crete but Venice won in the end. Herakleio was renamed Candia, a corruption of the Byzantine Handak, and it remained capital of Crete. The walls of the city were reconstructed and many fine new buildings were put up. These included the Doge's palace, the basilica of St Mark and the Loggia, the meeting-place of the nobility.

Crete beneath the emblem of Venice in an engraving by Boschini

The entrance to the Venetian castle of Rethymno

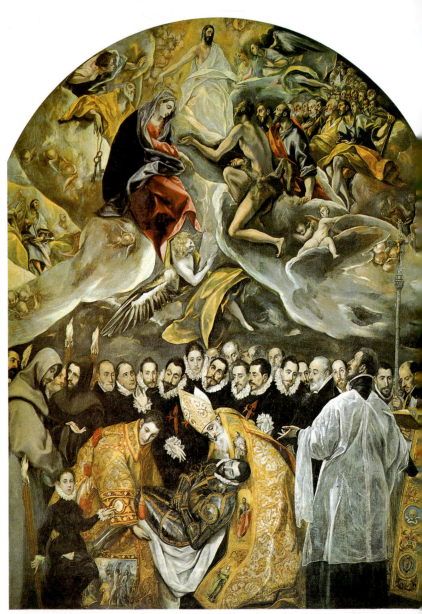

Domenico Theotokopoulos: The Burial of Court Orgaz, one of the most outstanding productions of an entire age and civilisation. It is to be seen in the church of St Thomas, Toledo. It is generally accepted that the knight looking out of the picture at the viewer is a self-portrait of Theotokopoulos (see p. 231)

Right from the start there was much discontent under Venetian rule, because the attempts to introduce the feudal system and displant Greek Orthodoxy in favour of Catholicism made large sections of the population resort to frequent armed resistance.

When Constantinople fell to the Turks in 1453, large numbers of Greek nobles and scholars took refuge in Crete. As a result, Byzantine culture and Byzantine art took on a fresh lease of life. The Monastery of St Catherine in Herakleio was a particularly important centre of Byzantine culture, where theology, philosophy, music and literature were developed.

The traditional Byzantine style of painting combined with elements taken from the Italian Renaissance to form a new school of art called the 'Cretan school'. Very few of the examples of this school are to be found in Crete itself: most are on Mt Athos, in the Meteora and in the large museums of Greece and other countries. Among the most famous painters of this period were Michail Damaskinos, Klontzas and Ioannis Kornaros, a large icon by whom belongs to the Toplou Monastery. The youthful works of Domenico Theotokopoulos, better known as El Greco, should also be seen as belonging to the Cretan school.

During the closing years of Venetian rule there was a flowering in Cretan literature, which produced a number of interesting theatrical works under the influence of the Italian poetry of the Renaissance. The epic by Vincenzo Cornaro *Erotocritos*, dating from early in the 17th century, occupies a predominant position in the literature of this time.

Turkish Rule (1669-1898)

Throughout the last years of Venetian rule, Crete was under the constant threat of invasion by the Turks. In 1538, led by the famous admiral Hayredin Barbarossa, they succeeded in occupying much of central and western Crete, but their attack was stopped by the walls of Candia.

In 1645, a Turkish army of 60,000 men landed west of Chania from a fleet of 400 ships. Chania itself fell before long, and in 1646 Rethymno and other castles were forced to surrender. By the end of 1648 the whole of Crete was under Turkish domination — with the exception of Candia. The siege of Candia, one of the most dramatic episodes in the entire history of the island, lasted 21 whole years (1648-1669). On 27 September 1669 the city was finally starved into submission after the siege had cost 117,000 Turkish lives and losses of nearly 30,000 among the Greeks and Venetians. Francesco Morosini, governor of Crete, handed Candia over after negotiating the right of passage for himself and the remainder of his men.

The Turks rebuilt the walls of the cities and converted most of the churches into mosques. In order to escape the barbarity of their new masters, many Cretans left the island and took refuge in the Ionian Islands. The years between 1770 and 1821, in particular, were among the darkest in the island's long history. And when the Greek War of Independence broke out in 1821, the Turks in their rage behaved with even greater cruelty to the Cretans. Mehmet Ali, regent in Egypt at the time, undertook the general

An engraved map of Crete by Dapper, 1688

UM PELAGUS.

ARCIPELAGO

PROFUNDISSIMUM

DI CANDIA

CARPATHIUM

DORIENSES
TRICHALCES

MARE
Nunc
MARE
DI
SCAR-
PANLO

COM MARE

DI BARBARIA

Inversa Isticcsis locorum nomina.

LOCA	POPULI	Lobeynes	SYAGNU
Adephs	Corene	Trien	Conysum
Adroua	Dryites		MONTES TEMPLU
Corium	Lyres	Asterysos	Boccos seu
Bagesrorori	Ocy	Ardeus	Diana
Coprobium	FLUVII	Corius Loson	INSULÆ
Topania	Amnisus	Ocheys	Alsicla
Trigolus	Oaxes	Sycracium	Kumasches

command of the Turkish forces and managed to recapture most of the island by 1840. In the last years of Turkish rule, Crete was shaken by successive rebellions.

The 'great Cretan rebellion' began in 1866 and lasted until 1868. This was the climax of the Cretan desire for freedom and union with the rest of Greece. During the course of the revolt, the Arkadi Monastery was destroyed (see p. 136) and it became a symbol of the indomitable will of the Cretans to be free. The Arkadi sacrifice sent a tremor of horror round the world. In the end, the rebellion petered out amid incalculable destruction and loss of human life. The Cretan problem, however, was taken up by the Great Powers, which compelled Turkey to make certain concessions.

Fresh fighting broke out in 1895-1896, after a period since the beginning of the decade when the old wounds had reopened and violence was an everyday occurrence. In 1897, Greek forces and volunteers reached Crete and gradually began to liberate the island, with the intention of uniting it with Greece.

The Cretans continued to struggle for their freedom, with the Theriso revolt of 1905 as the culmination. This rising led in 1913 to the union of Crete with Greece and elevated Eleftherios Venizelos to the stature of a leading Greek statesman (a popular depiction)

42

ΕΟΝ

1866-69
1878-1889
1896-97

ΣΠΑΝΑΣΤΑΣΕΙΣ

ΚΡΗΤΗΣ

ΚΗΡΥΤΤΕΙ ΕΝΩΠΙΟΝ ΘΕΟΥ ΚΑΙ
ΩΣΙΝ ΜΕΤΑ ΤΟΥ ΒΑΣΙΛΕΙΟΥ ΤΗΣ
Ν. ΣΥΝΤΑΓΜΑΤΙΚΗΝ ΠΟΛΙΤΕΙΑΝ
ΙΡΟΣ ΤΑΣ ΔΥΝΑΜΕΙΣ)

Autonomous Crete - the Modern Period

The fighting stopped in 1898, a year marked by the Turkish massacre in Herakleio. The Great Powers —Britain, France and Russia— recognised the existence of the autonomous 'Cretan State'. Prince George of Greece was appointed High Commissioner over it.

However, the struggle of the ordinary Cretans continued, culminating in the Theriso rebellion of 1905. That rebellion led to the eventual union of Crete with Greece in 1913 and made Eleftherios Venizelos a household name in Greece. He was the statesman who in the decades to come was to guide the fortunes of the nation as a whole.

The most recent heroic event in Cretan history occurred during the Second World War, when Crete became the theatre of hard fighting. In May 1941, as part of a large-scale attack on western Crete, thousands of German paratroopers were dropped on the island. British, Australian, New Zealand and Greek troops put up fierce resistance, with the aid of thousands of islanders, but the numerical superiority and much better equipment of the invading forces eventually won the day. Even today, historians are still producing unknown details of the Battle of Crete from the archives of both sides.

However, the people of Crete continued to resist the Germans even after the island had fallen. Perhaps the climax of the resistance movement was the abduction and shipping to Cairo of the German General Kreipe. German reprisals were severe.

YESTERDAY AND TODAY

During the 16th century, numerous European travellers visited Crete. They were impressed by what they saw, and recorded their descriptions later in chronicles and notes. The French geographer André Thevet (1556) wrote of the traditional liberalism of the Cretans:

"The Cretans used to be called Telchines, that is, people who have a dreadful way of life. It is precisely that way of life which creates in them an indomitable desire for liberty.

"The Cretans are good pilots and experienced seamen".

And Thevet added: *"They have a great idea of their hair and beards, and they would prefer to have their noses or ears cut off rather than lose their hair or beards. They regard this as insulting and humiliating".*

The British traveller Lithgow reported that the Cretans were the best archers in the East and were famous for their bravery on land and at sea, *"just as they were in antiquity"*. They were cheerful, boisterous and very hospitable:

"After dinner, the men, women and children of each family sing for an hour. It is a pleasure to hear them, so melodic and harmonious is their song.

"The truth is that when you visit kind Greeks they never allow you to leave empty-handed. They load strangers down with gifts and supply a man to carry them".

The Cretans' prowess with the bow was remarked on by a number of travellers. The Frenchman Belon (1546) wrote that:

"It is not a mistake to say that the Cretans worshipped Artemis in antiquity. Even today, they contine this old custom as if by instinct. They learn in childhood how to make perfect use of the Scythian bow".

The Italian monk and pilgrim Noe wrote that *"the Cretans have a great tolerance of hunger and hardship, and are very skilful archers".*

According to the French pilgrim Jacques de Saige, *"they are great archers, and when they pluck the string the arrows whistle".*

The European travellers were also impressed by the consumption of wine in Crete. The Frenchman Villamont (1672) wrote that:

"The Cretans do not put any water in their wine, however strong it may be, and I have witnessed this myself".

The Italian pilgrim Jerome Dandini (1599) remarked that:

"The good wine of Crete has made the islanders great drinkers".

The Catholic Archbishop of Athens L. Petit provides us with a brief description of the island and its inhabitants:

"This is a truly admirable race, which has discovered how despite the misadventures of forty centuries to preserve its national characteristics and pure language intact: bravery mixed with a sentiment of independence which sometimes verges on indiscipline, a vigorous wit, burning imagination, a language packed with images yet spontaneous and unaffected, a love for adventure of all kinds, an indomitable passion for freedom combined with a desire for advertisement which cannot be satisfied... This is a fertile land which has never ceased to produce most able men for the Church and the State, for the sciences and letters, for the economy and for war..."

What, then, was this Crete of yesteryear which the foreigner travellers of Venetian times tried so hard to describe, and who were the Cretans? And who are these Cretans today, and what makes them different?

One can gain some idea from a walk through the narrow Venetian alleys of Chania or Rethymno, or from a glance at a Cretan from a mountain village, in his broad cloth belt with a knife stuck through it by his side; the appearance is much the same as in the Minoan statuettes made four thousand years ago.

In any case, it is not yet a hundred years since Crete gained its freedom and was united with Greece. Before that time, there was only the smoke of war, with very few intervals of peace.

For eight hundred years, Crete fought against its enemies: Romans, Arabs, Venetians and last of all the Turks have left their traces here. And throughout those centuries Crete resisted, fought back.

No other part of Greece —and perhaps of the world— has seen so much fighting, so many sacrifices, such frequent revolution. For that reason one should not be surprised that the Cretans carry the remnants of a turbulent past deep within their souls.

A large part of the population of Crete has come to terms with reality as it is today. These are people who live in the big urban centres and often work in the tourist industry. However, one should not jump to any conclusions based on the towns, most of which are located on the north coast, from the tourist resorts or from the huge hotels which stand on the seemingly endless beaches.

Cretan tradition is still to be found very much alive on the island. But to find it, one has to travel inland, where the slopes of Psiloritis, of the White Mountains or of Dikte are to be seen. Up in those imposing mountains are villages which tourism has not touched. Here, people are different: they still live with their customs, their occuptions, their habits and the beliefs of the past, and they keep their traditions alive.

In these villages, the principal occupation of the population is farming and stock-breeding. Wine is regarded as an almost sacred drink, and the grape harvest, which begins in early September, provides seasonal employment for many people. Excellent raki is produced by the old traditional methods. The 'Kazanemata' —the days when the raki is being distilled— are an opportunity for feasting and drinking.

Ploughing, threshing, picking the olives —the island produces vast quantities of olive oil— grazing and *milking* are all part of the daily routine in the Cretan hinterland. For centuries the Cretans have been taking from the rich and fertile soil of their island whatever it is capable of giving them.

Although Crete is an island, **fishing**is not highly developed and has remained on what one might call an amateur level. This is because the sea is not rich in fish: there are no rivers to bring down food for the fish. Furthermore, the sea around Crete is very deep, which makes fishing difficult.

The patriarchal form of Cretan society, which relied on farming and the products of stock-breeding, was still very much alive until recently. The family was the nucleus of the entire social formation, and the senior members of the family took the decisions. No young man with unmarried sisters might himself marry until he saw them 'settled' first. Anything which happened in society, however serious —including murder— was a family matter and was nobody else's business. Sheep-stealing and the vendetta, both of which were essential for the smooth functioning of Cretan society, caused whole villages to be wiped out.

Sheep-stealing has a long history in Crete, and is the continuation of the heroism of those who fought against Venetian and Turkish rule. It was controlled by the community and never went beyond certain limits, since there were very specific rules as to how it was to be done, involving competition, conflict, settlements and alliances. Sheep-stealing was a form of social relations in this stock-breeding society, which accepted it as an institution for the proving of manhood and superiority, to be followed by negotiation and the redistribution of the community's wealth.

The *vendetta*, a relic of the very distant past, took on a new lease of life in Venetian times. The Venetians and the local nobility were above the law, and often eliminated their opponents by the use of hired killers: they knew they were safe from punishment. The only way in which justice could be administered was to take the law into one's own hands and deal out retribution: i.e., the vendetta. In the end, such acts were given a veneer of social values and were particularly esteemed as indications of honour and manliness.

Cretans are different. They lose their tempers over nothing and see insults where none was intended. Perhaps deep down they do not really believe that the storm is over, that the persecution and the massacres have stopped. It is as if they were forever on the alert to deal with danger. They are mistrustful, taciturn and brusque. But all of that is just at the beginning, until they have weighed up the stranger and decided he is a friend. Then everything suddenly changes. The angry faces soften, and broad smiles spread across them. A hand will be stretched out to clasp the stranger's; *"Come in for a glass of tsikoudia"*, will be the next step, and no more is needed. From then on, the stranger is a guest, under the protection of his host. The host will do anything for his guest; later, when he knows the stranger better and they have become close friends, he will even sacrifice his life if needed. It is difficult to refuse such hospitality; one's host will become angry, and the smiling face will cloud over again. *"Why don't you sit down and have something to eat with us?"* The tone of voice is disarming, as if the speaker were saying, *'here I am, opening my heart to you. Will you scorn me?'.*

That might be the voice of the typical old Cretan. Visitors will often see such old men in the market-place or in one of the cafes, even in the cities.

Dressed in his loose trousers (the 'vraka'), his knee-boots ('stivania') and with his black kerchief with the bobbles on his head, his face grave, browned by the sun and deeply wrinkled, he will sit in the corner of the cafe, thinking. What he has to say is wise; his mood is sometimes philosophical, sometimes jovial when circumstances demand; then, a good-natured smile will spread across his face and smooth out the wrinkles.

On the other side of the cafe may be a group of young men, whose height and bearing is often striking. On the Cretan feast-days, old and young join in celebration. Anyone who experiences one of these feasts will remember it for many years: when the Cretans decide to enjoy themselves, they do it in style. Engagements, weddings, christenings and personal name-days: these are all opportunities for dancing and song.

*"In fron he holds
A Cretan cypress tree,
And behind he pulls
A spring of crystal water."* mantinada

The Cretans have *dancing* in their blood. For them, the dance is a chance to let off steam, to externalise the restlessness and dynamism of their spirits. This can be seen most clearly in the leaping dance ('pidichtos', as it is called).

The best-known Cretan dance is the *'pentozalis'*, a very manly performance reminiscent of the 'pyrrichios', the war dance of the ancient Greeks, which also used to be danced by armed Cretans. The pentozalis is danced throughout Crete. The dancers stand in a circle around the lyre-player, whose central position emphasises the fact that he gives the dance its rhythm. The music starts slowly and gradually builds up to a frenetic speed, with a leaping beat. The lyre-player also decides when the dance will end, breaking off the music quite suddenly.

It is wonderful to watch the erect bodies, black-clad torsos hardly moving, while beneath the legs in their black boots move back, forwards, to the left and right with mastery and always in time to the rapid beat of the lyre.

The *'syrtos'* is a little milder, but the steps of the leading dancer are, if anything, more showy than those of the pentozalis. The Cretan syrtos generally resembles the dance of the same name performed elsewhere in Greece; there are local variations, of which the best-known is that which originated in Chania.

Among other Cretan dances are the *'Kastrinos'* or *'Maleveziotikos'*, a fast, leaping dance, and the *'sousta'*, which is danced by couples. The sousta does not have the pace of the other dances, but it has all their elegance and technique.

The *Cretan wedding* is the social event at which dancing reigns supreme.

The 'sousta' dance is performed by couples

The Cretans distinguish themselves in dancing even as children

*"Today there's going to be a wedding
In a pretty orchard;
today the mother will be saying
goodbye to her daughter".* (mantinada)

The *Cretan wedding* is the most important of all the feasts and celebrations. It combines all the crafts and daily occupations, and the Cretan traditions can been seen in it in their most lively and authentic forms. Anyone who gets a chance to attend a Cretan wedding should make the most of it; this is a custom whose roots lie far back in the centuries and which has survived intact in the hinterland of the island.

A wedding is a major event in village life. It begins with the *heralding*, done by the *herald* ('kalestis'), who goes from house to house and even from village to village announcing the forthcoming event. Everyone who happens to be living in the vicinity —whether Cretan or not— is invited. Preparations for the wedding take many days; the bride's trousseau is on show at her house, and everyone comes to admire it. It really is an admirable sight: delicately-worked woven goods, lace and embroidery rich in pattern and with harmonious colours, a large carved wooden chest and other utensils, also carved in wood. On the day before the wedding, the trousseau is moved to the bridegroom's house and *'mantinades'* (improvised couplets) about it are sung to the accompaniment of the lyre. On the same evening, the *'kaniskia'* —a kind of basket containing meat, wine, olive oil, cheese, potatoes, etc., a present to the couple from the whole village— is sent to the matrimonial dwelling. Those who carry the trousseau and the kaniskia are each given a handmade kerchief and a large wedding loaf.

These loaves are famous: before baking, the dough is richly decorated with naturalistic motifs which make the loaves look rather like examples of the wood-carver's art.

Great care is taken to ensure that tradition is followed to the letter, and also that everything is ready when the great day comes.

The wedding begins at the bridegroom's house, from which the groom sets out in procession with his retinue for the house of the bride. Everyone is wearing their best traditional costume, and it can be a wonderful sight to come across such a procession walking through the pretty lanes of the village or astride their proud horses, which are also decorated with plumes. The procession is headed by the flag on its pole, followed by the lyre-player, who keeps up a constant accompaniment. The songs he sings are in praise of the groom: he will sing of his bravery, his good nature and all his other advantages:

*"Open up your doors
To the east and west,
And welcome in the bridegroom,
Like a handsome cypress tree."*

The procession, firing rifles into the air, approaches the bride's house. But the door is closed. When the bridegroom and his friends reach the door, silence falls: it would seem that 'negotiations' are about to begin. A female voice from the group around the groom breaks the silence with a mantinada sung to a sweet and questioning tune: this is a request that the door be opened so they can see the bride:

"Open up your door
With its iron bolts,
And let us see your bride
About whom we've heard so much."

There is now an exchange of mantinades, in which those inside the house enjoin the bridegroom to take care of the bride and those outside reply appropriately, promising that he will. This procedure sometimes lasts quite some time. In the end, the groom is invited to step inside:

"Come in, bridegroom, and kiss
Your mother-in-law's hand;
For she brought up the basil plant
Which now she gives to you."

The door opens, and the bridegroom's parents enter, followed by the young man himself. The parents always come first: they will be the first to kiss the bride, who kisses their hands and the bridegroom as well. This part of the formalities is now over.

The women of the house hand round food, drink, walnuts, almonds and raisins. Under the influence of the strong wine and the continuing music, everyone is soon jolly — only the bride stands with bent head. She looks thoughtful; soon she will have to leave the house in which she was born and bred, to go to live in her husband's house. Her feelings are mixed, joy and sorrow together.

In the meantime, the wishes fly back and forth across the room, and glasses are raised to the groom, to the bride, to the families.

Through the hubbub the sound of the church bells can be discerned. The time has come for the religious part of the ceremony. Everyone now goes to the church, where the service differs little from the wedding formalities in the rest of Greece. The only real difference is that the relatives hand over their wedding presents or gifts of money at the end of the service, inside the church, as they pass the newly-weds and wish them happiness. As soon as the service is over and the congregation goes out into the church courtyard, a fresh opportunity for dancing presents itself. All the male relatives, and above all the groom, dance with the bride and there is friendly rivalry as to who will seize her kerchief: it usually goes to whoever dances with her last. After this the whole procession, headed by the lyre-player once more, heads for the bridegroom's house and happy mantinades, composed specially for the occasion, are heard. Here the bridegroom's mother follows the tradition of serving the bride honey and walnuts, and before the bride enters the house, her mother-in-law takes a knife and carves a cross high above the door. As the bride enters, a pomegranate is broken apart, signifying a wish that the couple will have many descendants. Before entering, the guests sing:

"Come out, mother of the groom
And mother-in-law of the bride
And receive the new husband
With his new wife".

The party sometimes goes on for as much as three days, with all the guests

The fireplace and the lantern were essential parts of any old Cretan house

eating, drinking, singing and —above all— dancing non-stop.

In the long years of the struggle for survival under the Turks, people were forced to confine their need to express themselves to the applied arts: weaving, embroidery and wood-carving. Every house in Crete had its own loom.

The *village houses* of Crete were simply built: as simple as the souls of those who created them. The main features are the thick walls, made of the toughest stone, the relatively low height, the lime-washed plaster, and the arch which separates the two rooms and supports the roof with the help of medium-sized beams. There were two main advantages to structures of this kind: on the one hand, short beams were better able to withstand the weight of the earthen roof, and on the other the trees of Crete are generally short and longer beams would have been difficult to find. As further developments, such a house would acquire a courtyard with an outside oven and a stable, a separate sitting-room, a proper kitchen and an outhouse which might also have an upper floor. The houses of Chora Sfakion have an additional characteristic in the outside arch in front, which forms a kind of roofed courtyard before the door.

Inside, one would be struck by the relative lack of furniture: the main feature is the *'pezoula'*, a platform which doubled as sofa and bed. Furniture as such was confined to a proper sofa (in more 'luxurious' dwellings with a sitting-room), the *'portego'*, (from the Latin porticus, a colonnade), the table, the chest in which the bride's trousseau was kept, and a few chairs. There would also, of course, be the loom. However, these few pieces of furniture were often masterpieces of wood-carving, proof of the skills of the local craftsmen. Many of the kitchen utensils —spoons, salt-cellars, cups, etc.— were also carved in wood.

Around the year 1800 some of the merchant classes began to build houses in the neo-Classical style, assimilating the Cretan elements into an architecture of which examples can still be seen in the commercial quarters of Chania and Rethymno. Scattered throughout the island are a few examples of Venetian or Turkish architecture, reminders of another age.

The Cretan loom, which for centuries has been weaving the motifs of Cretan life and nature

The traditional *woven goods* of Crete are still in great demand today. They are seen as a living continuation of the ancient tradition, filtered through the Byzantine style of gold embroidery. Apart from being technically complex and difficult, these woven goods are remarkable for the decorative motifs they incorporate — for their embroidery, in other words, which is added by hand or with a thick needle when the cloth is still on the loom. The women of Crete used their weaving to depict the nature among which they lived, with its strong colours (red and black predominate), its fascinating variety and its brilliant light, and also to show life in all its manifestations. Their innate taste had only one competitor: nature itself. Over the ages, patterns going as far back as Minoan times (such as lilies and geometrical shapes) were brought into the tradition and were used long before the murals of the palaces were rediscovered. These traditional themes were handed down from one generation to the next, as were the motifs with scenes of everyday life. The figures and shapes we see are those of a quiet, peaceful life, but there are also occasionally themes which were embroidered in pain and anguish:

revolution and cruel war often caused upheaval in life in Crete.

Today, the old looms can sometimes be seen standing next to their modern successors. From the shearing of the sheep to the making of wool, weaving in its traditional form employed all the family. Even today there are weavers who make their own natural dyes for the wool they use. Wool and cotton are the usual materials, and although silk was often woven in Venetian times it is much less common today.

— *An embroidered hem from a bridal blouse*

— *A Cretan sofa, decorated with embroidered covers and cushions*

— *Embroidery around the fire was an integral part of everyday life*

— *A piece of embroidery with a motif from a bridal procession*

The woven goods of Crete stand out for their vitality and expressiveness. Nowhere else will one find this tireless attention to detail and the filling in of empty spaces with traditional and modern motifs. There are countless items made in this style: blankets, rugs, covers, bags, bedcovers, skirts, capes, table-cloths, curtains and towels. Apart from incorporation into the woven goods, lace and embroidery is also made for purely decorative purposes in the house and as part of women's dress.

*"When the Cretan man gets dressed up
And puts on his best clothes,
All the world is pleased to see
How brave and manly he is".*

The *Cretan male dress* is as brave and manly as the dances performed wearing it, and it varies little from one end of the island to the other. There are two costumes: the simple one, for everyday wear, and the formal version. The simple costume consists of the 'vraka' (loose trousers) in blue or black linen cloth, a sleeveless waistcoat, a shirt with black sleeves and a broad belt of maroon cloth which is wound many times round the waist and can be up to 10 metres in length. The costume is accompanied by long leather boots ('stivania') and on the head a black linen kerchief with bobbles.

In the formal version of the costume, the vraka is pleated, the waistcoat is of felt and is specially embroidered, and the belt is silken. The whole costume is supplemented with a felt cape with a hood, lined in brightly embroidered silk. The stivania are white, the socks knitted and decorated and the black kerchief on the head is silken and keeps its bobbles.

The female costume is also found in two types: that of the towns and that of the mountain areas, of which the costume from the village of Anoyeia has come to be the most widely-worn. The town costume consists of a wide red skirt and the 'meidani', a kind of long-sleeved jacket, a variation on which is the embroidered jacket without sleeves which allows the silk blouse underneath, with its broad sleeves and silver belt, to show. The women wear high-heeled slippers or white stivania, and attractive veils in light or dark-coloured silk over the face. Jewellery is worn, with coins strung round the neck as a favourite decoration.

The way in which the brides of Anoyeia are dressed is of particular interest and charm. Across the forehead is placed the *'zoyia'*, a gold chain with gold coins hanging from it. On the crown of the head is the *'kapasti'*, a kind of wreath with gold braid. The blouse is white, of pure silk, with wide sleeves. An ornamental vraka is worn, and above it a skirt interwoven with gold thread caught at the waist with a silken belt; into this is stuck a little silver knife, a gift from the bridegroom. The stockings are knitted in white and embroidered, and shiny black shoes are worn. On the breast are pinned numerous brooches.

The making of pottery has been of particular importance in the Cretan tradition since ancient times. Among the triumphs of this art are the huge storage jars, whose capacity ranges between 128 and 500 kilos. These are famous for their design and their firing: the balanced mixing of the three kinds of clay (white, black and red) enables them to withstand the very high temperatures of the firing process without any danger of breaking. The village of Thrapsano, near Herakleio, is the centre of the jar-making trade.

Other pottery centres of importance are Margarites, in the Prefecture of Rethymno, and Kentri near Ierapetra, which is known throughout eastern Crete for its water-jugs. The ceramics workshops of the island also turn out fine flowerpots, jugs, cooking pots and other clay household utensils.

Cretan women do not forget their traditions

Basket-weaving is very much part of agricultural life; the main purpose of its products is to transport the farm produce of the island, but nonetheless it has developed into a real art. Different kinds of baskets are used for harvesting olives, grapes and vegetables, while for longer distances there are the large *'kofinia'*, which are made from reeds or the shoots of the willow or other trees.

Cretan folk art also extends into other areas: the making of *gold and silver jewellery*, for example, and the *making of knives*.

Even in Minoan times, knives were an important part of the Cretan costume. The constant invasions which followed increased the need for people to go around armed, but as the centuries passed knives ceased to be only weapons and were incorporated into the local costume as an essential element. Thus, the formal costume includes a knife with a silver handle and a silver sheath, to which coins are usually attached. The knife for everyday use is simpler, with a black handle and wooden or leather sheath. A mantinada is usually carved on the blade:

"Black-sheathed knife
With your silver carvings,
I'll wear you in my belt
For my whole life".

A Cretan knife, large or small and with or without artistic value, is a good souvenir of the island and tells us something about the Cretan soul.

Basket-weavers, wood-carvers and
saddlers are still to be found in Crete

*"The mountains make shepherds
And the wine makes drunks;
The school turns out educated men
And the lyre men who enjoy life".*

The *lyre-player* is an inseparable part of any group of Cretans, whether in joyful or sorrowful mood. Without a lyre-player, there can be no festivities, and no company of friends is really complete. He is the conveyor of the musical traditions of Crete.

The *traditional music* of Crete is one of the most interesting elements in the folklore and art of the island. It has a very marked individual character and great variety. The basic categories into which it is divided are dance music and music to be sung to. Its roots lie far back in the centuries; perhaps even in ancient Greece, the Greece of the Kouretes and their dance, the pyrrichios. There are certainly Byzantine influences in it, and at later dates the music of the whole Mediterranean had an impact. Even as far back as the 2nd century AD, shortly before the Byzantine era, we hear of a famous Cretan composer called Mesodemos.

The group of traditional instruments which accompany the dance or the song is dominated by the *Cretan lyre*, which can convey the spirit of Cretan music better than any other instrument.

It is made of wood, has three strings and is played with a short and slightly curved bow. In recent years, the traditional bow has often been replaced with a violin bow. The lyre-player rests the instrument on his left knee, holds it in his left hand and, with his fingers on the strings, plays and sings. His songs will often be familiar to all, but just as frequently he will improvise. Some of these lyre-players are very talented; they have to be singers as well as instrumentalists, and poets as too.

The lyre is accompanied by the eight-stringed lute or 'pasadoros', which is the forefather of the modern bouzouki and is played in much the same manner as a guitar. Among other instruments is the *'outi'*, another type of lute, the *'askobadoura'*, which is rather like the bagpipes, and the *'hambioli'*, a wind instrument played by shepherds on its own or as part of the askobadoura.

The *songs* of Crete express the proud soul of the Cretan people in a simple, austere manner. They are tightly structured and highly poetic, with great imagination and a richly poetic vocabulary. These songs fall into three categories: historical songs, mantinades and rizitika.

The *historical songs* tell of the wars and sufferings of the Cretans. They are detailed accounts of the rebellions which, under the Arabs, the Venetians and the Turks, could not be set down in written form. The people made them into songs which were passed down from generation to generation, just like the epics of Homer, to our own times. The historical songs are subdivided into narratives and dirges. They contain material of the greatest literary value and are sung cyclically: that is, the first singer produces a verse, which is then repeated by the others.

The lyre player is accompanied by the 'pasadoros' with his lute

The *mantinades* are rhyming couplets of fifteen-syllable lines. They are sung to simple old tunes, to the accompaniment of the lyre or a larger group of instruments, or without any accompaniment at all, because what is of importance here is the words. The lyrics of these songs are improvised, and there can be exciting battles between the *'rhymers'* as they try to outdo each other in skill and wit. These competitions, which often take place at weddings, christenings and other social events, are followed with intense interest by all those present. When the pentozalis, in particular, is being danced, the mantinades fly back and forth across the room as one singer answers the other and the song and dance are taken as an opportunity to reveal the erotic foibles of those present. The mantinada is to be found only in Crete, where it was born out of the need of the people to find a way to work out the everyday problems and issues of life. It is simple, human, true and emotional, exrpessing the philosophical thoughts of ordinary folk:

"This world
Is like a well;
When one bucket fills,
Its neighbour empties".

The mantinada sings of the passions, dreams and hopes of the people, and, of course, of love. Perhaps the mantinada love songs are finest of all:

"I'm not asking you to love me;
Love cannot be asked.
It comes to birth by itself
Is the secret places of the heart".

A mantinada sung throughout Crete has truths to tell about human suffering:

"You've built your nest too high
And the branch will bend,
And the bird will escape,
Leaving you only the pain."

The ancient custom of *mourning the dead*, exclusively a female affair, continued for many centuries in Crete. As described by foreign travellers, it must have been an awe-inspiring and unimaginable sight. When a death occurred, the women gathered and as soon as dawn broke they would begin to screech, to beat their breasts, to gouge their cheeks with their nails and to tear their hair; a shattering sight to anyone who saw them. However, in the 14th century the Venetians forbade this Greek custom in all their possessions (Crete, Corfu, Zakynthos, etc.) and perhaps this is why such an emotionally-charged custom gradually died out.

Cretans regard death as a disaster which provokes pain and grief. Although they know that the end of life is inevitable, they do not wait passively and fatalistically for it to come. As throughout their lives, they strive to keep death away, even though they know the fight is in vain.

"Death has put me to sleep
Among the roses,
And neither tears nor dirges
Can wake me".

A picture of the Cretan philosophy in the face of death is to be found in Kazantzakis' *Captain Michalis*, in which there is a scene where the brothers of the dead man drink raki and dance by his death-bed on the night of the wake.

Also to be found in the mantinades is the humour of the people of Crete: nothing which happens in life escapes comment, ironic or mocking, and the result is amusing but also good-humoured:

"Anyone who doesn't enjoy life
Would be better off dead;
In this world, all he's doing
It taking up space".

The *rizitika* songs used to be sung only in western Crete, and particularly in the mountain villages among the foothills ('rizes') of the White Mountains and Psiloritis, from which they took their name. These are songs with many verses and no rhyme. Their themes are manliness, love, nature, hospitality, and love of freedom:

"On a high mountain
At the bottom of a crag,
Sits an eagle
In the rain and snow,
Poor creature,
Watching
the sun Rise".

The rizitika songs of Crete are the creations of an indomitable and proud people. They are not the products of a momentary creative urge, as is the case with the mantinades, but songs which endure. Their composition, in terms of content and also of technique, is a centuries-long process, and there are very ancient elements to be discerned in them. Above all, they bear resemblances to the songs of the border guards of the Byzantine Empire. They are subdivided into *table songs* (which are sung during and after meals) and *road songs*, which have a much longer drawn-out, dragging rhythm to accompany a group of friends travelling.

The mantinades and rizitika songs are interesting specimens of the *Cretan dialect*. It is not only in pronunciation that Crete differs from the rest of Greece. The Cretan dialect has a very rich vocabulary which, among other features, contains more Byzantine words than any other dialect of Greece, a reminder that this island had very close links with Byzantium. It should not be forgotten that when the rest of Constantinople, capital of

Erotokritos and Arethusa in a painting by the naif artist Theofilos

In the three theatrical works by *Yeorgios Hortatzis* of Rethymno, who had studied in Padua, we can see how well the author knew the dialect of his island. Hortatzis, a far from negligible dramatist, had successes with his plays and revived the theatre in Crete. Other plays were produced by authors whose names have not survived. Two comedies written shortly before the fall of Herakleio to the Turks have come down to us in manuscript.

The most important figure on the poetic scene of the time, and one of the best-loved Greek authors, was *Vincenzo Kornaros* (17th century). His epic entitled *Erotocritos* is still sung and recited everywhere today. All we know of his life is that he was from Siteia and that he probably lived in Candia (Herakleio). His work dates from the final period of Venetian rule, between 1600 and 1660.

The epic tells of the love of Erotokritos for the princess Aretousa, daughter of the local ruler. The plot unfolds at an unspecified time, as in a fairy-tale. Love is the central theme which inspired the poet, but it is intertwined with adventure. The whole imaginary story is made more credible by plenty of realistic detail.

Byzantium, had fallen into Turkish hands, the Cretan soldiers in the Tower of Vasileios, Leon and Alexios were still fighting on. In recognition of their bravery, they were given free passage out of the city under the flag of the defeated Empire, with its double-headed eagle.

The language of Crete developed in a different manner to that of the rest of Greece. In the *literature* of the late 16th century we can see Greek being constantly enriched with words from the Cretan dialect, which made a triumphant entry into poetry at this time. The influence of the Italian literature of the time was of decisive importance in the selection of literary genres and models. The theatre, too, was revived under Venetian influence after an interruption of some two hundred years.

Under the Turks, poetry survived thanks to the people of Crete, who kept the works they liked best deep in their memories and passed them down orally from generation to generation. One example of the way tradition lived on was the shepherd Pantzalios, who produced a Cretan epic of a thousand lines on the subject of the rising of 1770; the work was not printed until 1947, under the title *"The Song of Daskaloyannis"*.

Cretan literature became world-famous after the Second World War with the work of *Nikos Kazantzakis* (1883-1957). This writer's books gained particular fame in Europe and America as a result of his *Alexis Zorbas*, which, filmed as *Zorba the Greek*, was a worldwide success. Many of his novels (such as *Captain Michalis*, or *Liberty or Death*) take the struggles of the Cretans against the Turks as their theme. In Greece he is best-known for other works, such as his monumental translation of the *Odyssey*, his verse drama and his travel books. Kazantzakis also produced good Greek translations of masterpieces of world literature, (Dante, Nietzsche, etc.).

Pantelis Prevelakis, born in Rethymno in 1909, was for many years overshadowed by the figure of Kazantzakis. In his novel *The Tale of a Town*, written in 1938, Prevelakis developed a personal narrative style in which the past of the town where he was born is bound up with its present.

The Italian influence on the arts in Crete during the period of Venetian rule was not confined to literature. It also had an impact on *painting*: Cretan painting consists of religious subjects recorded in portable icons and wall-paintings in the 850 or so churches of the island (approximately 300 are still in good condition). The wall-paintings were produced by the fresco method. We have records that in the period 1527-1630 there were some 125 painters in Candia (Herakleio).

The most famous icon-painters were Theophanes (1535, a Cretan monk and painter who founded the Cretan School of painting in the 16th century; he initially worked in Herakleio but moved as far as Mount Athos, where he painted the churches of the Megiste Lavra and Stavronikita Monasteries, and Meteora, where his work can be seen in the St Nicholas 'Anapafsas' Monastery), Zorzis (1544), Antonios (1545), Damaskinos (1520) and Tzanes (1615). Their basic themes were, of course, orientated towards the traditional Byzantine subjects, but they also adopted a host of expressive details from the West and particularly from the Italian artists, whose work they had seen. The natural rendering of the human figure, the sharp contrasts between light and shadow, the tragic expressions and the expressiveness of the faces of their figures were all taken from the West. This new trend in Byzantine painting came to be called the *Cretan School*.

The spread of the reputation of the Cretan School and of its works themselves was assisted by the commercial power of the Venetians, which was then at its height in the eastern Mediterranean. The portable icons became so valuable that their painters were able to sign simply "of Crete". Today, works by painters of the Cretan School can be seen in museums all over the world; the Ecclesiastical Museum in Herakleio has some excellent examples.

With El Greco (Domenico Theotokopoulos), Cretan icon-painting found its link to European art. El Greco was born in 1541 in Crete (perhaps at Fodele, near Herakleio), and learned his trade in Candia. At the age of 25 he emigrated to Venice and later moved to Spain, where he was to create the paintings which made him world-famous.

*"The Adoration of the Magi", by Michail Damaskinos (16th century),
a typical work by this artist, who is one of the principal representatives of the Cretan
School (Herakleio, collection of the St Catherine of Sinai church)*

Icons are an inseparable part of the Greek Orthodox religion, and as a result they are still painted today in the traditional manner. In his *"Tale of a Town"* Pantelis Prevelakis, who was for many years a teacher at the School of Fine Arts in Athens, has this to day about icon-painting in Crete today:

"The Christian painter is little different from the monk, even if he does live in towns and even if he does have dealings with the world. As the monk kneels to pray to God, so the icon-painter sits down on his stool and picks up his brushes to paint. His work is a prayer too, although rather than murmuring the words he paints them. Thus he must be pure in heart, his tongue must be free of vulgar words and his hands must be clean. Before touching his brushes and his paints, he must prepare: he must fast, he must read the brief life of the saint whose story he will be illustrating, and he must enter into the life and martyrdom of that saint. His soul must be clear as crystal, and only then will Divine Grace descend on him and the holy icon will flow from his brush. Here, the painter does not boast of his work, and he must not insert into it anything from his own things or the cares of his life, as other painters do. Here the icon is the gift of God, and the painter is the conduit of his spirit".

Perhaps it is surprising that icon-painting has revived during the 20th century, reproducing the old-established models with absolute accuracy, particularly when we remember that such painters have to subject their art to very strict rules. None of the elements which have emerged during the evolution of art in the 20th century are of any interest to the icon-painter. The anxiety of personal expression, the search for new kinds of symbolism and the contant renewal of style mean nothing to him. Western visitors, then, should not be surprised if, at first, they feel very foreign when they see these works.

One of the features of Crete is the large number of painters who have never studied art. They are often called 'folk painters', but this term hardly suffices to describe their work. Among the most notable practitioners of 'folk art' are *Alkiviadis Skoulas* of Anoyeia and *Antonis Markakis* of Tymbaki, who works as a custodian at the Ayia Triada archaeological site.

The wood-carving in churches developed in a manner similar to the painting of icons. There are some excellent carved screens: real masterpieces. Among the decorative motifs used in these screens is that of the vine with grapes. An exhaustive listing of these screens is impossible here, but we could mention those of the Asomaton Church in Rethymno, of the churches at Kato Chorio (Ierapetra) and Myrsini and Mouliana (Siteia), as well as that of the Toplou Monastery.

The carved wooden screen of the little church of St Minas, Heraklei

THE PREFECTURE OF CHANIA

The Prefecture of Chania occupies the westernmost section of the island and has an area of 2,375 km². Of this, 1,476 km² is mountainous country where wild hills are crossed by magnificent gorges. The vegetation is dense, consisting principally of holm oak, pines and chestnuts, and the sweet scent of the orange groves fills the air in spring. The steep mountain cliffs plunge down to superb beaches (Ayia Roumeli, Chrysoskalitissa, Sfakia).

Map of the Prefecture of Chania with place names including:

Akr. Spátha, Zoungrí 370m, Oiktýlo, Akr. Xironíssi, Mourí 747m, Rodopoú, Onithás 748m, N. GRAMVOUSSA, AGRIA GRAMVOUSSA, Akr. Voúxa, Xcrygi 225m, Gerąskinou 762m, KOLPOS KISSAMOU, Peloponnissos, Spitákious Rodí 646m, Afráta, Rodopoú, Astrátigos, Gonìàs, Kolympári, Áspra Nerá, Ravdoúha, Kamará, Koufós, Skoutelónas, KOLPOS, Tavronítis, Máleme, Paleó Geráni, Plataniá, Falássarna, Akr. Koútri, Azográs, Kalivianí, Néo Choríó, Trachilos, Nopigia, Kallidónia, Nohiá, Plakáliona, Méllssourgio, Sfiliá, Marathokefála, Kamisiana, Gerákiana, Youves, Xamoudohóri, Agia Marli, Kastélli, Piperiana, Agios Geórgios, Koléni, Drapanià, Polemári, Módi, Kladó, Loutráki, Vrísses, Patellári, Gramvoussa, Metóhi, Kalleriana, Vassilópoulo, Dìkona, Kalihéa, Sirli, Kiparissos, Xirokámbi, Kakoudiana, Paleokastro, Kotsianá, Faleliana, Ano Vouves, Horafákia, Mathiana, Psathógiannos, Plátanos, Fterolakka, Galóvaros, Rokká, Agios Andónios, Gardiomouri, Zounáki, Zaharianá, Maredianà, Pervolákia, Koukouthiana, Koufós, Gavranou, Akr. Kórukas, Loussakiés, Horéftiana, Sakopigádi, Kría Vríssi, Pigí, Néo Chorió, Manolìópoulo, Apothíkes, Aliki, Polyrrinia, Tsikliaria, Deliana, Katouros, Skonízo, Vatólakkos, Koukounara, Alikiannis, Zimbrágos, Kato Kefála, Vouigáro, Mouri, Kaídari, Fotokáko, Derés, Topólia, Kóilianá, Maláthiros, Ano Kefála, Sirikari, Sinenianá, Néara Essiana 1649m, Platáni, Pappadiana, Skineso, Agia Sofía, Kakopetro, Platániani, Hiarò, Sfinári, Ano Sfinari, Melissiá, Sássalos, Messávlia, Palea Roumáta, Katziana, Langós, Askordalós, Koutsomatádos, Kondoudiana, Kehrés, Mihaliana, Nea Roumáta, Orthoúni, Kares, Karános, Kámbos, Berpathiana, Plagia, Vlatos, Rógdia, Vavouledo, Hosti, Kourtaliს 107m, Aerinos, Flória, Sémbronas, Prassés, Kefáli, Amigdalokefáli, Louhi, Limni, Strovles, Spina, Pappadiana, Perivólia, Aligi, Apópladi 133m, Agia Irini, Omalós, Profitis Ilias 631m, Pigkaminá, Agios Díkeos 1182m, Dris, Vólos, Tirília, Elos, Ramhi Lakkos 1004m, Moustako, Vothlana, Kopeti, Trańiálakkos, Kándanos, Anissaraki, Skafi, Epanohóri, Tourli 1458m, Chrissoskalitissas, Sklavopoúla, Chóndros, Amohdiko, Grigoriana, Plemeniana, Kavalleriana, Argasteri, Prínes, Tsiskiana, Kalamias, Stavros, Vamvakádes, Pera Skafi, Kambanós, Languadás, Platánios, Barakina, Kakodiki, Kaniskádes, Maralia, Psiláfi, Maniatiana, Voutás, Agios Pávlos, Strati, Temenía, Maza, Rodováni, Maráilia, N. ELAFONISSI, Azogirés, Agii Theódori, Vlithiás, Kádros, Glímata 773m, Pappadiana, Elyros, Koustogeráko, Livadás, Obre 792m, Kalamos, Kondokinigi, Spaniakos, Asfendilés, Prodrómi, Agia Triáda, Anidrí, Vardu 561m, Lissós, Gialós, Akr. Kriós, Akr. Trachili, Paleochóra, Akr. Flomés, Soúgia, Akr. Tripiti, Akr. Kalotrividis

Inset map of Crete

In the north of the Prefecture is the large plain of Chania, protected on three sides by the White Mountains. In the fertile soil of this plain grow most of the Prefecture's 17 million olive trees, oranges in groves like forests and considerable numbers of vines.

Large hotels have been and are being constructed all over the Prefecture and the infrastructure for tourism is far enough developed to meet the requirements of even the most demanding visitors. By way of contrast to the archaeological interest of the other prefectures and particularly of Herakleio, Chania will compensate visitors more with its natural beauties and the magnificent variety of its landscapes. Nonetheless, there are archaeological sites, consisting mostly of Venetian and Byzantine monuments, and a number of historic villages.

Public transport within the Prefecture is served by the KTEL buses, while caiques ply between the villages of the south coast and sail out to the islet of Gavdos, the most southerly point in Europe. Chania airport, at Akrotiri (15 km from the city) has a shuttle service to Athens and daily flights to Thessaloniki. Suda Bay, Greece's largest natural harbour, is the departure point for the daily sailings to Piraeus. There are also less frequent sailings from Kastelli Kissamou to Monemvasia, Neapoli, and Yitheio in the Peloponnese, Ay. Pelagia and Kapsali on Kythera, Antikythera and elsewhere.

The Town of Chania

Chania is the second-largest town in Crete, after Herakleio, and it has a population of some 60,000. It is the capital of the Prefecture of the same name and is its commercial and administrative centre. During the period of Cretan autonomy and in the first period of union with Greece, Chania was the capital of the whole island.

Chania consists of the Old Town and the New Town, which blend harmoniously into an attractive, warm and friendly entity. There are old Venetian buildings —many of them now superbly restored— to take one backe to the magic and glamour of an earlier age.

The Old Town is surrounded by the fine Venetian walls, dating from the 15th century, a typical example of Venetian architecture. The nar-

row, labyrinthine alleys with their Venetian buildings —interrupted by occasional Turkish structures— suggest something of the conquerors who came this way.

The old inner harbour, with its long Venetian pier and its lighthouse, is a reminder that Chania was once an important commercial port.

Today, the old harbour is unable to meet modern requirements and shipping takes place via Souda harbour.

The New Town lies around the Old, and is divided into many different quarters.

This is a modern but attractive city; the streets are comfortably wide and the city is well tree-lined and every house has its garden; in the suburbs, flowers are even more predominant. It is with justice that Chania has been called 'city of the flowers'.

Plan of the Town of Chania

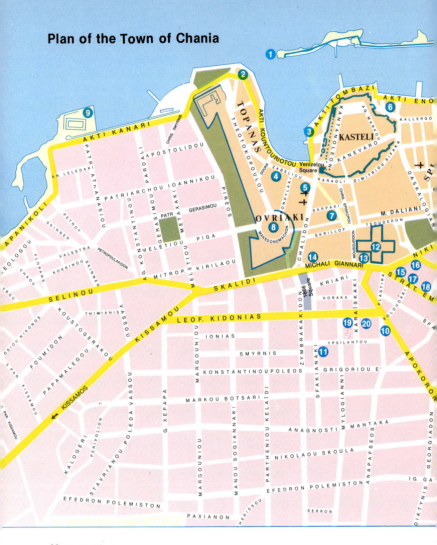

Key to the map

1. Lighthouse
2. Firkas - Maritime Museum
3. E.O.T. (Nat. Tourist Organisation)
4. Venetian Loggia
5. Archaelogical Museum
6. Customs House
7. The Cathedral
8. Chiavo Bastion
9. The Naval Club
10. Buses to Akrotiri
11. Bus Station for Rethymno, Herakleio, Samaria, Kasteli, Palaiochora
12. Municipal Market
13. Buses to Souda Port
14. Ionian Bank
15. National Bank
16. Bank of Greece
17. Post Office
18. O.T.E. (telephone company)

Chania stands on the site of the ancient city of Kydonia. According to the myths, the ancient city was built by Kydon, a grandson of Minos (or a son of Hermes), who was a protector of travellers: this perhaps explains the reputation of the local people for hospitality.

Archaeological investigations have shown that there was a Minoan settlement on this site. In the post-Minoan period, the powerful commercial town of Kydonia grew up in the same position and competed with the two other large cities of the period, Knossos and Gortyn. In 69 BC, Kydonia fell to the Romans and in 325 AD passed to the Byzantine Empire.

Under Byzantium, the history of Chania was much the same as that of the other Cretan cities: that is, it declined. In 823 it was taken by the Arabs, who gave it the name Chania.

Under the Venetians, it regained something of its former prosperity and power. In 1252, the Venetians began building the town they called 'La Canea' on Kastelli hill.

It acquired its first defensive wall around 1300, and the walls were extended in the 16th century to protect the new quarters of the growing city.

At about this time, the harbour was given a new breakwater and pier, but it was never able to because of the shallowness of the water and the vulnerability of the site to the north wind. Nonetheless, Chania flourished as a trading centre, and at one time was called the 'Venice of the East'.

19. Town Hall
20. Tourist Police
21. Stadium
22. Public Garden - Zoo
23. Olympic Airways Office & buses to the airport at Akrotiri
24. Historical Museum
25. Law Courts

Chania: the view from the castle

The new walls were unable to stop the advance of the Turks, and Chania became the first Cretan city to fall to them, in 1645, after a siege of 55 days. Remains of the Turkish period can be seen in the mosques with their minarets, the Turkish baths, and the latticed windows of many of the houses in the Old Town.

In 1850, Chania was declared capital of Crete. It retained this position throughout the period of Cretan autonomy (1898-1913) and even after union with Greece: in fact, Chania was the capital of Crete until 1972. In the period of autonomy, in particular, the city became very prosperous. It was the seat of the ambassadors from the Great Powers, of the High Commissioner and of the autonomous Cretan government.

The **Old Town**, with its narrow alleys and its Venetian and Turkish buildings, makes a good starting-point for our acquaintance with the city. The Old Town occupies an area about 700 metres square on the northern edge of Chania and a considerable portion of the Venetian wall has remained, with the bastions of Sciavo and San Salvatore.

Our tour begins in the district known *Splantzia*, at the end of Daliani St (behind and to the east of the Municipal Market, see the town plan). This is a typically Turkish neighbourhood, over which rises the minaret of the church of St Nicholas. In Venetian times, the church was a Dominican monastery, and colonnades with monks' cells have survived. We continue into the *Kastelli* district, where the Venetian aristocrats lived; some of their mansions have survived. At the end of the main street through this district is *Eleftheriou Venizelou Square,* which was once the centre of social and business life in Chania. The aristocracy gathered here to stroll, to drink coffee, to discuss politics and to arrange its social life. Where a hotel stands today there was, until the end of the 19th century, an establishment frequented by the officers of the Great Powers. Among the young ladies who ensured that the officers had no cause to complain of their treatment was the famous Madame Hortense, whom Nikos Kazantzakis brought to life most vividly in *Alexis Zorbas*. Later it was used as the Prefecture offices. Here, too, is the **Mosque of Hasan Pasha,** formerly used as a museum, and the *Tourist Pavilion.*

We continue along Koundourioti Quay, with its traditional shops, and enter the *Topana* district, which takes its name from the cannon ('topia') installed there by the Turks.

The end of the quay is overshadowed by the **Firka Fortress.** This castle, which consists of a group of buildings, was used by the Venetians as a place of incarceration for Greeks who had been condemned to death. Here the Greek flag was hoisted for the first time in 1913, in official recognition of unification with Greece.

The first building in the castle, which has been restored, houses the **Naval Museum.** The collection consists of nautical instruments, historical documents, models of ships and pictures showing the activities of the Greek Navy since 1821.

Among other sights in the Old Town are: the cathedral of Chania, known as the **Church of the Three Martyrs**, in Helidon St in the *Ovriaki* district; the church of *San Francesco*, the largest Venetian church in Crete, in the same street (it now houses the city's **Archaeological Museum**)). This is a fine Gothic building in the style of a basilica with columns.

The Archaeological Museum collection contains interesting finds from the vicinity of Chania and Western Crete in general, and covers the period from the Neolithic era to modern times.

Among the exhibits are vases, excellent mosaics, figurines, statues, old coins, tools and weapons, inscriptions in Linear B and pottery from Cyprus imported into Crete during the Late Minoan period. There are also interesting Roman finds, including statues and mosaics.

Looking from the Firka Fortress towards the old harbour with its Venetian lighthouse

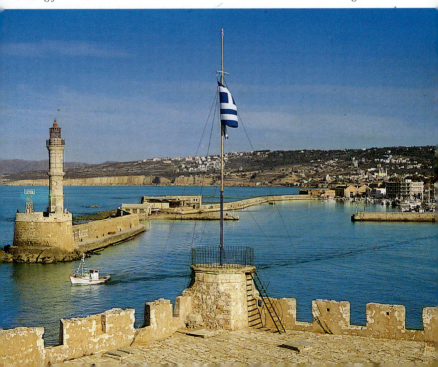

The east side of the old harbour, which is a continuation of Sintrivaniou Square

The Old Town is fronted by the *Venetian harbour* with its Egyptian lighthouse at the far end. The lighthouse was built by the Venetians in 1570, but in 1830, after a period in which it had been allowed to fall into disrepair, the Egyptians reconstructed it in its current form. Also near the harbour are the large vaulted chambers of the Venetian *shipyard,* where goods were stored and ships repaired. Of the 23 chambers, 7 have survived and are used as an exhibition centre today. To the east, the harbour ends at the impressive Venetian fortress.

The pretty cafes along the quay provide an opportunity to sit down; over one's refreshing drink, one's mind may drift back to an earlier age, when this place was the promenade of a bustling crowd of men and women in crinolines and frock coats.

The scene is constrantly changing at the harbour

The **New Town** lies around the old. The *Municipal Market*, in *Kotzabasi Square,* is a kind of link between the two. The Market was built in 1911 with the corresponding building in Marseilles as its model. It is cruciform, with four entrances; the roof is made of glass to provide lighting and the Market houses stalls and shops of all kinds. A stroll around, through the wealth of colours, aromas and sights, gives the visitor an idea of the wealth and variety of products which the island can turn out.

Close to the Market, to the right, is *1866 Square,* which is adorned with busts of the leaders of the armed bands who fought for the independence of Crete. In this vicinity is the *Nea Katastimata* district, which consists of new shops.

In Kydonias St, near the square, is the *Town Hall,* of impressive size and interesting architecture. The modern two-storey building occupies an entire city block and also houses the *Municipal Library.*

Also of interest is the pleasant *Municipal Garden*, laid out in 1870 under Reyuf Pasha along the lines of the European formal gardens of the day. A small zoo has recently been added to it. This is one of the city-dwellers' favourite places for calm and relaxation.

To the south of the Municipal Garden, at Sfakianaki St, is the **Historical and Folklore Museum**, housed in a fine neo-Classical building. The Museum has a large collection of exhibits showing the history of Crete, and also contains the **Archives of Crete**, often regarded as Greece's most important after the

Chania municipal market, built early in this century

The statue of Eleftherios Venizelos in front of his house at Halepa

General State Archives themselves. The archive collection was set up in 1920 and contains a wide range of other historic collections, the official correspondence relating to the Cretan rebellions, old documents and various other items from periods in the island's history. Here, too, is an important **Library** with 6,500 volumes including rare editions from Byzantine, Venetian and Turkish times and an extensive press archive with almost all the publications produced in Crete since 1831.

To the south east of the Municipal Garden, at the end of Sfakianaki St where it joins Dimokratias St, is *Dikastirion Square*, where fine neo-Classical buildings house the Courtrooms and the *Prefecture*.

The attractive and aristocratic suburb of **Halepa** is on the eastern edge of Chania, on the road towards Akrotiri. The suburb stands on a hill; during the period of Cretan autonomy, the administrative buildings were located here, together with the luxurious residences of the ambassadors and consuls. Among other residents were Prince George, the High Commissioner, and Eleftherios Venizelos. The neo-Classical Venizelos house, in the square of the same name which also contains the statesman's statue, is of interest. Note, too, the *church of Mary Magdalene*, built in a 'Russian-Byzantine' style in 1903 by the Grand Duchess Maria, sister of Prince George.

Chania is also a modern coastal town with a full range of tourist facilities. To the east and west of the town are good beaches with modern amenities, suitable for swimming and also for sea sports of all kinds. Chania is a very suitable place to base oneself for getting to know the whole island.

An interesting nearby place to visit is the village of **Mournies**, 4 km. from Chania. In the village is the house in which Venizelos was born; today it is a museum. Nearby is the famous *Koukounara villa*, a marvellous example of Venetian architecture, with fine gardens and fountains; the chief decorative motif is the winged lion of St Mark.

The village of **Theriso** is of considerable historical interest, as well as being a beautiful place. However, since its geographical position does not permit it to be included in our 4 routes in this part of the island, we present it separately as a short trip from Chania.

Chania - Theriso (16 km)

Theriso is a place of natural beauty which is also the starting-point for the ascent of the White Mountains. It was a landmark in the modern history of Crete.

We leave Chania in a westerly direction, towards Kisamos. At 1.3 km from the town we take the turning to the left (signposted). The road runs through extensive groves of fruit trees amid trees and bushes, which emit a vast variety of aromas and are brilliantly coloured.

The road runs through the impressive Theriso gorge, 6 km in length and quite deep. Two kilometres before the end of the ravine, at the spot known as Gaidouromori, is the **Kato Sarakina** or **Elliniko cave**. Finds from the Neolithic and Minoan periods testify to the use of the cave as a shrine.

We leave the gorge and enter a densely-vegetated plain across which we can see the village of **Theriso**.

The village stands among the foothills of the White Mountains, at an altitude of 500 metres. Walks are organised to the highest peak of the Mountains, Pachnes, at a height of 2,452 metres.

Standing as it does in a strong position on the foothills of the White Mountains, Theriso was able to take part in all the struggles of the Cretans for freedom.

Under Turkish rule, the local inhabitants were in an almost constant state of revolt and some fierce battles took place. In 1866 the village was burned by Mustafa Nahayile Pasha, and many of the villagers, including the mother of future Prime Minister Eleftherios Venizelos (the politician was then aged 2), were forced to take refuge in Kythera and the Peloponnese.

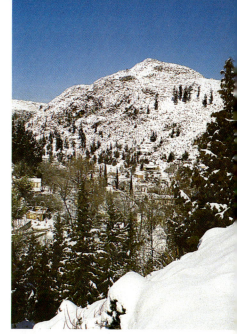

Theriso under snow

The village acquired its greatest historical importance during the period of Cretan autonomy, with the revolt organised by Eleftherios Venizelos against the appointment by the Great Powers of Prince George as High Commissioner. In 1905, Eleftherios Venizelos gathered his supporters there and proclaimed the outbreak of a revolution against the regime of Prince George, forcing him to resign and preparing the way for the union of Crete with Greece.

In the village, one can see the 'Headquarters', that is, the house which was used by Venizelos. It is a picturesque two-storey building with potted flowers and an outdoor oven in the courtyard. High up on the right-hand corner of the house is the following inscription:

"HEADQUARTERS
OF ELEFTHERIOS VENIZELOS
DURING THE THERISO
REVOLT, 1905".

ROUTE 1

Chania - Maleme
Tavronitis - Kandanos
Palaiochora - Gavdos
Souyia - Rodovani
Alikianos

The first route is our introduction to the Prefecture of Chania, crossing the island amidst a verdant landscape to reach the southernmost point in Europe, the islet of Gavdos. This itinerary provides an opportunity for sight-seeing with quiet beaches and short trips by caiques.

We leave Chania to the west, along Kisamou St.

2.5 km Ayii Apostoli: A coastal village. To the left of the road is the monument to the German paratroopers killed in the invasion of 1941. It is in the form of an eagle and is locally known as the 'Evil Bird'.

5.5 km: Turning, left, for **Daratso** and **Galatas**.

In 1645, the Turks made their camp here when preparing for their two months' siege of Chania. During World War II there was a particularly murderous battle, known as the 'Battle of the Giants', between Greek and New Zealand forces, on the one hand, and German paratroopers.

The surfaced coast road continues past the beaches of **Glaros, Kalamaki, Stalos** and Ayia Marina.

Stalos, to the west of Chania, is one of a series of fine beaches

These particularly attractive beaches have helped the area to develop, in recent years, into a modern tourist resort with large hotel units and complexes.

Close to the shore off Ayia Marina is the islet of **Ayii Theodori** or **Thodorou**. This is a National Park (landing is forbidden) where the Cretan ibex is bred. According to the ancient Greek myths, an enormous sea monster with its newborn offspring was swimming towards Crete when the sea-god Poseidon turned it into a rock to prevent it from swallowing up the whole island. The islet was important in history, too: This was the first heroic act of self-immolation in Cretan history, 200 years before the Arkadi monastery. It was the first point to be attacked by the Turks in 1645. The Venetian commander of the islet with 70 men, was forced to blow up it up, taking with him many Turkish troops.

11 km Platanias: A tourist resort on a little hill, with a panoramic view. The sandy beach is 3 km long and 39 metres broad.

16 km Maleme: Maleme used to be the site of Chania's aerodrome, and it was the first spot to be subjected to attack during the German airborne invasion of 1941. The fierce fighting between Allied and German forces has gone down in history as the Battle of Crete. The road to the left leads to a **German Cemetery**, where the remains of those who fell have been gathered.

On the side of the hill, at the spot known as Kafkales, a Late Minoan tholos tomb has been discovered. Although it had been robbed, it yielded two cylindrical seal-stones and depictions of wild goats running.

Today, this area is an important centre for tourism.

The beach of Ayia Marina, with organised facilities and the nearby islet of Thodorou

The German cemetery at Maleme

19 km Tavronitis: The village stands on the banks of the river of the same name. At the crossroads, we turn south for Palaiochora, while the other road continues west to Kasteli (see p. 93).

26 km Voukolies: This is a large village at an altitude of 110 metres on the west bank of the Tavronitis. It took its name from the 'voukoli' ('shepherds') who made up the bulk of the local population. The road continues south, passing through **Kakopetro**, where a turning to the left leads to the village of **Palaia Roumata**. Continuing along the main road, we cross a fertile plain where the little River Kandanos flows all the year round. The plain is covered with olive trees and chestnuts. Naturally enough, the landscape is verdant and the area rich in the production of grain, wine and other produce.

We now climb to the highest point on the route, the village of **Floria** at 580 metres. This village, with its panoramic view, is a cool and shady place to enjoy a cup of coffee or a glass of tsikoudia, the Cretan raki.

After Floria the road begins to run downhill, continuing in a southerly direction.

58 km Kandanos: This is the chief town of the Eparchy of Selinos, and it has a population of approximately 400. It stands on the site of ancient Cantanos, built in the 10th century BC after the Dorian invasion. In the Byzantine period, it was the seat of a bishop. The town has numerous interesting churches with wall-paintings dating from this period, such as those of St Kyriaki, the Archangel Michael, St Anne at Anisaraki, 2 km from the village, etc.

Under the Turks, Kandanos was a janissery post and the seat of the 'kaymakam', the local governor. It has its place in modern history, too: on 23 May 1941 the local inhabitants, almost unarmed, dispatched a number of Nazi troops, but two days later the occupying forces entered the village and razed it. They also installed a plaque, which can still be seen today. It reads: "This is the site of KANDANOS, which was destroyed in atonement for the murder of 25 Germans". The village was rebuilt after the War.

We leave Kandanos and continue south across a thickly-planted plain.

64 km Kakodiki: This is another village with a number of Byzantine churches, one of which has wall-paintings dating from 1387. There is a medicinal spring and the area produces large quantities of olive oil. We continue south, passing **Sarakina** at 66 km from Chania and **Vlithia** at 69 km. The latter village takes its name from a kind of wild radish found in the area. The road runs on to Palaiochora.

76 km Palaiochora: This is the southernmost town in the Prefecture of Chania, on the Libyan Sea. It has a population of 1,500, most of them former residents of Sfakia or Gavdos. The town straddles a peninsula on the southern end of which, in 1282, the Venetians built their Castelo Selino, which gave its name to the whole district. On the outside, the castle is quite well preserved.

Palaiochora has numerous churches and the ruins of buildings from both ancient and Roman times.

On both sides of the peninsula there are excellent beaches, with fine sand and stands of tamarisks. The fine climate, the long spells of sunshine and the high temperature of the sea make this spot ideal for winter swimmers. The western beach, with fine sand and plenty of shady trees, is

The Palaiochora peninsula, with its Venetian ca

marginally better. It is 2 km long.

There are more sandy coves to be found along the road to Yialos, at a distance of 7 km.

The beach on the eastern side of the peninsula has no fresh water; there are pebbles and it is less busy. Still further to the east there are more little coves with sand and pebbles.

Two boat trips are possible from Palaiochora. The first is to the little islet of Gavdos, and the other to the pretty coastal village of Souyia. Another caique route is to the islet of Elafonisi (see p. 98).

(see p. 98)

In Palaiochora we can also decide whether to return by the road along which we came or to continue to Souyia along Rodovani, and then turn north for Chania.

the east and a long beach to the west

The passage across to **Gavdos** is accomplished by caique. This islet is the most southerly inhabited extremity of Europe, lying 28 miles from Crete and approximately 150 from the shores of northern Africa. It is triangular in shape, with an area of 37 square kilometres. The 80 inhabitants are shared out between the four hamlets, Kastri (the 'capital'), Vatsiana, Ambelos and Karaves, a tiny harbour.

According to some, this is the mythial Ogygia, Calypso's island, where Homer says Odysseus was shipwrekecd. As evidence, the supporters of this theory point to the cave at Errikia, on the north-east cape of the island as the place where Calypso had her palace and kept Odysseus captive for seven whole years.

The ruined lighthouse on Gavdos

Souyia, with its long pebbly beach behind

The primitive and isolated nature of the island, together with its sandy beaches shaded by scattered cedars and bushes, attract numerous visitors each summer, when the quiet aspect of the island changes completely.

We return to Palaiochora. There are regular caique sailings from here to Souyia (70 km from Chania). The village stands on the site of ancient Syis, which was the port for ancient Elyros. There are some remains of walls, tombs, altars and an aqueduct. An Early Christian (6th century) basilica with painted mosaics has also been discovered, and there are churches with 13th century wall-paintings. Souyia was the birthplace of numerous Cretan military figures.

Today, Souyia is a quiet, pretty village with an excellent sandy beach, 1.5 km in length, where the swimming is very good.

We leave Souyia in a northerly direction. After passing **Moni** at 65 km from Chania, we come to the little upland village of **Rodovani** (60 km). Here there are outstanding wall-paintings. Nearby, on Kefala hill, are the remains of ancient Elyros. This was one of the most important Doric settlements in western Crete. It had Syis and Lessos as its outlets to the sea. Sections of wall have survived, together with the remains of the aqueduct, the theatre and other buildings. The city struck its own coins, and during the Byzantine period was the seat of a bishop. The city was destroyed by the Saracens in the 9th century.

From Rodovani, a turning to the left leads to **Temenia**, with a fine Byzantine church which has good wall-paintings. The track which leads straight on from here goes back to Palaiochora, and it could be used by those who would prefer to avoid the sea-voyage to Souyia.

We return to Rodovani and turn right (north). We pass the village of **Maralia** and, 53 km from Chania, come to **Kambanos**. This village stands in the western foothills of the White Mountains, half-hidden amongst forests of pine, cypress and lofty olive trees. It has a number of churches decorated with Byzantine icons.

46 km Epanochori: A pretty village with a panoramic view from the White Mountains to the Libyan Sea. Here the verdant gorge of Ayia Irini begins.

43 km Ayia Irini: A little village on the banks of the seasonal Ayia Irini river, which flows down to the sea at Souyia.

After Ayia Irini, a passable road 10 km in length crosses the White Mountains and leads up to Omalos; it is one of the three routes of access to the plateau.

31 km Prases: An upland village, at an altitude of 480 metres.

26 km Nea Roumata: Another upland village.

15 km Skines: A village in the midst of an enormous expanse of orange trees (100,000 of them). In the spring, there is a special orange festival here.

12 km Alikianos: A verdant village with many orange trees. There are ruins of the tower built by the Venetian nobleman Damolino and a 12th century Byzantine church with extremely interesting wall-paintings by Provatas.

From Alikianos, a turning to the left leads to the picturesque village of **Vatolakkos**, in a fertile area where there are many Byzantine churches.

Continuing along the main road, at 10 km from Chania we come to **Ayia**. The swamp here was used as a site for a rural prison. During the Occupation, the prison was used by the Germans and hundreds of Greeks lost their lives there.

The road returns us to Chania.

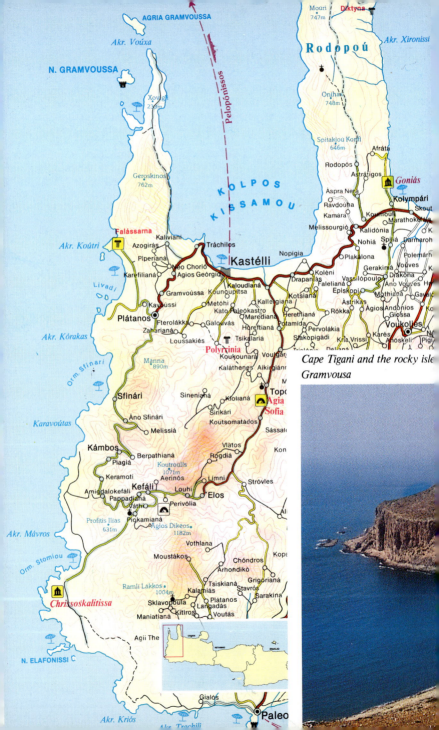

Cape Tigani and the rocky isle Gramvousa

ROUTE 2

Chania - Kolymbari
Kasteli - Falasarna
Chrysoskalitissa Convent
Elafonisos - Elos
Topolia Gorge

In this second route, we shall be touring the western side of the Prefecture, which is occupied by the sub-prefecture of Kisamos. We will start with visits to Kolymbari and the Gonia Monastery before going to the two north-westernmost extremities of the Prefecture, capes Rodopou and Gramvousa. We then cross the fertile plain of Kisamos and, after acquainting ourselves with the local capital, Kasteli, and ancient Phalasarna, reach the southernmost point of our route at the Chrysoskalitissa Monastery and Elafonisi.

Chrysoskalitissa Monastery

e Tigani and the rocky islet of Gramvousa

Kolymbari stands in a sheltered spot at the head of the Gulf of Chania

We leave Chania in a westerly direction, along (see route 1, p. 85) Kisamou St.

We cross the River Tavronitis and enter the Eparchy of Kisamos. Kisamos occupies the north western corner of Crete. Thanks to its abundant supplies of water, it is densely vegetated, with numerous olive groves and fine chestnut woods. This verdant landscape, the interesting caves and, above all, its excellent beaches, have made the area of considerable importance for the tourist trade.

19 km: In the village of Tavronitis, a turning to the left leads to the villages of Kantanos and Palaiochora.

23 km: A fork off the main road to the right leads to the coastal village of **Kolymbari**. The village stands among dense greenery at the head of the Gulf of Chania. It is a major wineproducing centre for Kisamos wine.

One kilometre to the north, on a fine site, stands the **Gonia Monastery**, a stavropegic foundation (one with special privileges granted by the Ecumenical Patriarchate of Constantinople). It has a domed main church with a narthex and chapels surrounded by a spacious courtyard. Around the courtyard are the cells of the monks, the abbot's quarters, the refectory and storehouses. The Monastery is devoted to Our Lady Hodeghitria and has its feast on 15 August.

The Gonia Monastery has an important collection of post-Byzantine icons, relics of the saints and other religious treasures. Numerous inscriptions are built into its walls. Today, it is the seat of the Orthodox Academy of Crete.

At 23 km from Chania along the main road, a turning left leads to the villages of **Marathokefala**, where there is the cave of St John the Stranger, **Spilia**, which has a church of Our

Lady with wall-paintings from the 14th c., **Drakonas**, with its 9th c. Byzantine church of St Stephen, and **Episkopi**, which has an impressive rotonda church dedicated to the Arch. Michael.

25 km: Turning, right. A surfaced road leads in 5 km to **Rodopou**, which was once one of the largest and most important villages in Eparchy of Kisamos. The road continues along the eastern edge of Cape Spatha, where there are the ruins of **Diktyna**, an ancient sanctuary and one of the most important centres for the worship of the Cretan goddess Diktyna.

Returning to the main road, we head south for Kasteli Kisamou. Soon we have a view of the coastal plain, with its myriad olive trees, and the town of Kasteli in the distance.

37 km Kaloudiana: A turning to the left leads to Topolia and Elafonisi. We head straight on.

A portable icon of St Nicholas (15th c.), from the Gonia Monastery of Kissamos, seat of the Orthodox Academy of Crete

42 Kasteli Kisamou: In antiquity, Kisamos was the most important maritime and commercial centre of western Crete. It was the port of ancient Polyrrhenia, but it was autonomous and minted its own coins which depict Hermes on one side and a dolphin on the other. The city reached the height of its importance under the Romans, as can be seen from the ruins of its acropolis, its theatre, its aqueduct and the statues which have been found. In early Byzantine times the seat of the local bishop was moved to the village Episkopi. The town took its name (which means 'little castle') from its Venetian fortress.

After being destroyed a number of times, the fortress was eventually rebuilt from the foundations up by the Turks. It contained barracks, a church and a prison. Whatever is still standing of the castle dates from this period.

Today, Kasteli is the chief town of the Eparchy of Kisamos and has a population of 2,800. It is a commercial centre, and the agricultural produce of the surrounding area is shipped out from its harbour. Wine and chestnuts are the most important products. There are ferry sevices from Kasteli to Yitheio in the Peloponnese.

Off the northern extremity of Cape Vouxa is the islet of Gramvousa with its Venetian castle, subsequently a lair of pirates. Gramvousa was an important place in the history of Crete under the Turks, acting as a base for Greek armed bands which organised attacks on the Turks.

We continue west from Kasteli, towards Phalasarna. The road runs downhill and, 53 km from Chania, we arrive at **Platanos**, a modern village with extensive cultivation of fruit an vegetables.

Kasteli Kissamou, famous for its wines

In Platanos we bear right. In the distance, to the right, we can see the fertile plain of Phalasarna, which runs down to one of the best beaches in Crete, with clear greenish-blue water and a sandy shore. The road to the beach is surfaced. At the end of the beach, one can see the steep, rocky hill on which ancient Phalasarna stood. The surfaced road ends here, but a track continues to the ancient acropolis. Near the beginning of this road is a throne cut into the rock. Where the track ends, at the western extremity of Cape Gramvousa, we can see the remains of the ancient city, the most westerly in Crete.

Phalasarna was built in historical times, was independent and autonomous and struck its own coins, which show a female head on one side and the letters 'PHA' on the other, framed by a trident.

Gramvousa: the Venetian castle

Sunset at Falasarna

Phalasarna was another of the ports of ancient Polyrrhenia. Its harbour was enclosed, meaning that it was walled in and that entry was effected through a narrow channel. Thenks to its safe harbour, impregnable castle and fertile plain, Phalasarna became an important commercial and maritime centre.

The city was entered from the sea side, and it was built on a number of levels, as can be seen from the surviving remnants of the walls, which were built using square untrimmed stones. There are also ruins of a temple of Artemis or Apollo, and even the foundations of houses can be seen.

Today, the harbour is 100 metres back from the coast and the channel is a cultivated field, for the level of the beach has risen (see the karstic phenomena, p. 7).

We return to the village of Platanos. The surfaced road continues south, towards the coastal fishing-village of **Sfinari**. At the south end of the village the road becomes a good track and crosses a fertile plain where the landscape is dominated by greenery, streams and plane trees. We pass through the village of **Kambos**, at an altitude of 340 metres, the largest village in the area. The village is full of arbutus trees and produces raki. At the village beach there is a pretty 13th century chapel to St Paraskevi.

The track continues in the direction of **Keramoti** and reaches **Kefali**, which is a point of intersection for a number of roads. We tern south for the village of **Vathi**. After Vathi the road becomes very poor, running south until, after a total of 73 km, it reaches the south coast at the **Chrysoskalitissa Convent**. The fortress-like convent is built high up on a steep cliff over a narrow bay, with a wonderful view south over the Libyan Sea. There are 90 steps up to the convent and, according to tradition, seven of them are gold, though sinners cannot see them. This is the origin of the name (which means Our Lady of the Golden Staircase).

The convent was built under Venetian rule, on the site formerly occupied by a monastery of St Nicholas. Another possible origin of the name is that it comes from an icon, of Our Lady preserved in the convent; the icon is more than 1,000 years old and is gilded and carved. The double-aisled main church is dedicated to the Dormition of the Virgin and to the Holy Trinity. Its feast day is on 15 August. The foundation was formerly inhabited by monks, but since 1940 it has been used by nuns. One kilometre from the convent there is a fine sandy beach, but access to it is quite difficult.

Continuing about 5 km south west from the convent, we come to the beautiful islet of **Elafonisi**, which is joined to the body of Crete by a shallow reef some 800 metres long. This is easy to cross when the weather is calm. The landscape is warm and welcoming, with brilliant white sand and the calm sea. There is no hint of the frightful waves which the south wind can whip up — some of the fiercest in the Mediterranean. Nor is there any reminder of the catastrophe of 24 April 1824, when, on Easter Sunday, the troops of Ibrahim slaughtered 40 Greek fighters and 600 women and children. Only a plaque on the summit of the island bears witness to their terrible end.

We return to Kefali and take the road in the opposite direction to that along which we came, for the valley of chestnut trees. At 57 km from Chania, we come to the chestnut-producing village of **Elos**, at an altitude of 560 metres, the highest on the return route. After a further 5 km, a turning to the right leads to the village of **Strovles**, immersed in greenery and with abundant streams and plane trees, and on to Kandanos.

The main road continues north. At 50 km from Chania we come to the village of **Karstomatado**, with its plane trees and wild olives, though which the **Topolia Gorge** runs. The wild and imposing ravine has walls which reach heights of 300 metres, with deep cavities in the rock. The road runs along the left-hand side of the gorge and passes through a tunnel. The gorge is 1,500 metres in length, and the drive through it is most striking.

Shortly before the end of the gorge, 2 km to the south of the village of Topolia, the cave of **St Sophia**, with a chapel, is to be found 80 metres above the road on a hill. This is one of the finest caves on Crete, with rows of tall stalagmites.

We leave the gorge and, at 46 km from Chania, reach the fertile village of Topolia in its densely-wooded valley. The village has numerous springs and thick vegetation. There are quite a number of Byzantine monuments in the area, as well as the double-aisled church of St Paraskevi.

The road continues north, through a number of attractive villages, including **Voulgaro** and **Potamida**.

We reach the main Chania-Kasteli road at the village of Kaloudiana, 37 km from Chania, and turn right to return to our starting-place.

The crossing to Elafonisi

ROUTE 3

Chania - Omalos Plateau
Samaria Gorge
Ayia Roumeli - Loutro
Chora Sfakion
Frangokastelo - Vryses

This route has not been chosen by us as a way of getting to know Crete, as is the case with the other itineraries. It has developed into a standard route organised by travel agencies in Greece and abroad. Indeed, there are many visitors who come to Crete purely and solely for the pleasure of this itinerary.

Here, the main section of the route is a 6-8 hour walk through most unusual scenery in the finest gorge in Europe (awarded the 1st Prize of the Council of Europe for landscapes throughout the continent, in 1980). However, the walk through the gorge, which starts at the Wooden Stair and, having marked the division between the main bulk of the White Mountains and the Volakia range, ends on the Libyan Sea, is not the route's only attraction. It also has swimming from incredible beaches and plenty of interesting visits to offer. The round trip can be done in one day —this is the way the travel agencies normally organise it— but for those who have more time, two or three could be filled with ease and just as much interest.

The drive from Chania to the **Wooden Stair (Xyloskalos)**, as the entrance to the gorge is called, is 43 km in length. Apart from the travel agencies, there are also regular bus services (KTEL). Those who intend to go down the gorge will find private transport useless, since the return journey cannot be done in one day; indeed, the climb up the gorge is extremely arduous and is recommended only for seasoned and fit walkers.

We leave Chania to the west, along the Omalos road. We pass first through the Keritis valley, a pleasant run through orange groves. At 12 km from Chania we pass a turning for Alikianos and Souyia.

The road continues through the lush landscape with its thousands of orange trees until we see **Fournes**, 15 km from Chania. Here the climb begins, as we snake up the side of the White Mountains. The route takes on a beauty of a different kind as the landscape changes entirely. Gone are the orange trees and their green and gold tranquillity; here the land is wild and imposing. At 24 km from Chania, we reach **Lakki**, a village of much historical importance for Crete. Thanks to its inaccessible position high up in the mountains, this settlement was able to play a leading part in all the island's struggles for independence and freedom.

We continue to the highest point on the route, 1,200 metres above sea level, which we reach at 39 km. Here we have a superb view of the Omalos plateau, ringed by mountains. The Omalos plateau, a legendary place of which many songs have been written, was for centuries the base of the fighters for the freedom of Crete, and many heroic pages in that struggle were written here.

When will the stars shine clear,
When will February come,
And I can take my musket,
Inheritance from my father,
And go up to Omalos,
To the Mousouri road,
And make mothers without sons,
Wives without husbands.   (rizitiko)

The Omalos plateau has a diameter of 4 km and three entrances: from Lakki, which at 1,047 metres is the

Omalos plateau

The Wooden Stair (Xiloskalos), entrance to Samaria Gorge

lowest point, from Ayia Irini and from Ayia Roumeli. Also here is the **Tzanis Cave**, the deepest in all Greece at 280 metres.

The road runs across the plateau, and after a further 5 km ends at **Xyloskalo**, the highest point (1,227 metres) and the entrance to the **Samaria Gorge**.

Before entering the gorge, we should perhaps know that it is the longest in Europe, at a total length of 18 km, though the path through it is only 14 km long. The width varies from 150 metres to 3 metres at its narrowest point, Portes ('Gates'). It has been declared a national park in an attempt to preserve its rare flora and fauna. Thanks to the wild and precipitous terrain, this is the only place in Crete where the native wild goat (agrimi or kri-kri) still lives. There are also many rare species of birds and all along the gorge there is a vast variety of herbs (including *Origanum dictamnus*, wild dittany)

and flowers. For that reason it is forbidden to hunt, to light fires, to pick flowers and herbs or even spend the night in the gorge. There are rangers all along the route and muleteers who, for a fee, are prepared to carry visitors for whom the walk has proved too much to the end of the route. Each visitor is issued with a ticket, for a minimal charge, when entering the gorge. This must be returned at the bottom so that the safe passage of all the day's visitors can be checked. In the winter, the gorge is impassable, and entrance is only permitted from May to October. The walk takes between six and eight hours, depending on one's walking abilities. Visitors should have with them strong shoes or boots and something to eat. There is no need to carry water, as there are frequent streams of cool, clear water. The time of sailing of the last boat from Ayia Roumeli, where the gorge ends, to Sfakia should also be ascertained.

The **Xyloskalos**, at the top end of the gorge, is a narrow path with a wooden parapet to facilitate and protect those descending. As one goes down the path, the predominant feeling is one of awe; tall mountains tower to the right and left, while the gorge, seemingly endless, stretches out in front. There are countless shades of green to be seen, and in the distance another high mountain looms.

The descent is four kilometres in length, and the landscape alternates plunging depths with *high trees, springs of running water, and enormous rocks* which look as if they are about to block the path.

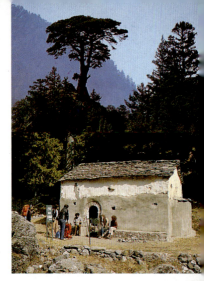

After about 30 minutes there is a slight change in the view, as we pass *the little chapel of St Nicholas, on our right, with tall cypresses, and two doors in the pronarthex.* Now we are at the bottom of the gorge, and mountains whose peaks are close to 2,000 metres tower all around.

At this point the path becomes flatter. Every so often, smaller gorges run into the main one. The gorge begins to open out and quite suddenly the water disappears underground.

Here, half-way along the gorge, is the village of Samaria, uninhabited today because the wood-cutters and shepherds who used to live here were moved elsewhere when the area became a national park. The 14th century Byzantine church which survives has numerous icons and wall-paintings. It is dedicated to the Blessed ('Osia') Maria of Egypt, whose name was gradually corrupted to Sia Maria and thence to Samaria, giving the area its name.

Samaria, with its springs, is ideal for a rest and a picnic. Now, in any case, we are halfway along the route.

Now the landscape changes. The gorge narrows, and the towering walls of rock come closer and closer. Shortly before the Gates, on the right, there is a little stream and a flat spot.

A little further along we come to the Gates themselves; a truly magnificent spectacle. The walls of the gorge are only three metres apart, towering to 600 metres on each sidde. And through the narrow opening the blue sea can be glimpsed in the distance. Now the path runs along a dry stream-bed, on round stones. Gradually it widens out again and we come to another deserted village, Ayia Roumeli. One further kilometre over the same stones brought down by the torrent in winter will bring us to the modern village of **Ayia Roumeli**.

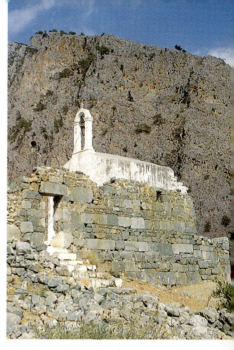

The deserted village of Ayia Roumeli, as seen from its castle

The exit from the gorge is another of its pleasures. A swim in the Libyan Sea is the ideal epilogue to a long walk; there is an excellent beach with coarse sand, black pebbles and a clear blue sea.

Ayia Roumeli is a modern settlement consisting of two sections, Apano (Upper) and Kato (Lower) Roumeli, built on the ruins of the ancient city of Tarra. This was a small but independent city known for its oracle and destroyed by earthquake in 66 AD.

It issued its own coins showing the head of a Cretan wild goat on one side and a bee on the other. A religious centre, Tarra had many temples to Apollo. It flourished during the Roman period, as witnessed by the numerous 4th and 5th century BC tombs and considerable amounts of jewellery found here. When the Romans discovered that the city had a temple to Britomartis, protector of flocks, they rededicated it to Romelia, their equivalent goddess, and when Christianity arrived it adopted the pagan goddess and turned her into St (Ayia) Roumeli. This ancient temple is now the Byzantine church of Our Lady, of which only the rounded part is open today.

Communications between Ayia Roumeli and the rest of Crete take the form of little boats. There are frequent sailings in the summer, either west to Souyia and Palaiochora (see Route 1, p. 91) or, more frequently, east to Loutro and Chora Sfakia.

The voyage to Sfakia is most

As we leave the gorge, Ayia Roumeli lies at our feet

impressive, with the mountains rising sheer out of the sea or forming little bays with tiny beaches, the haunt of nature-lovers. Shortly after leaving Ayia Roumeli, we see the little Byzantine church of **St Paul**. At the mouth of the little Aradaina gorge, is a idyllic spot, **Dialiskari** Beach.

In the next bay, at the neck of Cape Mouri, is the little village of **Loutro**, a pretty settlement on a tiny beach between steep cliffs. It stands on the site of the ancient city of Phenicas (Katopoli), and got its name from the baths (of which ruins can be seen) which supplied water to Anopolis. A narrow strip of land on the seaward side and a small island protect the village from the worst of stormy weather.

Our boat trip continues beneath the steep mountainside as far as Sfakia or, as it is usually known to-day, **Chora Sfakion**, where the boat moors in the small safe harbour. The village rises above us, nestling into the rock face. The houses, one above the other, are arranged amphitheatrically, with a superb view out over the Libyan Sea. Gavdos can be seen in the distance.

The landscape is wild, harsh and grand, dominated by the White Mountains. The whole area is criss-crossed by gorges, ravines, difficult passes and wild mountain peaks. Even the beaches are hard to get to, and boats find it difficult to moor there. The name betrays this feature of the terrain; it comes from the word 'sphax', which means 'chasm in the earth' — the land of gorges, that is.

The pretty village of Loutro can only be reached by sea

Thanks to this position and to the bravery of its inhabitants, Sfakia was never conquered by the Turks and always played a leading role in the fight for Cretan independence.

The wildness of the terrain also caused the Sfakiots to turn their backs on the land and devote themselves to the sea. During Turkish rule, they were the only Cretans who carried out sea transport and trade — and piracy as well, an occupation in which even the Turks had to admire their prowess. The dense forests of the mountains which surrounded their home provided the wood from which their ships were made. The wealth the Sfakiots accumulated in this manner can be seen in their mansions, some of which are well into their fourth century of life. They are fine stone-built one or two-storey houses, with enclosed courtyards where the dominant element is the outdoor oven, and small door and window openings. All these houses were burned and looted in the aftermath of the Daskaloyannis revolt of 1770 and again in 1821, on the the war of the independence. The locals came back, one by one, and repaired the houses again, but Sfakia never regained its economic position or the full glory of its buildings.

The difficulty of life in the mountains and in this harsh landscape can be seen in the faces and bodies of the Sfakiots — and in their personalities as well. Authentic descendants of the Dorians, they are tall and fair-haired, with eagle eyes and lithe bodies. The women of Sfakia, too, are among the island's most beautiful. Both sexes are celebrated by the popular muse:

Do you wish to see and enjoy
Handsome young men?
Strong and terrible young men
Like lions?

Chora Sfakion with its castle and its harbour, from which there are frequent cai

Then go to Frangokastello
And go to St Nikitas,
You'll see blond men,
Men with curly hair,
Handsome tall young men.
And you'll see pretty girls, as well,
Pretty as the pearls,
Girls with eyebrows like pencil lines
And pretty blonde ones too.

Restless and hard to tame by nature, the Sfakiots are a proud and self-obsessed breed who are inclined to believe that they are superior to Cretans from more milder areas, and that the laws do not apply to them. That is why it is not surprising to find that the custom of the vendetta (see p. 47) took even firmer root here than it did in the rest of the island. Whole villages have been laid waste by the vendetta, with some of the inhabitants being killed and the others fleeing to escape vengeance. Fortunately, the

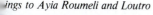
...ings to Ayia Roumeli and Loutro

custom is beginning to die out today.

The Sfakiots are much attached to their primitive habits and customs. Even their speech retains many traces of its Doric origin. They are very superstitious, as perhaps is natural in a place whose landscape, with its caves and ravines, is easy to associate with demons and fairies. At the same time, however, they are very pious and extremely hospitable; it is a social obligation to treat strangers, and any refusal to accept will be taken as an insult.

A walk around the cobbled streets of Chora Sfakion will reveal the daily life of these people, unaltered down so many centuries. In the multi-coloured throngs of summer visitors, **the traditional costumes of the Sfakiots and their proud deportment still stand out. They stand like ancient kouroi, bringing other memories to mind** and making the thoughtful visitor wonder whether and for how long they will be able to resist the 'polish' of civilisation.

111

From Sfakia, we can return directly to Chania — there are frequent connentions by bus. At the same time, there are two trips to the made in the vicinity: to the upland village of Anopolis and to Aradaina, which was once inaccessible, and to the imposing historic castle of Frangokastelo.

From Sfakia we turn west and then north, where a passable road leads 12 km to **Anopolis**. This village stands on the site of an ancient city of the same name, on a small but fertile plateau, half-hidden among vines and dense greenery.

In antiquity, there were two cities, Anopolis and Katopolis, which was better known as Phoenicas and stood on the site occupied today by Loutro.

Ancient Anopolis was an independent city, and issued its own coinage. It flourished in Byzantine times, as can be seen from the large number of churches which were built in Anopolis then, with fine wall-paintings.

As part of the Eparchy of Sfakia, it shared the fate of Chora Sfakion during the period of Turkish rule. Ioannis Vlachos, known as Daskaloyannis, was born here. As early as 1770, he envisaged a free Crete, but the revolt which he initiated was drowned in blood and he himself came to a terrible end.

Today, it is a picturesque upland village with a healthy climate. The inhabitants are mostly employed in stock-breeding.

Between the Anopolis plateau and the Aradaina plateau lies the imposing **Aradaina gorge**. This starts in the foothills of the White Mountains and ends 7 km later at Dialiskari beach. *The two plateaus have recently been linked by a steel bridge built across the awe-inspiring gorge.*

We return to Sfakia, from which we head north in the direction of Chania.

At the crossroads, we turn right for the village of **Komitades**, which is heavily planted with olive trees, and continue for Frangokastelo.

Frangokastelo stands on a large bare plain. This Venetian fortress has survived in excellent condition. It is square in plan, with a tower at each corner. Over the gate is the lion of St Mark, emblem of Venice, between the Quirini and Dolfin coronets. On the seaward side of the castle is the ruined chapel of St Charalambos. The castle is associated in history with some of the fiercest battles fought by the people of Crete.

It is also associated with a unique and unexplained phenomenon. On or about 18 May Old Style (6-7 June New Style), the shadows of men in black appear at dawn; they are armed, wear helmets and carry swords; on foot or on horseback, they advance from the chapel of St Charalambos towards the castle and are visible for about 10 minutes.

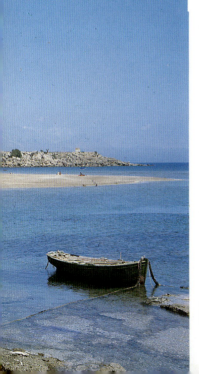

The Venetian castle of Frangokastelo, and its fine beach

If approached, they retreat and disappear into the sea. The locals call them 'the Drosoulites', from 'drosia', 'dew', because of the time in the morning at which they appear. They believe that the shadows are the ghosts of the Epirot soldiers of Hadzimichalis Dalianis and of the Cretans who fought with them, a force which was wiped out defending Frangokastelo in May 1828 against a Turkish army which was far superior in numbers (see Spanakis, CRETE, vol. 2, p. 388). Some have attributed the phenomenon to a mirage, claiming that the figures are actually a reflection of soldiers exercising in Libya, but it is strange that the same phenomenon should be visible on the same date each year, thus implying that the atmospheric conditions are similar. One wonders why modern science has so far failed to explain it.

Near Frangokastelo is the very old church of St Nikitas. An annual festival was held here on the saint's day, with dancing and athletic competitions. Efforts are being made to revive it.

From Frangokastelo, the road along the south coast continues as far as Rethymno.

We return to Sfakia. After the village of Komitades, we turn right on to the Chania road.

Shortly after this begins the narrow, winding road which climbs through the **Imvros gorge**. The gorge is 6-7 km in length. The sides are high and steep, and in some places come so close together, that it is rather like passing through a tunnel. The trip is an enchanting one, with pines, cypress trees and ilexes on both sides and in the distance. The gorge is the route by which Chora Sfakion is linked with the Askyfou Plateau.

As we emerge from our parallel route through the gorge, we see the attractive little village of **Imvros**.

We continue across the fertile **Askyfou Plateau**. This large cultivated area is surrounded by the peaks of Kastro, Trypali and Angathes, and it is believed that it was once a lake. Even today water gathers there in the winter and slowly drains away to the north, at Chono. The fields are very fertile and potatoes, grapes and fruit are grown.

Shortly before we leave the plateau, we pass through the attractive and historic village of **Askyfou**. Because of its position, controlling the sole overland access route to Sfakia, Askyfou played an important part in Greek risings against the Turks. Today, it is known for its production of cheese, and all sorts of different varieties are on sale. The cafés sell cheese with honey, an ideal tit-bit to accompany a glass of tsikoudia.

We now pass into another, shorter, gorge, the **Langos tou Katre**, 2 km in length. It is narrow and steep-sided, and its flanks are covered with ilexes trees.

After the gorge, the landscape changes once again and becomes calm and bewitching. A green sea of wild olives, and ilexes stretches out in front of us. This is the **Krapi Valley**, the natural border between the Eparchies of Sfakia and Apokoronou.

By the time we reach **Vryses** we are only 33 km from Chania. The village, a modern settlement, stands on the banks of the River Vrysanos, a shady place of plane trees and running water.

To the east of the village on the road to Rethymno, there is a Greco-Roman bridge over the Vrysanos.

We now take the old National Road to the north and west, returning to Chania.

The fertile Askyfou plain

The verdant village of Vryses, a major crossroads in the area

ROUTE 4

Chania - Akrotiri
Souda - Yeorgioupoli

Starting once more from Chania, this route takes us around the Akrotiri headland (also known as Kýdonia).

Apart from the attractive villages with their old-fashioned architecture, we shall also be visiting two most important monasteries, Gouverneto and Holy Trinity.

There are also plentiful good beaches for swimming. After touring the headland, we shall visit Souda and the surrounding archaeological sites, after which we shall head east through pretty farming villages on our way to Yeorgioupoli. From there, we shall visit Lake Kourna, the only lake on Crete, and enjoy the marvellous view from the village of the same name. The route ends in the beautiful town of Rethymno.

This is our last tour round the sights of the Prefecture of Chania, and it introduces us to the Prefecture of Rethymno.

Yeorgioupoli

Cape Akrotiri (Kydonia): This is the headland which rises to the east of Chania and protects Souda Bay from the storms of the Aegean. In ancient times, the settlement of Minoa was located on its western side. In 824 the Arabs landed there. In more modern times, the area played an important part in Crete's fight for freedom.

Chania airport, one of the best in Greece, lies on Akrotiri at a distance of 15 km from the town.

A surfaced road climbs up out of Chania town to the east, with good views over the town, and after 6 km comes to **Profitis Ilias**. This is the historic hill where the revolutionaries of 1897 first massed, and here the Greek flag was first raised over Crete in February 1913.

The beach of Kalathas

Beautiful beaches at Stavros

This is also the site of the **tombs of the Venizelos family**; there is a panoramic view over the town of Chania.

We continue, straight on, through a fertile landscape, and pass through the village of **Kounoupidiana**. The road forks here: the right-hand road crosses Akrotiri before ending at the airport, while the left-hand road leads to the beach. We continue straight on, and soon see on our left **Kalathas bay**, with tourist installations: a very busy place. We continue for the village of **Chorafakia**, where there is a crossroads. The road to the right goes to Ayia Triada. We continue straight ahead for **Stavros**, which stands on a well-protected inlet on the north-west point of the headland. There is a good sandy beach.

Shortly after the junction at 9 km and left (15 km from Chania), stands the **Monastery of the Holy Trinity (Agia Triada) 'Tsangarolon'**. We see the imposing entrance to the monastery, finely sited, across a fertile plain of olive trees and vines. The monastery impresses both with its size and with its appearance and is in very good condition. It was built in 1612 by the monks Laurence and Jeremiah, who belonged to the Greek Orthodox Venetian family of the Tsangaroli, of Cretan descent, which gave its name to the monastery. It is said that the site on which the Tsangaroli brothers built their monastery was formerly occupied by a chapel to the Holy Apostles.

The monastery church dates from 1634 and is cruciform with a dome. The influence of the Renaissance on its architecture is very clear.

The main church of the Holy Trinity Monastery, and the lintel of its doorway

The entrance and the bell-tower to Ho...

The facade is imposing, with Doric columns. There are two chapels, to Our Lady Zoodochos Pighi and to St John the Divine. The high and impressive bell-tower was built in 1864.

During the War of Independence of 1821 the monastery was burned by the Turks, and it lay waste for many years before being restored by the local monks Callopis and Gregorius. There is a library, a collection of Byzantine icons attributed to the painter Skordilis, and a number of codices, one of which dates from the 9th century.

From the monastery entrance (left) a very poor track continues. However, it is worth taking the trouble to drive along it, as it leads to a monument of great historical interest on a site which will fascinate nature-lovers: the **Gouverneto** or **Our Lady of the Angels Monastery.** The monastery stands at a height of 260

Monastery

The Gouvernetou Monastery

The main church of the Gouvernetou Monastery

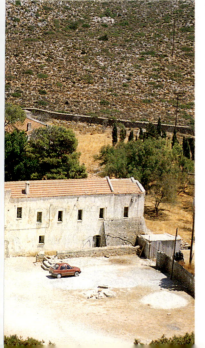

metres and is one of the oldest on Crete, possibly dating back to 1537. It is said to have been built by monks from the Katholikon monastery, which was so close to the sea that it was forever at the mercy of pirates.

From the outside, the monastery resembles a fortress, with a strong Venetian influence. The church is rectangular, with a vaulted ceiling and turrets at each of the corners. The turrets have special slits through which guns and bows might be fired. The facade of the church is excellent, with fine Venetian carvings. There are a total of fifty cells, arranged on two floors. The monastery is dedicated to the Purification of the Virgin, or Our Lady of the Angels. There are also two chapels, to the Ten Saints and St John the Stranger. The monastery was destroyed by the Turks in 1821, but it was restored later and amalgama"ed with the Holy Trinity monastery.

The beach at Almyrida

18 km Kalyves: A coastal village with a marvellous beach stretching for 18 km. The village stands on a fertile site with abundant supplies of water and dense vegetation. The village is divided into two parts: the old settlement, with traditional stone-built houses, and the new quarter, with more modern structures. Nearby are the ruins of the Venetian fortress of Apicorno, which gave its name to the whole area: Apokoronos.

20 km Almyrida: A pebble beach with good, clean water.

27 km Gavalochori: A village with numerous churches and chapels. The 30 wells, famous throughout Crete, from which the village once drew its water, have also survived.

30 km Vamos: Chief town of the Eparchy of Apokoronos, an administrative and commercial centre. The town takes its name from the Arabic 'vamos', meaning pass or crossing. Today, it is a quaint village with traditional houses, steeply-raked tree-lined streets and shady squares with enormous plane trees. There are numerous Byzantine churches, including one to the Dormition of St George. Every August, the local Cultural Association organises a kind of mini-festival.

The road continues through more pretty villages before reaching **Yeorgioupoli**, 39 km from Chania.

This is a coastal village on the Armyros plain. It used to be called Almyros or Armyroupoli, but was renamed in honour of Prince George, High Commissioner of Crete. The river Armyros, which rises in Lake Kournas, flows into the sea here. There is an enormous square with tall eucalyptus trees. The village has an exceptionally good beach, 9 km long with fine white sand, which is completely protected from the northwest winds that can make bathing on this coast hazardous. Thanks to its beach, Yeorgioupoli has recently developed into an important holiday resort.

It is possible to visit Lake Kourna from Yeorgioupoli. We cross the main road across a bridge and, after 6 km, a track leads to the lake and the village of the same name.

Lake Kourna, the only lake in Crete, covers a total area of some 15 acres. The circumference of the lake is 3.5 km, its surface area 1.2 square kilometres and its depth up to 25 metres. In antiquity it was called Cornesia and there was a sanctuary to Athena Cornesia. The current name comes from an Arabic word meaning 'lake'.

The landscape around the lake is wonderful. There is dense vegetation, with bushes, reeds and brambles. The south eastern bank is covered with olive trees. Beside the lake here there is a strip of white sand where a café serves tsikoudia and coffee and where a swim in the lake can be enjoyed.

To the south of the lake, at Keratide, is the Kourna cave. This cave, discovered in 1961, has richly decorative stalactites and stalagmites and natural pillars. There are labyrinthine passages on a number of levels.

We can now climb to the village of Kourna. From the highest point of the road, the view of the lake is magical. The colour of the water can be seen changing from light green to dark blue, with the wild mountains all around reflected in the calm surface of the lake.

Kournas is built on the slopes of Mt Dafnomadara. It has many churches, including a 14th century church to St Irene.

We return to the main road and head towards Rethymno. To the left, soon before we reach the town, is the beach of Petre. There is an excellent view of Rethymno just before we enter the town.

Lake Kourna

Behind, Almyros bay, and, below, Yeorgioupoli with Almyropotamos

THE PREFECTURE OF RETHYMNO

The Prefecture of Rethymno lies to the east of the Prefecture of Chania, between the White Mountains and Mt Psiloritis or Ida, which towers over the eastern side of the district and acts as the spinal cord of the island. Its highest peak is Timios Stavros (2,456 m). The Prefecture has an area of 1,496 square kilometres, of which only 596 square kilometres are suitable for agriculture; the remainder consists of high mountains and barren hillsides, for Rethymno is the most mountainous of the four prefectures of Crete. The population amounts to approximately 63,000, and their main occupation is stock-breeding, given that of the approximately

858,000 sheep and goats on Crete 193,000 are in the Prefecture of Rethymno.

Apart from the products of stock-breeding, the Prefecture also produces olive oil, olives, vegetables and carobs; in the case of the latter product, much consideration has recently been given to ways of making better use of them.

The Prefecture has excellent beaches

such as Bali in north, Plakias and Ayia Galini in south. Along the southern coast, are some of the best beaches in western Crete and comfortable resort centres are now coming into existence as new and modern tourist units spring up almost daily. Despite this, the Prefecture is in many ways one of the most traditional parts of the island, and increasing tourism has not encroached upon the agricultural and stockbreeding occupations of the inhabitants.

However, half of the beauty of Crete is in its mountains. As one climbs the sides of Mt Psiloritis, one's sense of the harshness of the upland scenery gradually dies away. Nature has en-dowed the rocks and the mountain peaks with such forms that, with a little imagination, one can see in them recumbent human figures, dancers or a human face.

The Prefecture is not famous for its archaeological sites, but it does have the famous Idaean Cave, where according to the myths Zeus was raised and where the spades of the archaeologists have brought to light offerings and Minoan finds. However, there is no shortage of sights, given that the Prefecture of Rethymno contains the heroic Arkadi Monastery, symbol of liberty, and the historic Preveli Monastery as well as a number of historic villages, including Anoyeia.

Communications between the Prefecture and the rest of Greece consist of a daily ferry sailing to Pireaus. There are also buses to Souda, where large car ferries serve the Chania-Piraeus line. From Chania airport at Akrotiri, Olympic Airways buses connect to Rethymno. In the summer, there are launch departures for Santorini and there are caique services from Ayia Galini to Matala in the Prefecture of Herakleio.

Inside the Prefecture, KTEL buses link the town with the villages and beaches.

The Town of Rethymno

Rethymno is the smallest of the three historic cities of Crete, with a population of 18,000. It is the capital of the Prefecture by the same name and is the commercial and administrative centre for the surrounding area. It lies along the sea-shore approximately half-way between Chania and Herakleio. For that reason, the Venetian rulers of the eastern Mediterranean used it as a way-station and a refuge in time of trouble.

Rethymno is a most attractive little town which has never been damaged by earthquake and which has managed to retain both its oriental magic and its western grandeur. As one walks through its narrow Venetian alleyways with their little old houses with wooden covered balconies ('sachnisia'), their mosques and minarets, their Venetian mansions with magnificent flights of steps, coas-of-arms and Latin inscriptions, one has a strong sense of being carried back through time to the magic of another age. The Fortezza, the superb Venetian castle, the Venetian loggia and fountains and the Turkish mosques stand harmoniously side-by-side today, but they are testimony to the turbulent past of the town. The picture is completed with the picturesque Venetian harbour, where the fishing-boats moor today, and the modern harbour next to it for larger vessels. To the east of the town is a huge beach with fine golden-greyish sand, which stretches for a total of 12 km.

Rethymno has a long tradition in scholarly and artistic matters, going back to Venetian times. Even then there were schools in Rethymno, teaching philosophy, mathematics and logic. Rethymno was the starting-point for many learned men, including Hortatzis, the poet of *Erophyle*, Tzanes, Prevelakis and others. Today, the town continues to have a lively academic and artistic scene, with arts centres, folklore and historical associations, theatrical performances and other events. Since 1974 the Faculty of Arts of the University of Crete has been based here.

In recent years, tourism in Rethymno has been on the increase. Thanks to the mildness of the climate, the tourist season here lasts for 8-9 months of the year. Modern tourist amenities stretch along the beach to the east, providing all the facilities necessary for a pleasant stay, for an acquaintance with Cretan cooking, genuine Cretan music, song and dance and for water-sports of all kinds.

Rethymno stands on the site of a very ancient city called Rithymna. This city was autonomous and independent and it issued its own coins, which depicted Apollo. In 1947, a Late Minoan tomb was excavated at Mastaba, to the south of the town. Roman mosaics have been found within Rethymno itself, at the foundations of new buildings.

Rethymno was at the height of its power and wealth in the Venetian period. At this time, indeed, it became a city and acquired its harbour, called Mandraki. In the 13th century the Venetians began fortifying the town, beginning with the wall to the west of the harbour.

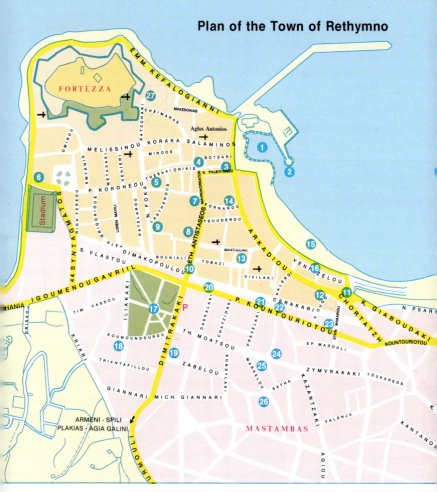

Plan of the Town of Rethymno

Key to the Map

1. Venetian Harbour
2. Lighthouse
3. Loggia
4. Rimondi Fountain
5. Our Lady of the Angels (The little Ch. of the Virgin)
6. The Prefecture (Iroon Square)
7. Neraje Cami
8. San Francesco
9. Turkish School
10. Great Gate (Entrance)
11. Iroon Square (Bus terminal)
12. Kara Musa Pasha Mosque
13. Cathedral ('Big Church of Our Lady')
14. Tourist Police
15. Public beach
16. E.O.T. Nat. Tourist Organis.
17. Public Garden
18. Hospital
19. Olympic Airways Offices
20. Church of the Four Martyrs
21. Telephone company
22. Town Hall
23. Post Office
24. Buses to Chania-Herakleio
25. Buses to Ayia Galini-Plakia
26. Veli Pasha mosque
27. Archeological Museum

Rethymno gradually grew into a major urban centre in which the Greek element was predominant in the population. It was the seat of a Venetian Prefect.

In the years 1540-1570 the Venetians strengthened the town's defences by building an outer wall to plans by the famous military architect Sammicheli. Only a short length of this has survived, together with the Great Gate. During this period, the town was attacked by various raiders and suffered damage. In 1538 it was sacked by the pirate Hayredin Barbarossa, and in 1567 the corsair Uluc Ali captured it and burned it after looting it. In 1571 the Sultan Selim's fleet sacked the town once more.

In the years which followed, the fine fortress called the Fortezza was built on Palaiokastro hill. Among other buildings of the time were the Loggia, the Rimondi fountain, and the clock. Yet despite all the fortifications, the Turks captured it on 3 November 1646 after a siege of only 22 days. Under the Turks, Rethymno was the commercial port and administrative centre for the whole of western Crete. In the uprising of 1821 it suffered the same fate as the other Cretan towns, with massacres of the unarmed Christian population and looting. This did not prevent it from being a hotbed of resistance to the Turks. Between 1897 and 1909 it was occupied by the Russians, as part of the general occupation of Crete by the troops of the Great Powers.

The **Old Town** of Rethymno has kept its medieval character, and the buildings are all scheduled. Its boundaries are the 'ring road' (which starts from the old harbour, runs round the Fortezza and ends in Iroon Polytechniou Square, where the Prefecture stands), Dimakopoulou St, Yerakari St, Iroon Square and the Venizelou esplanade (see the town plan, orange markings).

The *Venizelou Esplanade* leads west to the attractive **Venetian Harbour**, a bustling little place with shops of all kinds. Today, fishing-boats and other small craft anchor there. The large lighthouse on the end of the north pier was built under the Turks, while the vaulted ground floors of the buildings which line the harbour front are Venetian. These were used as storerooms. The wall around the harbour is also Venetian.

The old town of Rethymno, and a section of its long beach

The Venetian harbour of Rethymno

The Venetian loggia

The Rimondi fountain

Close to the harbour, on the corner of *Palaiologou* and *Arkadiou* Sts, is the fine Venetian **Loggia**. This is a 16th century building, which has survived in excellent condition. The Loggia was the place where the local nobility gathered to discuss political, economic and commercial matters and also to indulge in gambling. The Loggia housed the **Archaeological Museum** until 1991, when it was moved to the Fortenza.

The Museum collection contains finds from all over the Prefecture, arranged in chronological order and covering all the periods in the history of the area.

There are figurines, tools, jewels and pottery from the Neolithic period, seal-stones, statuettes and votive offerings from the Minoan and Late Minoan periods, and interesting Egyptian finds —seals, scarabs and jewellery— which show how close were commercial contacts between western Crete and north Africa.

The Museum also contains exhibits from the Hellenistic, Roman, Byzantine and Venetian periods. One exhibit to note is the life-size Roman statue of Aphrodite, hewn out of local marble and possibly dating from the time of the Emperor Nero. There is also a female statue from Eleutherna.

The Museum contains an important numismatic collection with coins from many Cretan cities and a number of different periods.

Opposite the Loggia stood the **clock-tower**, a fine piece of architecture which has not survived.

The minaret of the Neranje Mosque

On *Palaiologou St*, which runs into *Petychaki* or *Platanou Square*, is the **Rimondi Fountain**. This was constructed in 1588 and rebuilt by Rimondi in 1626. Its architectural decoration is impressive: the water spouts are in the shape of lion's heads, and its columns rise to Corinthian capitals.

In Petychaki Square we come to the beginning of *Thessalonikis St*, the street with the largest number of enclosed balconies ('sachnisia'). Where Thessalonikis St meets *Nikiforou Foka St*, which is also known as *Makri Steno*, is the church of **Our Lady of the Angels** or the **Little Church of the Virgin** (to distinguish it from the Cathedral, which is called the Big Church of the Virgin). This is a three-aisled building without a dome, built in late Venetian times and dedicated to Mary Magdalene.

To the west of Our Lady of the Angels, on the western outskirts of town, is *Iroon Polytechniou Square*, dominated by the massive neo-Classical **Prefecture** building.

To the east of Our Lady of the Angels, on the corner of *Venardou* and *Ethnikis Antistaseos Sts*, is the **Neraje Cami**. This was the church (Santa Maria) of an Augustinian monastery, and it was converted into a mosque in 1657. Perhaps the minaret, which was built in 1890, is more important than the mosque itself. Today, the building houses the town conservatoire.

We continue along *Ethnikis Antistaseos St* to the **Church of San Francesco**, a single-aisled basilica with a chapel which is striking for its decoration and also for its architecture. On the same side of the street, further west, is the **Turkish school**, which has a superb double-arched doorway.

Ethnikis Antistaseos St, which is also called the *Megali Agora* ('big market') because it contains a large proportion of the town's shops, and particularly its food stores, ends at the **Great Gate** or **Porta Guera**, which was the central opening in the Venetian fortifications. The opening of the gate —2.60 m. in width— is flanked by hewn slabs leading up to a semi-circular arch. The Great Gate and a short stretch of wall are all that is left of the fortifications. The lion of St Mark in relief which used to adorn the pediment of the Gate is now in the Archaeological Museum.

On the eastern extremity of the Old Town is *Iroon Square*, where some of buses leave from. This is also the beginning of *Arkadiou St*, the

A mosque in the Fortezza fortress

town's second most important commercial street, known as 'Mikri' ('small') Agora'. *Arkadiou St* has most of the finest Renaissance houses and mansions in the town. Where it intersects *Victor Hugo St* is the **Kara Musa Pasha Mosque**, with a vaulted fountain. Further along *Arkadiou St*, where it intersects with *Ayia Varvara St, is the* **Cathedral Church of the Presentation of the Virgin**, or **'Big Church of Our Lady'**, with a square in front of it.

The Church was built in 1834, and takes the church of Our Lady in Tinos as its model. Inside, there is a fine carved wooden screen and a portable Byzantine icon of Our Lady of Passion. Next to the church, the outstanding belfry was built of rectangular blocks of red limestone in 1889. To the south of the church is the **Bishop's Residence**, an imposing neo-Classical bulding with a fine symmetrical facade.

The esplanade, officially known as *Eleftheriou Venizelou St*, runs parallel with Arkadiou St. The esplanade is the part of town where most of the tourist facilities are located, with the municipal beach and a host of attractive cafes and restaurants.

We continue along the esplanade to complete our acquaintance with the Old Town by heading in the direction of the entrance to the most important monument in Rethymno, the fortress.

The **Fortezza** was built between 1571 and 1600 on Palaiokastro hill in accordance with the precepts of the military architecture of the time. It has three bastions on its southern side and one on the east, connected by battlements.

The *main gate*, through which we enter today, is on the eastern side of the fortress. There were also two auxiliary gates, through which supplies and ammunition could be delivered, on the western and northern sides. Among the buildings to be seen inside is the *church of St Theodore*, a single-aisled vaulted structure.

On the southern side of the castle were the soldiers' barracks, the cannon store, and the artillery storerooms. In the centre was an open space on which stood the *cathedral*, a building which the Turks converted into a mosque. On the north side were the *gunpowder stores*, with more storerooms on ground level and beneath. *Water tanks* which supplied the Fortezza in the event of a siege can be seen scattered throughout the entire area.

The walls of the Fortezza provide a superb view of the town and the sea which embraces it. A small open-air theatre has been built inside the walls, and various events are held there every summer.

The **New Town** is an extension of the Old Town to the south. After 1970, the needs of a modern town and the growth of tourism caused Rethymno to spread out to the east along the coast, as far as the village of Perivolia. Most of the buildings in the New Town are new, and many of them are blocks of flats. Down by the sea, there are large hotel complexes.

Apart from the Venetian wall, which ran along what is today called *Koundourioti Ave.*, the New Town also contained the Turkish cemetery, which has now been converted into a spacious **Municipal Garden**. The Garden is almost directly opposite the Great Gate. It covers an area of 25,000 square metres and also contains a small zoo. Every July a Wine Festival is held in the Municipal Garden.

Further to the east along *Koun-*

dourioti Ave. is *Tessaron Martyron Square*. Here, in 1824, the Turks beheaded four Christian martyrs. In memory of them, the **Church of the Four Martyrs** was built; its feast day is on 28 October. Almost opposite the square is the old girls' high school, a fine neo-Classical building, while on the same side of the square on *Kountourioti Ave.* are the telephone company, the Town Hall and the Post Office.

To the south of *Kountourioti Ave.*, on a hill, is the *Mastabas* district, where the archaeologists have brought Minoan finds to light. In this district are the old boys' high school and the long-distance bus station. To the south of the bus station is a minaret and the **Veli Pasha mosque**.

To the east of *Kountourioti Ave.* is the district called *Kolonaki*a, with fine neo-Classical houses.

The new town of Rethymno seen from the breakwater

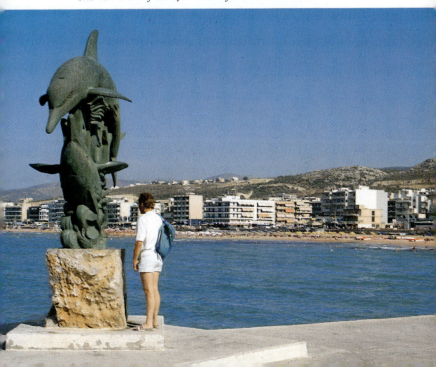

Rethymno

Rethymno - Arkadi Monastery
(22 km)

Our acquaintance with the Prefecture of Rethymno begins with a visit, or rather a pilgrimage, to the Arkadi Monastery, symbol of Liberty and Self-sacrifice.

Our trip begins in Rethymno, and we take the Herakleio road. After 5 km there is a turning, which we take, for the village of **Adele**. The road runs through verdant scenery, and Adele itself stands among vineyards and olive groves. The village was bilt in Roman times and took its name from the first settler, whose name was Adel. This was the birthplace of K. Yamboudakis, who blew up the Arkadi Monastery. His house can be seen in the village, and his bust stands in the village square.

The road continues through the villages of **Loutra** and **Kyrianna**, the latter of which has Venetian buildings and a 14th century church dedicated to the Dormition of the Virgin and St Paraskevi.

We begin to climb, and after 18 km from Rethymno come to the village of **Amnato**, which has an excellent view. To the west towers **Mt Vrysakas** (see p. 151). To the north east an enormous forest of olives stretches all the way to the sea and to the south we can see the height on which the Arkadi Monastery stands.

This village has been inhabited since Venetian times, as can be seen from the Venetian houses and the inscriptions on the gates. In the revolt of 1866 many of the villagers were among those who who barricaded themselves in the Arkadi Monastery, including the heroine Charikleia Daskalaki and her two sons. Her bust stands in the square.

From Amnato, a narrow winding road climbs up through a green gorge with dense olive groves to the Arkadi Monastery (5 km).

The historic **Arkadi Monastery** stands on a fine site amid dense greenery, with an excellent view down the thickly-wooded gorge and out to the azure sea.

The date of its foundation is not known with exactness. According to one source, it was founded in the late Byzantine period (10th-13th centuries) by a monk named Arcadius, or alternatively it may be as late as the 16th century date on the belfry. It consists of a fortified building with two main entrances, a guesthouse, a refectory, a gunpowder store and cellars. The main entrance was destroyed in the fighting of 1866 and was rebuilt in its original form only four years later. Opposite the entrance was a windmill, which in 1910 was converted into an ossuary. The church was completed in 1587. The fine facade of the church, in a Renaissance style, dominates the whole complex of buildings, with their vaulted cells and Gothic windows. The church itself is a double-aisled basilica and it is dedicated to St Constantine and to the Transfiguration. Under the Venetians, the monastery was a very wealthy foundation, with 300 monks according to the traveller R. Pococke. In the 18th century it was known for its embroidery in gold thread and there was a workshop which turned out embroidered vestments.

The inaccessibility of the monastery and its castle-like structure, with high, thick walls, were to be of decisive importance in its history.

The imposing facade of the main church of the Arkadi Monastery

ROUTE 1

Rethymno - Kourtaliotiko Gorge - Preveli Monastery Plakias - Damioni Kotsyfou Gorge Asi Gonia - Myriokefala

This route is an opportunity to pass through the imposing Kourtaliotiko Gorge, make the acquaintance of the historic Preveli monastery, and visit a number of picturesque and heavily-wooded villages. We shall also be descending to the magical coastline, with its fine sandy beaches and beautiful clear water. The Kotsyfou gorge, to which we shall also be going, is a miniature version of the Samaria Gorge.

Our acquaintance with the western part of the Prefecture of Rethymno will end with a supplementary route from Rethymno to Asi Gonia, as far as the upland village of Myriokefala.

In Rethymno, our road starts on the eastern side of the Municipal Gardens in Dimitrakaki St., heading south towards the higher ground in the centre of the Prefecture. As we climb, the landscape is bare and rocky. However, the view down to Rethymno with the Fortezza and the blue sea which embraces it, is marvellous. We soon run into olive groves and oak forests, and at 11 km arrive at the village of **Armeni**. This village, at 380 m. above sea level, was first settled in the year 961 by Armenians who served in the army of the Byzantine Emperor Nicephorus Phocas which liberated Crete from the Arabs. Near the modern village, 167 shaft tombs hewn out of the rock have been discovered in an oak wood.

At **19 km** we come to a fork. The road to the right leads to the village of Ayios Vasileios and the Kotsyfou gorge by which we shall be returning. We continue along the main road to Spili.

21 km. We turn off the main road for Spili and Ayia Galini and head right, for the **Kourtaliotiko Gorge**.

23 km Koxare: After the village, the road travels through the impressive **Kourtaliotiko gorge**, formed by the mountains of Kouroupa (984 m) and Xiro Oros (904 m). The gorge begins in Koxare village and continues along the course of the Kourtaliotis river. When a strong wind is blowing, it whistles strangely among the recesses in the rocks; since the noise produced is a kind of rattling ('kourtala' in the local dialect), it gave the the gorge its name. The gorge is narrow and wildly beautiful. On its bare sides are numerous springs and caves. The Kourtaliotis river which flows through it rises at five big springs, which form a waterfall 40 m. high.

Tradition says that this was the area chosen as a hermitage by a monk called Nicholas, with a companion, who was unwilling to stay there, because, he said, there was no water. So the monk laid his hand on a rock and water immediately began to bubble out from the five points where his fingertips had touched. Today there is a church to St Nicholas in the gorge, together with a little chapel to St George. It contains a wall-painting showing the Holy Trinity, in which the Holy Spirit is shown emerging from the mouth of the Father. This treatment of the subject is unique in Greece.

Crossing the Kourtaliotikos Gorge

We continue, passing through the village of **Asomatos** (altitude 230 m) and at 33 km come to a turning (left) for the historic **Preveli Monastery**.

The **Lower Preveli Monastery** appears quite suddenly out of the greenery to the west of the Kourtaliotikos river. It stands by a bridge over the river. Today, the monastery is deserted. Its main church is to John the Baptist, and its belfry bears the date 1594.

A further 3 km brings us to the **Upper Preveli Monastery**, which is the more important foundation today. The main church is dedicated to St John the Divine and the bell-tower is dated 1629. The monastery stands on a rocky site with such a fine view that many visitors come to admire that alone. Among

The historic Preveli Monastery, built in an idyllic setting

them was the British admiral Spratt, who later wrote that *"this is the Paradise of Crete, a proper hermitage for those who wish to be relieved of the cares and responsibilities of life"* (Spratt II, 269).

The foundation was established in the 16th or early 17th century, and the double-aisled main church was erected in 1836, under the Venetians. It was destroyed in 1866 and restored in 1911. The current abbot's quarters were built in 1900, together with twenty new cells, and the old abbot's quarters were converted into a guesthouse. The monastery served as a base during all the struggles of the Cretans to gain their independence, and in more recent times it was used as an escape route for Allied troops.

Inside the Monastery is a gold Crucifix incorporating pieces of the True Cross and precious stones, which is regarded as miraculous. The museum contains books, vestments, property registers and the sigil of the Patriarch Gregory V, of 1789, by which the monastery was afforded the special protection of the Ecumenial Patriarchate. There is also a library.

From the Lower Preveli Monastery, a path leads down through an idyllic landscape to the coast near the point where the Kourtaliotikos river runs into the sea. Here the river forms a little lagoon surrounded with palm trees before joining its waters with those of the sea. The gorge is worth exploring along the river-bank path.

The river, the beach and the palm trees at the exit of the Kourtaliotiko Gorge

The scenery is exotic, with the palm trees all around and the green waters of the river flowing quietly or more rapidly through pools or over little waterfalls. The gorge ends at the beautiful beach, with rocks to the right and left and crystal-clear water.

We return to Asomatos and head left for **Mariou**. The road continues west to **Myrthio**. This village has a fine view over Plakias Bay, 4 km away, and out to the Libyan Sea. There is a church of the Transfiguration with wall-paintings depicting the torments of the damned.

Now the road runs downhill, and we reach the pretty coastal village of **Plakias**, on the bay of the same name. This is the one of the most beautiful spots on the whole south coast of Crete. Until just a few years ago, Plakias was a sleepy fishing

In the Kourtaliotikos Gorge

The long beach at Plakias, with the village behind

village with a few houses around a shady square. Now, thanks to its sandy beach (1,500 metres long) and the mountain which, like a stage set, towers behind it, it has become a busy resort. Its mild and dry climate make it an ideal spot for off-season holidays.

From Plakias, there are boat trips to Frangokastelo, the Preveli Monastery and Ayia Galini.

To the east of Plakias is the coastal settlement of **Damioni**, on a pretty cove. There is a good beach of fine white sand, 600 metres long, and the water is most inviting.

We return to Myrthio. After the village, to the west there is a crossroads. The road to the left leads to **Sellia**, along a superb route with views out to the sea. We then come to **Rodakino**. To the left at the entrance to the village, a road leads in 2 km to the attractive beack of **Korakas**. Rodakino, standing on a semi-circular

site amid dense olive groves, consists of two parts: **Ano** ('upper') and **Kato** ('lower').

The road continues to the west after Rodakino, and leads to Frangokastelo and Chora Sfakion.

The other road from the Myrthio crossroads turns north east and leads to the end of the Kotsyfou gorge.

The **Kotsyfou Gorge** is formed by the mountains of Kouroupas and Kryoneritis. In many ways, the gorge resembles the Samaria gorge on a smaller scale, and the passage through it is most attractive. For most of the year there is a stream down the centre of the gorge. The end —that is, strictly speaking, the entrance— of the gorge is near the upland village of **Ayios Ioannis** (460 m). The road then continues to **Ayios Vasileios** (310 m), the village from which the surrounding Eparchy takes its name, and then at 19 km returns to the road to Rethymno.

ROUTE 2

Rethymno - Vrysinas
Amari Valley
Ayia Galini - Spili

This itinerary runs right through the verdant Amari valley.

The valley of Amari, which has an average altitude of 400-500 m., lies between Mt Ida (or Psiloritis) to the north east and Mt Kedros to the south west.

In the middle of the valley, the height called Samithos or Samitos splits the area into two separate valleys, the Asomathianos valley, so called from the Asomati Monastery which stands there, and a much smaller one, which takes its name Smylianos valley from the village of Smyle. The spring waters from both these valleys form the Amarianos or Platys river, which runs down to the sea at Ayia Galini. The Amari valley is green with vegetation all year round, and has mountain villages, old monasteries and interesting chapels. We shall return to Rethymno from Ayia Galini in a northwesterly direction, through the densely-vegetated plain of the Eparchy of Ayios Vasileios. This area extends over the far side of Mt Kedros (that is, Mt Kedros rises to the north east of Ayios Vasileios) and is crossed by the Kourtaliotis river.

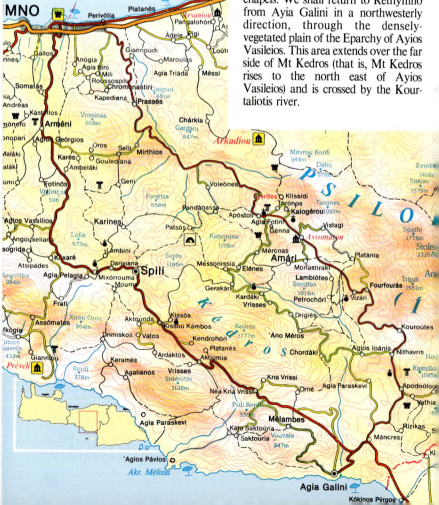

We leave Rethymno along the road to Herakleio. After 3.2 km, in the suburb of **Misirgia**, there is a turning, right, for Amari. From the Amari road, a further turning right will bring us in 7 km to the village of **Chromonastiri**, one of the largest in the area in Venetian times.

Nearby, at a spot known as **metochi tou Perdiki**, hidden amongst olive groves, is the important church of St Eutychius, which preserves 11th century wall-paintings. The area is ideal for walking and climbing on Mt Vrysinas.

The main road climbs, with bends, and after 11 km brings us to the village of **Prases**. This pretty village, with its many Venetian houses, stands on the slopes of a densely-wooded gorge. The church in its cemetery, dedicated to Our Lady 'Myrtidiotissa', has wall-paintings

Asomaton Monastery, in the Amari Valley

dating from the 14th century. From the exit to the village there is a fine view, from above, of a verdant valley with Mt Psiloritis towering to the left.

Now the road descends, with bends, crossing a narrow old stone bridge with three arches. Behind us is the wild **Prasano gorge**. Shortly after the bridge, a turning to the right leads to the villages of Myrthio, Seli, Oros and Kares. This road embraces the southern slopes of Mt Vrysinas and afterwards joins the main Spili road (see p. 158).

Mt Vrysinas rises to the south of Rethymno (858 metres). Its slopes are densely vegetated, thanks to the numerous springs ('vryses') from which it takes its name. From its conical peak, the whole of the sub-prefecture of Rethymno is visible, with the 21 villages which nestle there. Thanks to its position, it was frequently a battle-field, notably during Crete's long struggle for freedom.

During antiquity, Vrysinas was a sacred mountain, and on its peak, where the church of the Holy Spirit stands today, was a sanctuary dedicated to the goddess Artemis Diktyns, who was worshipped throughout western Crete. It is believed that the ancient city of Osmis stood on the Onithe plateau.

We continue through **Potami** (21 km). The surrounding area is fertile and quite heavily cultivated. After Potami, a further turning to the right leads to the villages of **Voleones, Pantanassa** and **Patsos** (31 km).

In the Patsos area is the cave of Ayios Antonios, with a church to the same saint (Antony) dating from the 16th century.

In antiquity, Hermes Cranaios was worshipped here, and remains from the Late Minoan, Geometric and Roman periods have been found. Three hundred metres further north is the Fournare cave.

The surfaced road runs on to **Apostoli**, 30 km from Rethymno. Built in the Byzantine period, this village stands at an altitude of 500 metres. In the year 249, the Ten Saints were arrested here, and since then the village has borne the name Apostoli ('apostles'). It has numerous churches, notably that of St Nicholas, with 14th century wall-paintings, and that of St Spyridon.

The road continues to **Ayia Fotini**, where there is an important crossroads. The main road continues straight ahead for the Asomaton Monastery. The turning to the right leads to the villages of the Smylianos plain, and that to the left will take us to the picturesque villages of Thronos and Kaloyerou. If we take the right turning, the following villages can be visited: **Meronas**, with an excellent view and churches with 14th and 15th century wall-paintings; **Yerakari**, standing at an altitude of 680 metres on the foothills of Mt Kedros, a centre of agricultural production famed for its cherries; **Smyle**, a small farming community which has given its name to the whole area; **Vryses**, a densely-vegetated village with numerous streams and wonderful gardens; **Ano Meros**, another thickly-wooded village with the old **Kaloeidena Monastery**, of which the Asomaton Monastery was once a dependency; and **Ayios Ioannis**, an upland village after we rejoin the main road at **Nithavri**.

The road to the left at Ayia Fotini leads, after 1 km, to the village of **Thronos**. Thronos stands on a hill called the Throniani Kefala, and has a wonderful view across towards Mt Ida, while the green Amari valley lies spread out beneath it. This was the site of ancient Syvritos, some remains of which have survived. Syvritos was built on a number of different levels; it was an independent city and reached the height of its prosperity and influence in Roman times. It issued its own silver coins, which depicted

The Byzantine chapel of Our Lady 'Thronia

Hermes. Its outlet to the sea was called Soulia, a town which has been identified with modern Ayia Galini. In the early Byzantine period, it was the seat of a bishop, whose throne ('thronos' in Greek) gave its name to the village. It was razed by the Saracens, but the name of Syvritos continued to be used in the castelans, the administrative divisions into which the Venetians separated Crete.

The village has a Byzantine church of Our Lady of Thronos, dating from the 14th century, with rich wall-paintings and decoration. The church probably stands on the foundations of the cathedral erected when Syvritos was a bishopric.

We continue through the upland village of **Kalogerou**. The church of St John, in the countryside near the village, has wonderful wall-paintings. The church has its feast on 29 August.

From a point between the villages of Thronos and Kalogerou, a passable track leads through verdant scenery to the Arkadi Monastery (see p. 138). The walk takes about 2 hours. At the start of this track and near the hamlet of Klisidi, is the **Petra spring**, known for many centuries for its therapeutic properties.

The road continues after Kalogerou, bending back to merge with the main road to the Asomaton Monastery.

The village of Kaloyerou in the Amari Valley, with Mt Psiloritis in the background

The Byzantine chapel of St Paraskevi, under the shadow of Mt Psiloritis

Near the monastery is the interesting Byzantine church of **St Paraskevi**. A cruciform church with a dome, it was restored in 1888. In the north wall of the interior is a tomb, which rises to an arched recess with paintings of the saints.

35 km Asomaton Monastery: The monastery stands in a beautiful position, with a fine view over the highly-cultivated valley with its olives, vineyards, fruit trees, enormous plane trees and ancient oak trees. In the centre of its courtyard is a fountain, from which crystal-clear water flows in abundance. The monastery was founded in the 9th or 10th century and it is dedicated to the Archangels Gabriel and Michael. It was destroyed by the Arabs, but rebuilt in 1682 by the monk Macarius. The Turks burned it in 1821, but spared the main church. During the period of Turkish rule, the monastery played an important role in scholarship and education. In 1833, the abbot Joseph, who is thought of as the founder of the monastery in modern times, set up at Monastiraki a secondary school, the Hellenic Academy, the only place in the Eparchy of Amari where higher education of any form could be acquired. Its main church preserves icons of the Holy Trinity (dating from 1619) and of the Archangels, the latter being the work of the abbot Manassis and dating from 1755. It has a library of theological works. Since 1927, the Asomaton Monastery has operated without interruption as an Agricultural School, with particular emphasis on stock-breeding.

From the Asomaton Monastery, a turning to the right leads to **Monastiraki**. The name ('little monastery') comes from a church which had cells around its courtyard, like a monastery, and which was an offshoot of the Asomaton Monastery. This was the site of the Hellenic Academy founded by Abbot Joseph.

The village itself was first settled around the 9th century. Archaeological investigation of the area around the village brought to light quantities of Minoan pottery, which would seem to indicate that there was an ancient city somewhere in the vicinity. The Byzantine church of the Archangel Michael, with wall-paintings, can be seen.

From the village, a road leads to the left across the slopes of Samitos hill. It goes to the pretty mountain villages of **Lambiotes** and **Petrochori**, which look across to Mt Psiloritis.

Another road leading off to the right from the Monastiraki goes, in 5 km, to **Amari**. This little mountain village (altitude 460 m) is the chief settlement in the Eparchy of the same name. It was first settled during the later Byzantine period. Even in Venetian times this was the principal village in the locality, while the Turks distinguished it from the surrounding villages by adding to its name the prefix 'Nefs', which means 'principal'. There are ruins of a small Venetian fortress on a site high up above the village, and many Byzantine churches with wall-paintings.

Thanks to the numerous streams near the village, the whole area is densely planted with fruit and olive trees. In fact, the whole district is a major producer of olives, those known as 'throumbes' being particularly good.

We return to the main road at the Asomaton Monastery. The road to the left will take us to the villages of **Vistagi** and **Platania**, while the main road continues straight on and begins to climb up to Vizari.

41 km Vizari: The village flourished during Venetian times. It contains the ruins of a mansion whose frontage boasts a sundial with Latin numerals. The villagers of Vizari founded Fourfouras.

44 km Fourfouras: This pretty and well-vegetated village stands on the top of a cliff (altitude 460 m) among the foothills of Mt Ida. It looks like a fortified village (which is one version of the origin of its name: from 'frourio', fortress). The most interesting church in the vicinity is that of **Our Lady 'Kardiotissa'**, dating from the Byzantine period. At one time it was a nunnery, and it has excellent 14th-15th century wall-paintings.

After some bends and having crossed a verdant plain, the road reaches **Kouroutes**, at an altitude of 510 m. According to the myths, it was here, at the foot of Mt Ida, that the Kouretes (young warriors) brought up Zeus. In the summer, groups of walkers start from here for the ascent of the highest peak (Timios Stavros) of Psiloritis at 2,456 m.

A little further down, at an altitude of 500 metres, is the village of **Nithavri**. The village takes its name from the elision of the two words Nitha (Mt Ida) + vris (you find), meaning that Nida, the plateau on Psiloritis where the Idaean Cave is located, is accessible from there. Graves found in the area show that it was inhabited as far back as the 2nd or 3nd century AD.

At Nithavri, a turning to the right leads through the villages of Ayios Ioannis, Ano Meros and Ayia Fotini (see p. 152).

We continue straight ahead and, at a distance of 55 km, come to **Apodoulou**. The village is quaint, with fountains and pretty gardens. It owes its name to its first inhabitants, who were liberated slaves (apo = 'from', douli = 'slaves'). It flourished during Venetian times.

Near the village, a Middle Minoan tomb with four sarcophagi has been discovered. A building with a golden axe was also found, together with inscribed libation vessels. All these finds are on display in Rethymno Museum. Nearby is the church of St George, with wall-paintings and a carving dating from 1496.

After Apodoulou, a road to the left through marvellous scenery and a verdant landscape leads to the villages of **Platanos, Lochria** (which is the most easterly village in the Prefecture of Rethymno and is a major handicrafts centre today) and **Kamares** (see p. 202).

The road straight on (south) through Apodoulou soon comes to a crossroads for Ayia Galini. The road to the left crosses the Mesara plain on its way to Herakleio (there is a bus service once a day along this route).

The turning to the right twists steeply down towards **Ayia Galini**, which it reaches after 6 km of wonderful views out across the Libyan Sea.

The pretty harbour of Ayia Galini stands on the sheltered bay of Messara, on the Libyan Sea.

Its attractive beach, 1 kilometre long, has pebbles of various sizes and, thanks to the mildness of the climate, the temperature of the sea is 18 degrees centigrade summer and winter.

This is what has made Ayia Galini such a popular holiday resort.

Along the coast to the west there are hidden caves, accessible only by boat, with wonderful light effects as the sun plays on the water inside. One of the caves is called the **Cave of Daedalus**, and according to tradition this is where the mythical craftsman had his workshop.

Narrow cobbled streets run up from the harbour into the town. The old-fashioned houses perch one above the other against a steep cliff, with panoramic views out to sea. The village stands to the west of a small but fertile plain formed by the Amarianos or Platys river, which flows into the sea to the east of the village.

In antiquity, the site of the village was occupied by a coastal settlement called Soulia or Soulena, the port for ancient Syvritos. The goddess Artemis was worshipped at a temple here. The city was destroyed by the Saracens in 640 AD. When the old religion was succeeded by Christianity, a church of Christ in Peace

('galini') was erected on the foundations of the temple of Artemis. The town cemetery has a church of the Dormition of the Virgin, which was once a monastery church. According to one version of the story, it is to this church —and its male saint— that the village owes its name, which ought properly to be Ayios Galinis. However, the name might also be derived from ancient Greek words meaning 'peaceful harbour'. Archaeological investigation of the seabed has brought to light a Roman shipwreck of the 3rd century AD, from which were taken figurines, lanterns, busts and copper utensils which can now be seen in the Archaeological Museum at Rethymno. From Ayia Galini there are frequent excursions by sea: east to Matala, and west to Preveli, Plakia, Frangokastelo and Chora Sfakion.

Ayia Galini, one of the most popular resorts in Crete

To the east of Ayia Galini is the beach and the estuary of the Amarianos river

Ayia Galini lies at the middle of our route. It is 67 km from Rethymno through the Amari Valley route and 61 km via the Ayios Vasileios district. Ayia Galini is 69 km from Herakleio via Mesara.

We take the road which will return us to Rethymno. After 5 km there is a turning, left, for the village of **Melambes**. This settlement stands between Mt Kedros and Mt Vouvala, at an altitude of 570 metres, in a fertile and productive area.

The road continues and rejoins the main road to Rethymno. At this point there is a turning on the left, leading in 12 km, after the village of **Sachtouria**, to the beach of **Ayios Pavlos** on Cape Melissa. We continue along the main road, and after 1 km come to a turning (right) to the upland villages of **Kyra Vrysi** and **Orne**. The road leads through most attractive scenery to **Akoumia** (22 km), which stands on the slopes of Mt

Kedros (530 metres), the location of the spring of the Akoumianos river, which flows into the sea to the west of Cape Melissa. The village has a church of the Transfiguration, with wall-paintings, dating from 1389. In one corner are the icons of the founders, depicted in traditional Cretan dress of the 14th century.

After 9 km, the main road leads to **Spili**, the chief town of the Eparchy of Ayios Vasileios.

Spili stands on a rise above the southwest foothills of Mt Kedros. It has numerous streams and is in a thickly-wooded area, where plane trees are very common. The village is an ideal spot for relaxation. In its little square, there are 25 water-spouts in the shape of lions' heads, from whose mouths cool water pours out. From the square, quaint alleyways lead to the upper village, which has pretty houses, courtyards full of flowers and a panoramic view.

The little cave ('spilia') called Skisma, at Peristere, has given its name to the village as a whole.

Spili has old churches to the Sts Theodore, St George and the Transfiguration, with exceptionally fine wall-paintings of the damned.

Still heading back towards Rethymno, we pass through the villages of **Dariviana** and **Mixorouma**, the latter of which took its name from the confluence ('mixi') of a local stream and a river flowing down from Spili. A Minoan settlement has been discovered in the vicinity of the village. At Mixorouma there is a turning to the left for the Preveli Monastery and Plakias.

We continue through Armeni (see p. 141), from which the road runs downhill and we can see Rethymno.

A picturesque alley and the square with the 25 fountains in Spili

ROUTE 3

Rethymno - Perama
Anoyeia - Idaean Cave
Melidoni Cave
Panormos - Bali

This route takes us through the, verdant Mylopotamos valley, with the Kouloukonas range to the north east and the northern slopes of Mt Ida to the south. The visits on this itinerary and the deviations from it complete our tour of the Prefecture of Rethymno.

From Rethymno, we take the Old National Road for Herakleio, passing through the suburbs of **Perivolia**,

Mysiria (both of which have fine beaches) and **Paralia Adele** before reaching **Stavromenos**. In recent years, this area has been much developed for tourism. Large hotel units have sprung up all along the coast, which in the summer hums with life and coming and going. At Stravromenos which has a good beach, the Old National Road crosses the new highway before reaching Perama. **Perama** is the chief town in the Eparchy of Mylopotamos, and it owes its name to the fact that it is situated on a river crossing ('perama'). Today, it has developed into a major commercial centre for the surrounding area. At the same time, it lies at the heart of a communications network.

Picturesqueness from Anoyeia

From Perama, a surfaced road leads south (5 km) to **Margarites**, a village which was important in Venetian times.

In the 9th century it was burned by the Saracens, but it had been fully restored within 100 years. Quite a number of Byzantine churches with wall-paintings have survived. Abbot Gabriel of Arkadi Monastery was from this village.

The villagers make pottery, notably the huge storage jars seen all over the island. Even today, the pots are thrown by hand, using techniques which date back, literally, thousands of years. Preparations for the firing of the pots begin in June, while the firing itself takes place in July and August, in large ovens at the top of the village. Most of the pottery workshops are to the south, on the main road.

The road continues to **Prine**, a village which stands in a wood of cypress and olive trees, and after 12 km, to Eleftherna.

Eleftherna stands on the site of an ancient city by the same name. It was a city-state of importance in Classical and Roman times, though it was first built much earlier, about 800-900 BC. It stood in terraces on the side of a hill, and had a surrounding dry stone wall.

At the top of the city was its acropolis, which was enclosed by circular walls. There was only one narrow entrance, and that was guarded by a high, square tower which is traditionally said never to have fallen to an enemy. The tower stood on the Prine river side. There was also a gorge and two seasonal rivers, the Classical stone bridges over which have survived.

The city was also named Satra or Apollonia, the latter name indicating that Apollo was worshipped here, along with Artemis, who is depicted on the city's coins. Traces of the temple of Apollo have survived, with a church of St Irene —itself ruined today— built over them at a much later date. Ruins of temples and houses cover the slopes of the hill. Around the hill were large, roomy shaft graves hewn out of the rock-graves. On of them was later converted into a church of St Anthony. The irrigation and water-supply system was extremely well designed. The acqueduct has survived, together with two communicating water-tanks hacked out of the rock, with large entrances. The channel along which the water flowed into the tanks, also carved from rock, can also be seen. From one of the tanks, an underground pipe led the water down to the town. All the evidence points to a city-state of great importance.

Eleftherna's port was Pantomatrio (on the site occupied by Fodele today) and it owned large areas of land. Once a rival of Knossos, Eleftherna was later allied with the city to the east. Under Byzantium it was the seat of a bishop.

Among archaeological finds in the area are idols and animal statuettes from the Geometric, Classical and Hellenistic periods. The torso of a female statue, carved in Parian marble and assigned to the 'Daedalian' period (7th century BC) was also found. All the finds are in the Herakleio and Rethymno Archaeological Museum.

Among the sons of Eleftherna were the poet Ametoras —said to have been the first poet to accompany love songs on a lyre— the philosopher Diogenes of Apollonia, the sculptor Timochares and the poet Linnos.

A road has recnetly been built from Eleftherna to the Arkadi Monastery.

We return to Perama, from which we start our main itinerary in an easterly direction. After the village of **Mourtziana**, (34 km), there is a turning south from the Old National Road for Garazo, Axos and Anoyeia.

Garazo is a pretty village whose

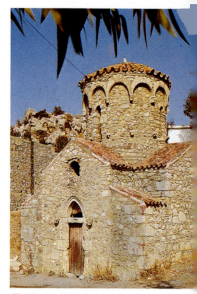

The Byzantine church of St Irene, Axou

square is shaded by an enormous oak tree. We continue after Garazo across a verdant plain, where the landscape is dominated by the colour green in all its possible shades. The plain is crossed by the Oaxos or Yeropotamos river, which also flows through the village of **Axos** (46 km), and gave it its name. The land around this village is very fertile; there is abundant water and the climate is good. The village, in the midst of which is a spring with crystal-clear water, is built on the site of the ancient city of Axos or Oaxos. Oaxos stood on the side of a hill, on a number of terraced levels, and it had a well-fortified acropolis. Its port was at Astali, on the bay where Bali stands today. The city was rich and powerful and continued to thrive under the Romans and Byzantium. It issued its own coins, which showed the head of Apollo or Artemis. In the Roman period it continued to mint coins. Of the 46 churches in the area in Byzantine times, only nine have survived.

To the east of the village, on the road to Herakleio and at the bottom of a deep valley are the ruins of an ancient wall some eight metres high. It is believed that this formed part of the aqueduct which brought water from the Skafidia spring down to the tank at Axos, covering a distance of 3 km. Rather crude idols, a copper headband, Late Minoan tablets and a marble statue of the goddess Demeter have also come to light.

When the inhabitants of Axos were persecuted by the Venetians, many of them fled eastwards and founded a new village, the Axika Anoyeia or Xinganoyeia.

Anoyeia, as the village is more simply known today lies on the north slopes of Mt Ida, on the side of a rise known as Armi.

It is to this site that it owes its name, which means 'high place'. The village is one of the major handicraft and cottage industry centres in Crete. The goods produced are of extremely high quality, with motifs unique to the village. Woven and embroidered articles are the most popular with visitors. It was here that Greece's first women's co-operative was set up. Anoyeia also produces fine singers and lyre-players.

Anoyeia is 55 km from Rethymno, and 36 km from Herakleio. The village stands on three different levels. The road from Axos brings us to the first level, the idyllie **Perachori**, with its plane trees and crystal-clear spring. After this, a wide bend uphill leads to Armi, the centre of Anoyia, the level first settled by the inhabitants of Axos, and the third level, the attractive **Metochi**.

The proud village of Anoyeia stands on the northern slopes of Mt Ida

The people of this village differ from the other Cretans —even from those of nearby areas. The centuries of almost complete isolation up on the mountain mean that they have preserved their traditions in dress, custom and dialect. However, they are notably hospitable and make a great fuss over their visitors. Here, too, in bygone days games, feasts and other celebrations would be held in honour of visitors, in the square of St John with its 12th century church and wall-painting. In his poem on the battle of Lasithi of 1867, Ioannis Konstantinidis describes the men of Anoyeia as follows:

"... They have the feet of hares,
the heart of lions,
They have slim waists,
the trunks of cypress trees.
In days of old,
when they had no knives,
They fought the Turks with the staffs
in their hands.
Now they have swords,
and rifled muskets."

Anoyeia took part in all of Crete's struggles for liberation. Under the Turks, it was forever in revolt. In World War II it was a major centre for the resistance movement. Here, in 1944, the guerillas kept the German General von Kreipe prisoner before smuggling him out to Africa. In retaliation, the Germans killed all the men they could find in the village and burned down all the buildings with the exception of the church of St John. Anoyeia was rebuilt after the Occupation. Every summer there is a festival of the arts.

From Metochi, a passable road climbs up the side of Mt Ida. At **Zomynthos**, about 6 km along the road, recent excavations have brought to light a Minoan villa. After a drive of about 20 km, we come out

Sheep-shea

above the barren but impressive **Nida plateau**, where there is a pavilion run by the NTOG. This is a good spot to rest, enjoying a piece of 'mizithra' (cheese) from Anoyeia or perhaps some spit-roasted goat.

The climb continues along a steep path which leads to the **Idaean Cave** or, as the local shepherds call it, 'the shepherd girl's cave', at a height of 1,538 metres. West of the cave, a ski-ing centre is currently being constructed.

This was a shrine from prehistoric times until the Roman period, and a place of study of mystical doctrines. Another name for it is Arkesio, from the ancient word 'arkesis' = help, since the cave helped Zeus to survive.

The cave entrance is on a spacious slab of rock where there is a carved rectangular altar. The slab is surrounded by a low wall, sloping amphitheatrically, which is also hewn out of the rock.

Inside, there were three chambers and the sanctuary. The second

Mt Psiloritis

chamber acted as the sanctum of the shrine, where the cult statues were placed. Initiation of the faithful took place in the depths of the cave, in the sanctuary. Steps carved in the rock have been excavated all round the cave and copper statuettes have been found.

Exploration of the cave is quite difficult, because the sloping entrance is covered with snow even into the summer.

Inside, objects made of bone and ivory, iron weapons and tools, copper figurines and idols, utensils (trays, tripods and kettles) and votive offerings of shields showing hunting scenes dating from the 8th-7th century BC have been discovered. All are on display in Hall XIX of the Herakleio Archaeological Museum. The finds show us that man was using the cave for the purposes of worship as far back as late Neolithic times.

According to the myths, Rhea brought her son Zeus here, after giving birth to him in the Diktaean Cave, so as to hide him and prevent his farther Kronos from swallowing him (see Mythology, p. 15). In the cave, the nymphs Adracteia and Ida nurtured the infant on milk from the goat Amaltheia and wild honey. Outside, the Kouretes danced the Pyrrhicheios war dance and banged their swords on their shields whenever the baby cried, so that Kronos could not hear him.

In Minoan times, the god of fertility, who dies and is reborn each year, was worshipped in the cave. His cult was succeeded by that of Zeus, who for the ancient Cretans was not immortal, either.

The birth and death of Zeus followed the cycle of nature, suggesting the winter and the spring. Every year there were special festivals to mark the birth of Zeus, and fire sprang from the cave in a ritual which has been compared to the way in which Christ, in the Greek Orthodox celebration, is crucified and resurrected every Easter. During these festivals, those who wished to be initiated into the cult of Zeus —and who came here from all over the Greek world— were taught the mysteries and left offerings to the god.

King Minos himself, so the story goes, came up to the Idaean Cave every nine years to renew his royal mandate and to receive the instructions of the god. The great Pythagoras came to the cave and was initiated into the mysteries of the Idaean Rings.

We return to Anoyeia. The road leads east, through Gonies and Tilyssos (see Herakleio, Route 3) before reaching Herakleio.

We retrace our steps to Axos. Here, a turning to the right leads to the village of **Zoniana**.

Sunset at Panormos

Near the village is the superb **Sendoni Cave**, whose name comes from a freedom fighter or perhaps a robber whose lair it was. The scenery is most spectacular; on the one side is the cave, flanked by rocks, with Mt Ida in the background. A small spring and the infinite distances visible in the other directions complete the scene. The cave, too, is spacious and impressive.

We continue through the village of **Livadeia**. The village is sited in the midst of a plain of olive trees, vineyards and carobs. Livadeia was on this site as far back as the 3th century, as witnessed by the church of the Annunciation which stands there, and it was once called Leventochori ('village of brave men') because the Turks never settled in it. We pass through these last villages among the foothills of Mt Ida and make our way back to Perama.

From Perama, we head north east this time. The road is surfaced and the pleasant route, with views over the plain, leads to the **Melidoni** or **Yerontospilio cave**, which is near the village of the same name. In Minoan times, the cave was a place of worship and tablets and a double·axe have been found there. Among the deities worshipped were the giant Talos, to whom, according to the myths, King Minos entrusted the implementation of the laws, Hermes Talaios and Zeus Talaios.

In modern times, the most important event was the suffocation in the cave of 370 villagers who had taken shelter there. The Turks set fire to various materials and threw them into the entrance of the cave when the villagers refused to surrender, and so they choked to death on the smoke. Their bones have been preserved in a mausoleum near the cave.

We now leave Perama heading north. A surfaced road leads in 8 km to the coastal village of **Panormos**. The village is built on a fine and densely-vegetated site between two bays, and it has developed into a notable tourist resort. It also acts as a centre for trade and fishing in the area. It is believed to stand on the site of ancient Panormos, which was the port for Eleftherna.

Coins which have been found in the area and which depict the head of a goddess on one side and a palm tree on the other have been assigned to Panormos. In early Byzantine times it was the seat of a bishop. A large Early Christian basilica which had a wooden roof has been excavated. In the village, a number of mansions with tiled roofs, many windows and stone-carved decoration have survived.

We now take the new National Road for Herakleio. As we travel east, a branch road at 33 km takes us down to the pretty fishing village of **Bali**. The village stands at the head of a little bay, on the site of ancient Astale, port of Axos. The heights around the bay form small valleys and little cones. Thanks to its natural position, which is protected from the north west wind, and also to its fine pebble beach, Bali is an excellent place for swimming.

Near Bali, on the slopes of Mt Kouloukonas, is the restored **Atali Monastery**, dating from the 17th century and dedicated to John the Baptist.

We return to the National Road, which continues to the east and passes through the village of **Sises** before arriving at Herakleio.

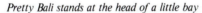

Pretty Bali stands at the head of a little bay

THE PREFECTURE OF HERAKLEIO

The Prefecture of Herakleio lies between Mt Psiloritis and the Lasithiotika Mountains and is the largest administrative division of Crete. It has an area of 2,641 square km and a population of approximately 250,000. The area is full of contradictions; there are peaceful and fertile plains of considerable size (the largest being that of Messara), and high and imposing mountains, sometimes bare and sometimes smothered in a riot of cypresses and holm oak. The hills are covered with fruit trees: chestnuts, date palms, banana trees.

And along the coast are inviting sandy beaches and secret coves where the water is crystal-clear.

Both the coastal and the inland parts of the Prefecture have been inhabited without interruption since prehistoric times, and so the area is the richest in Crete in terms of archaeological sites, with the marvellous Minoan palaces at Knossos, Phaestos and Mallia and even the town of Herakleio itself. From the point of view of tourist facilities, the Prefecture has a complete range of services.

There are daily car-ferry sailings from Herakleio to Piraeus. Herakleio international airport is fully capable of meeting the considerable air traffic demands. There are domestic flights to Athens, Thessaloniki, Rhodes, Mykonos, Paros and Santorini.

Inside the Prefecture, there are town and long-distance (KTEL) bus services to all the villages, beaches and archaeological sites.

In the summer, there are ferry sailings to the Cyclades, while cruise liners operating out of Venice link Herakleio to Limassol in Cyprus and Haifa in Israel.

The City of Herakleio

According to Strabo, the modern city of Herakleio stands on the site of Herakleia, one of the ports of Knossos in antiquity.

The settlement continued to bear the name Herakleia throughout the Roman and first Byzantine periods, but its real history does not begin until 824, when it was captured by the Arabs. They fortified the town, built walls and dug a large moat round it: 'handax', in Arabic, thus giving the town the name it bore down to the 19th century.

The Arabs made Handak or Candia the base for their pirate raids and it was the largest slave-market in the eastern Mediterranean.

After a total of six unsuccessful campaigns, Candia was eventually retaken for Byzantium by Nicepho-

rus Phocas in 961, marking the end of Arab dominion in Crete and eliminating the corsairs who had been the scourge of the whole Mediterranean. The town was destroyed in the siege, but it was rebuilt and new, strong walls constructed.

The Byzantines remained until 1204, when the Byzantine Empire was broken up by the Crusaders, and in their time the name Candia became internationally known and externded to the whole island: 'Isola di Candia', it was called. The locals knew it as 'Kastro' ('castle') or 'Megalo Kastro' ('great castle').

In 1210, Candia was taken by the Venetians and became capital of the island. During the four centuries of Venetian rule, the wonderful walls were built: work on them started in 1462 and took more than a century to complete.

The design was by the famous

A copper engraving of Herakleio (N. Visscher, 1682)

military architect Sammicheli, and the walls of Candia were the supreme example of fortificatory architecture of their time.

The Venetians also built the harbour and adorned the town with magnificent public and private buildings, churches, fountains, etc., simultaneously making it an important commercial centre.

At this time, Candia flourished in the arts and letters under the influence of the Italian Renaissance, which was then in full swing. After the fall of Constantinople in 1453, many scholars and artists took refuge in Candia, further strengthening learning there.

The Monastery of St Catherine on Mt Sinai set up a school in Candia, where theology, law and philosophy were taught.

The strength of the walls can be seen in the fact that although it took the Turks only two years to conquer the rest of Crete, Candia held out for 21 years of bitter siege (1648-1669). When they eventually captured the town, they gave it a very oriental look: the ruined houses were rebuilt, churches were converted into mosques, and the walls were repaired. Many Christians left the area, under the threat of massacre, and those who stayed were constantly in a state of rebellion; this state of affairs continued until the longed-for day of liberation arrived.

After the departure of the Turks the town was given back its ancient name, Herakleio, by the Assembly of Freedom Fighters which met at Armeni.

Although Herakleio has been destroyed and rebuilt on a number of occasions, it still has many interesting monuments and sights.

Plan of the
Town of Herakleio

Key to the map

1. Gule
   (Venetian Fortress)
2. Venetian Harbour
3. Port Authority
4. Buses to Lasithi
5. Commercial School
6. Archaeological Museum
7. E.O.T. (Tourist
   Organisation)
8. Eleftherias Square
9. Olympic Airways
10. Public Garden
11. St Mark
12. Venizelou Square
13. Morosini Fountain
14. Loggia
15. St Titus
16. O.T.E.
    (Telecommunications)
17. El Greko Park
18. Historical Museum
19. Holy Trinity
20. St Catherine
21. St Minas (Cathedral)
22. Kornarou Square
23. The New Gate
24. Tomb of Kazantzakis
    Martinengo Bastion
25. Sports Field
26. St Andrew
27. Chania
    or Pantokrator Gate
28. Buses to Western Crete
    Rethymno - Chania

Herakleio today is a modern city, capital of the Prefecture of the same name and, since 1972, of the whole of Crete. It is the island's largest city, with a population in excess of 110,000. This is the seat of the Church of Crete. It is also the focus of the economy of the island, with much trade and industry. Thousands of visitors arrive each year at its harbour and at Herakleio airport, which is the island's largest.

Herakleio consists of the **Old Town**, which is that part lying within the walls (although little has been done to preserve it) and the **New Town**, which spreads outside the walls. The walls cover a triangular area, with the sea as its base and the Martinengo Bastion as its vertex. There were seven bastions: *Sampionera, Vituri, Jesus, Martinengo, Bethlehem, Pantocrator* and *St Andrew*, and four gates: the *Mole Gate* (demolished by the British), the *St George Gate* or *Lazaretto*, where today there is a bust of Kazantzakis, the *Pantokrator* or *Chania Gate* and the *Jesus* or New Gate.

Our tour of the Old Town, which has not been preserved like those of Chania and Rethymno, begins at the *Venetian harbour*, where yachts and fishing-boats moor today. The entrance to the harbour is protected by the *Great Gule*, an impressive two-storey fortress which is a representative example of Venetian architecture. Its rooms were used for storing foodstuffs and military supplies, as the residence of the Venetian captains and as prison cells for the Greek rebels whom the Venetians managed to catch.

Herakleio with its harbour and the Gule fortress. Mt Youchtas dominates the background

Although the **Gules** has a Turkish name, it was built by the Venetians, in 1303. It was destroyed by earthquake and rebuilt in 1523-40. The port was used by merchant vessels, and also by the warships of the Venetians. On the quay were the boat-building sheds, and the position of the modern Customs house was occupied by the vaulted arches for the Venetian galleys. Together with the vaults which we see today, these made up the Arsenal.

To the west of the harbour, in the *Bentenaki* district, in *Kalokairinou St*, is the neo-Classical building which houses the **Historical Museum of Herakleio**. This was founded in 1952 by the Society for Cretan Historical Research and it contains exhibits of historical, religious and folklore interest dating from as far back as the Early Christian period. Its halls contain Byzantine, Venetian and Turkish sculpture, inscriptions, engravings, Byzantine icons, local costumes, furniture, woven goods, documents, wood-carvings and musical instruments. One hall is dedicated to the great Greek author Nikos Kazantzakis.

The harbour is the beginning of *Martyron 25 Avgoustou St*, which takes its name ('Martyrs of 25 August') from the massacre on that date of numerous Greeks and British by the Turks. It leads to the centre of town and it is one of Herakleio's busiest commercial thoroughfares. On this street stands the *church of St Titus*, patron saint of the city. The church was severely damaged but was rebuilt in 1557. Under the Turks, it was called the Vezir Cami and it was a mosque. In 1856 it was demolished by an earthquake, but it was reconstructed once again on its old foundations. The skull of St Titus is kept in the church, with other treasures.

Opposite the church is the *Town Hall* and the restored *Loggia*, an elegant and magnificent building which was first erected in 1626-28 and acted as a club for the nobility.

On the next block is the *church of St Mark*, protector of the Venetian Republic. The church was first built in 1239 as a three-aisled basilica with a wooden roof. The Turks converted it into a mosque. The Society for Cretan Historical Studies returned it to its original form in 1956, and now it is used as a lecture and concert hall. It also contains a permanent exhibition of copies of 13th and 14th century murals.

In front of St Mark is *Eleftheriou Venizelou Square.* In Venetian times this was the centre of the city, and even today it is a meeting-place and the heart of Herakleio beats here. All day long there are crowds of people in its cafes, restaurants and souvenir shops. The square was designed along the lines of the Piazza San Marco in Venice. On one side was the huge Venetian mansion of the Duke of Crete, which housed the courts and other departments of the administration. Some vaults have remained today. In the centre of the square is the *Morosini Fountain,* or 'the Lions', as the local people call it. The fountain was built in 1628 by Francesco Morosini, Governor of the island.

Scenes from everyday life in Herakleio harbour

Since Herakleio had a very erratic water supply, its Venetian governors decided to put down their names in posterity by building aqueducts and fountains. Morosini built an aqueduct through which water was piped from Mt Youchtas to the city. This aqueduct ended at the Morosini Fountain, which is adorned with coats-of-arms and fine scenes from Greek mythology —Tritons, nymphs, dolphins, etc.— and flanked by four lions.

Martyron 25 Avgoustou St ends in *Nikiforou Foka Square*, or the *Meidani*, from which many of the town's main streets radiate out. This is the start of *1866 St,* along the side of which is the city's central market, with its wealth of agricultural produce on display in an atmosphere of constant bustle and coming and going.

Herakleio market

The Morosini fountain, at the centre of the town

1866 St ends in *Kornarou Square*, where stands the ruined church of the Saviour. In the square is the earliest Venetian fountain, the *Bembo Fountain* built in 1552-54 and decorated with coats-of-arms and figurative scenes. The adjacent Turkish pavilion was refurbished in 1982 and is now one of the most attractive cafes in Herakleio.

From Nikiforou Foka Sq. we take *Kalokairinou Ave.,* also known as *Megali Strata.* Where this crosses *Ayiou Mina St* it forms *Ayia Ekaterini Square*, in which stands the basilica of St Catherine. This church was a dependency of the monastery of the same name on Mt Sinai, and in the 16th and 17th centuries it housed a school which was of the greatest importance for the intellectual life of the island.

To the north of the church is the *Ayii Deka* ('ten saints') chapel, which today houses the **Ecclesiastical Museum.** There is a collection of religious art from all over Crete: wall-paintings, church vessels, and six 16th century icons by the famous icon-painter Michail Damaskinos. Of these icons, that portaying the *Adoration of the Magi* is particularly representative of Cretan art of this time (see p. 65).

Also here is the **Cathedral of St Minas,** one of the largest churches in Greece. Completed in 1895, it is cruciform with a dome and has two tall bell-towers. On its north western side the old church of St Minas and the Presentation of the Virgin has survived in excellent condition. Also on this street are the offices of the Archbishopric of Crete.

The Venetian loggia

The Bembo fountain

The Koumbes café

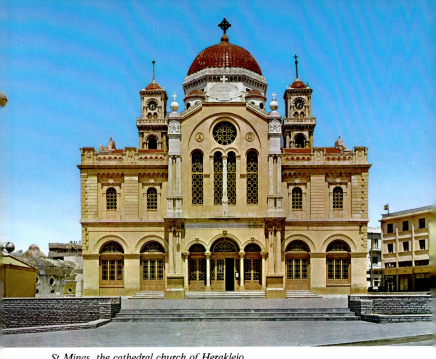

St Minas, the cathedral church of Herakleio

The Chania Gate

Kalokairinou Ave. ends at the **Chania Gate** (also called the Pantokrator Gate from a church which stood there), through which Herakleio's communications with western Crete pass. The gate bears a winged lion of St Mark, above which is a relief bust of the Pantokrator. To the left of the Chania Gate is *Plastira Ave.* with the *Bethlehem Bastion.*

Plastira Ave. leads to a staircase from which one can mount to the highest point in the city, the *Martinengo Bastion;* this is the only place at which the top of the walls is accessible. The view is panoramic: to the north lies the Old Town, with the New Town spread out to the south and the deep green vineyards of **Finikia** behind.

In this idyllic spot is the *tomb of Nikos Kazantzakis*. It consists of a simple slab of stone and a wooden cross; on the plain white slab are carved the words of the great author: *"I hope for nothing. I fear nothing. I am free"*.

Where Plastira Ave. joins *Evans St* is the *New Gate* or *Gate of Jesus*, which, as its name suggests, is the most recent of all the entrances into Herakleio.

We take Evans St and cross Kornarou Square and Nikiforou Foka Square before reaching *Dikaiosynis Ave.,* where the public buildings of the *Courtroom,* the *Prefecture*, the *Tourist Police* and the *Tax Office* stand. The *bust of Daskaloyannis*, leader of the 1770 rising, stands between the Prefecture and the Courthouse.

The harbour by night

Dikaiosynis Ave. leads to *Eleftherias Square*, which is also known as *Tris Kamares* ('three arches') because of the three vaulted arches of the aqueduct which stand there. Across them passed the water pipe which ended at the Morosini Fountain.

Here there is a bust of Kazantzakis, on the spot occupied until 1917 by the Gate of *St George* or *Lazaretto*. The facade of the gate was decorated with coats-of-arms and a marble frieze showing St George on horseback, which is in the Historical Museum today.

On the other sided of the square, in a modern building, is the **Archaeological Museum**, which houses one of the most important such collections in Greece. *Bofor St* runs from here to the long-distance bus station and the new harbour.

The Archaeological Museum

The **Archaeological Museum** is housed in a two-storey building in the neo-Classical style, constructed in 1937-40, situated on the NW side of Eleftherias Square. The collection of objects it contains was started in 1883, when the Herakleio Educational Association began to collect antiquities with the purpose of founding a museum. After a number of temporary homes, the building we see today was eventually built. In designing the building, provision was made for its use as a museum: it is aligned north to south, and so there is natural light throughout the day.

The Museum is unique of its type in that it contains only exhibits from Crete, covering the entire course of Cretan civilisation from the Neolithic period to the end of the Helleno-Roman era.

Eleftherias Square. In the background, to the right, the Archaeological Museum

The Ladies in Blue, a fresco from Knossos

The exhibits are organised and arranged in absolute chronological order, thus allowing visitors to follow the development of the island's great cultural tradition without any specialised knowledge of archaeology or even history. On the ground floor are the exhibits from the palaces at Knossos, Phaistos and Mallia, dating from the prepalatial, early palatial and late palatial periods and extending into the Greek and Geometric eras, and there is a special hall dedicated to sarcophagi.

On the upper floor are the frescoes, the Yamalakis collection and sculpture and smaller objects from the Greek and Helleno-Roman periods.

The jewellery, frescoes and exceptionally beautiful vases from the Minoan palaces are of the greatest artistic value. Among these exhibits, perhaps the faience figurine of the goddess with the snakes —a fertility symbol (see p. 23)— stands out.

The halls of the Museum are arranged in units in terms of their contents. The Latin capital numbers correspond to the dates of the exhibits.

Among the most important exibits are the following:

Gallery II: Finds from the Early Palace period (2000-1700 BC). Kamares ware with multi-coloured decoration.

Gallery III: Finds from the Early Palace period. Case 41: the famous Phaestos Disc, with writing in a script that has not as yet been deciphered.

Gallery IV: Exhibits from the Late Palace period (1700-1450 BC), found at the palaces of Knossos and Phaestos. Case 50: two statuettes of the Minoan snake goddess. Case 56: Ivory figures relating to the bull-leaping ceremony. The figures are shown in the act of leaping.

Gallery VII: Finds from the Late Palace period. Case 94: the incomparable Harvester Vase, from Ayia Triada. The farmers return home, in a procession of thanksgiving for a good harvest. Case 101: gold necklace with two bees (see photo. p. 32).

Gallery VIII: Late Palace period finds from Kato Zakros. Case 111: a rhyton in the shape of a temple.

Gallery XIII: Minoan sarcophagi from a variety of all periods.

Gallery XX: Sculpture from the Greek and Roman periods.

Upper floor: Minoan frescoes (wall-paintings) from Knossos, Amnisos and Ayia Triada.

Gallery XIV: case 171: the famous Ayia Triada sarcophagus decorated with frescoes — one of the finest examples of Minoan painting. On the walls are the incomparable frescoes of the Toreador, the Prince of the Lilies from Amnisos and the Wild Cat from Ayia Triada.

Gallery XV: La Parisienne, a wonderful fresco from the Knossos Palace. Fragments of a relief showing acrobats (see photo. p. 29).

Gallery XVI: the fresco of the monkey gathering saffron in a field, and the Blue Bird fresco.

Gallery XVII: the Yamalakis collection. Case 175: the Neolithic fertility goddess.

1

Exhibits in the Museum:

1. *Clay figurine (Petsofas, 1950 BC)*
2. *A faience ibex (Knossos, 1600 BC)*
3. *The Labyrinth on a coin from Knossos*
4. *Part of a gold bracelet*
5. *A model of a sanctuary with a figurine of a goddess* 6. *A Kamares ware spout*
7. *A rhyton of mineral cyrstal (Zakros, 1450 BC)*

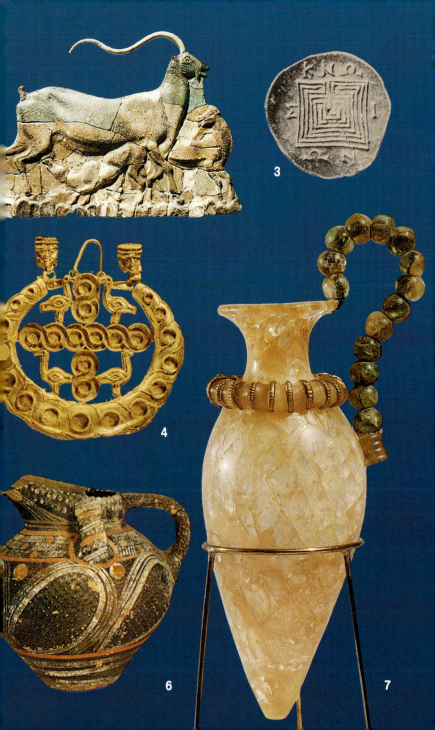

3

4

6

7

KNOSSOS
(5 km from Herakleio)

We begin our acquaintance with the Prefecture of Herakleio by visiting Knossos, the most important of the Minoan palaces. Because of the importance and the size of the palace, the archaeological site does not form part of our basic routes.

Knossos is, of course, Crete's most famous monument: the largest, strongest and most impressive of the island's Minoan palaces. Knossos is a must for every visitor to Crete. As Kazantzakis put it, in Knossos one's heart beats with a different rhythm and one's mind is flooded with questions. When these ruins were a Minoan palace, they were inhabited by a king, Minos, descendant of the mythical Minos who sprang from the union of Europa and Zeus. Minos was the founder of Cretan naval power, he was the scourge of pirates; he was also a wise legislator and the head of the Minoan religion.

The purpose of the Minotaur myth (see Mythology) was to show the might of Minos and Athens' subjugation to the island power. In addition, in the Labyrinth we find a hint of the number and complexity of the rooms in the palace, where it would be easy for a stranger to lose himself.

This was the famous palace of Knossos, the most ancient and most renowned city of Crete, around which the Minoan civilisation grew and prospered. The site was first inhabited in Neolithic times, around 5000-6000 BC, and this is the first city-state which can be called Greek, home of the first Greek religion and the first Greek art.

The palace stands on the hill now known as Kefalas, next to the river

Kairatos in the midst of a fertile plain. It had a total area of some 22,000 square metres, and around it stretched a city whose population has been estimated at between 80,000 and 100,000.

Its outlets to the sea were at Amnisos and Herakleio, while its territory on Crete extended from Mt Ida to Lyttos on the western slopes of Mt Dikte.

After the glories of the Minoan age, Knossos prospered once again in historical times (8th-6th centuries) and was the leading city on Crete, though by this time it had rivals in Gortyn and Lyttos. In the 3rd century BC it joined the alliance of Cretan cities which campaigned —unsuccessfully— against Lyttos. Later, however, when the Lyttians

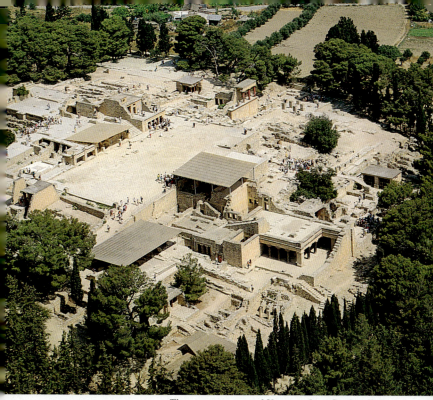

The eastern aspect of Knossos, from Profitis Ilias

were off warring elsewhere, the alliance took their city and destroyed it. In 166 BC it allied itself with Gortyn to destroy Raucos, near the modern village of Ayios Myronas.

In 69 BC it was taken by the Roman Metellus and, although still important, lost its leading position on the island to Gortyn. In Early Christian times Knossos was the seat of a bish—p, later losing this distinction to Raucos. It was finally destroyed by the Arabs; weeds grew over the site and it was forgotten. Under the Venetians, a small village grew up here, by the name Makryteichos.

Knossos minted a large variety of coins. Most show the Minotaur holding a stone in its hand. The Labyrinth is also a favourite theme; sometimes it is shown as square and sometimes circular, with the word ΚΝΩΣΙΩΝ. Another theme is the head of Athena, the goddess who founded the dynasty of Knossos, and Demeter is shown to mark the city's pride in its boast of having been the first place where wheat was used as food.

However, whatever the motif on one side of the coin, the other always depicted the Labyrinth. Apart from its connection with the mythical home of the Minotaur, the word labyrinth also means 'the house of Labrys' — that is, of the double axe, since labrys is derived from a Lydian word meaning precisely that. The double axe was the most sacred symbol of Minoan religion and as a decorative motif is to be found everywhere in Knossos.

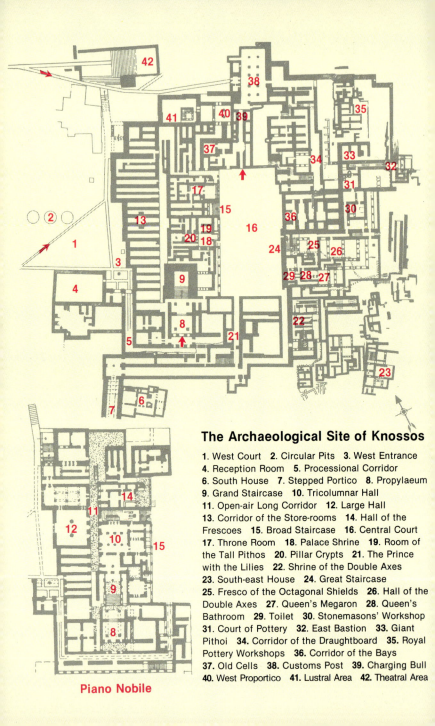

The Archaeological Site of Knossos

1. West Court **2.** Circular Pits **3.** West Entrance
4. Reception Room **5.** Processional Corridor
6. South House **7.** Stepped Portico **8.** Propylaeum
9. Grand Staircase **10.** Tricolumnar Hall
11. Open-air Long Corridor **12.** Large Hall
13. Corridor of the Store-rooms **14.** Hall of the
Frescoes **15.** Broad Staircase **16.** Central Court
17. Throne Room **18.** Palace Shrine **19.** Room of
the Tall Pithos **20.** Pillar Crypts **21.** The Prince
with the Lilies **22.** Shrine of the Double Axes
23. South-east House **24.** Great Staircase
25. Fresco of the Octagonal Shields **26.** Hall of the
Double Axes **27.** Queen's Megaron **28.** Queen's
Bathroom **29.** Toilet **30.** Stonemasons' Workshop
31. Court of Pottery **32.** East Bastion **33.** Giant
Pithoi **34.** Corridor of the Draughtboard **35.** Royal
Pottery Workshops **36.** Corridor of the Bays
37. Old Cells **38.** Customs Post **39.** Charging Bull
40. West Proportico **41.** Lustral Area **42.** Theatral Area

Piano Nobile

The first archaeologist to work at Knossos was a Greek, Minos Kalokairinos, in 1878, but it was not until 1900, when Sir Arthur Evans arrived on the scene, that excavations were at all systematic. The palace we see today is not the first built on the site (which, like all the other palaces on Crete, was flattened by the earthquake of 1700 BC). It is the second palace, rebuilt after the destruction of the first. Its magnificence marks the resurgence of Minoan Crete in the period until the final catastrophe in around 1400 BC.

The archaeological site: The numbering of the site will help visitors find their way around, and the numbers correspond to those on the diagram.

We enter the archaeological site of the Palace by the *West Court* **1**, where the upward-sloping corridors and the altar bases indicate that this must have been the starting-point for processions. On our right is a bust of Evans, the reconstructor of Knossos.

On our left are three *Circular Pits* **2**, as much as five metres deep; at the bottom can be seen the remains of the houses which were built on this site before the palace and were later used as granaries or as dumps for the remains of sacrifices. This latter view is supported by the ceremonial implements and animal bones found there.

We follow the corridor south. We enter the palace proper via the *West Entrance* **3**. On the stone base which has survived was a wooden column. This is followed by the guard-house and a *reception room* **4**, in which there was a throne.

We continue along the narrow *Processional Corridor* **5**, in a southerly direction. The corridor takes its name from the frescoes which were found there, showing a procession of hundreds of young men and women, almost life size, bringing offerings to the gods. At one time, the corridor, which ran in parallel to the western facade of the Palace, turned to the east and ended in the Central Court. Today it is not possible to follow it for all its length and for that reason we leave it at an earlier point and turn through the door on our left and head for the *South Propylaeum*.

To the south west of the Processional Corridor, on the edge of the Palace, can be seen the remains of the *South House* **6**. This was built in about 1600 BC, after the destructive earthquake, in the vicinity of the *Stepped Portico* **7**, which lies to its west, and must have been the property of a nobleman.

A little further down the stream we can see the foundations of a bridge built in the Early Palace period, which linked the Stepped Portico to the *Caravanserai*. This building was used as a purification area: it had running water and baths where visitors entering the palace at this side could wash before presenting themselves before the priest-king.

A wide paved road began here, and led to the southern coast of the island; along it, commercial traffic set our for Egypt and the East. In the Caravanserai was found the famous fresco of the *partidges and hoopooes*, a copy of which has been installed in its original position. This building faces on to the south side of the Palace, which was crowned by the consecrational horns and where the *South Entrance* was located.

Now we enter the palace by the imposing *Propylaeum,* **8**, where there were frescoes of a procession of young men carrying vessels. Here too was found the famous *Cup Bearer*, which is in Herakleio Museum today.

We continue to the *Grand Staircase* **9**, which was flanked by rows of columns and which led to the upper floor, the *Piano Nobile*, where the official apartments were. The Grand Staircase was completely destroyed by the earthquakes and has been restored by the archaeologists. At the head of the staircase we pass through an entrance with an antechamber and then into the *Tricolumnar Hall* **10**, where the procession of young men may have ended. To the south was the Treasury; its items of value and the gifts brought to the Sanctuary had fallen through on to the ground floor, where they were found.

The Piano Nobile is bisected by the open-air *Long Corridor* **11**, which let light into the rooms on either side of it. After the Corridor, on the left, is the large *Hall* **12**, of the Two Columns and a smaller one with six columns, which may have been a shrine. From here we can see the ground-floor store-rooms, where many enormous storage jars for wine, olive oil, grain and honey were found. The total number of jars found in the palace store-rooms was about 400, with a total capacity of 78,000 kilos; there were 21 store-rooms, of which three, on the southern edge of the palace, were no longer in use. The most important finds produced from this area of the palace, however, were the piles of clay tablets in Linear B script, containing inventories of the palace fittings and products, together

with the names of the men and women who lived there.

It seems that this Great Hall must have been the palace accounting department; the tablets had fallen through on to the ground floor. There used to be a wooden staircase which led into the *Long Corridor* **13** of the store-rooms, which unlike the Piano Nobile corridor, was quite dark. When the staircase burned down in a fire it was not replaced.

We now enter the *Hall of the Frescoes* **14**, which is above the Throne Room and communicates with it by a spiral staircase. This hall contains a series of copies of frescoes found in the palace and in a neighbouring house. Here we can ad-

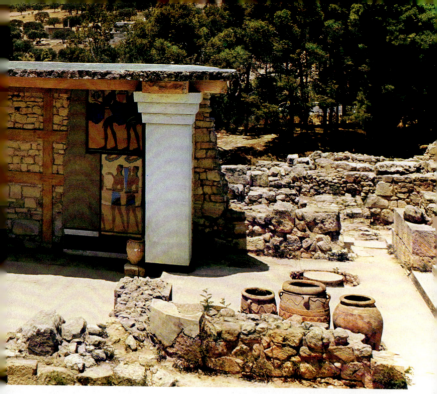

The south Propylum

mire the *Blue Ladies* and the *Miniature Frescoes* from the cell area, the *Leader of the Blacks* from the House of Frescoes and a whole series of representations of the plant and animal kingdom.

On the south side of the Hall of the Frescoes, at right angles to the Long Corridor, a *broad staircase* **15** leads down to the Central Court. The traces of more steps on our left testify to the fact that the palace also had a second floor at this point.

The *Central Court* **16**, measuring 50×20 m, which was paved, separates the official chambers on the western side from the private apartments on the east. As in all the Minoan palaces, it is the nucleus of the

whole building; it was used for religious ceremonies, athletic performances and contests, and other activities. In addition, it provided light and fresh air for the surrounding rooms.

On the western side of the Central Court, under the Hall of the Frescoes, was the *Throne Room* **17** set amid a group of rooms dating from the Late Minoan period. The Throne Room consists of an antechamber with stone benches (blackened by the fire which destroyed Knossos), and contains a wooden throne which is a copy of that in the Throne Room itself. Here the archaeologists have placed a large purple limestone vessel.

The throne room

We now come to the *Throne Roome* **17** proper, which is protected by a wooden railing. On the north wall is Minos' alabaster throne; hawks, symbols of power, are painted on the walls to the right and left. Directly opposite the throne is a small *Lustral Area*.

After the Throne Roome is a small *Shrine* with a high step on which cult objects were found. Next to this is a room equipped with a kind of grill which, it is believed, was a *Kitchen*.

To the south of this group of buildings was the *Palace Shrine* **18**. One of the Miniature Frescoes shows the arrangement of this area. A few steps down lead to the *Lobby of the Stone Seat*, an open area, beyond which is the *Room of the Tall Pithos* **19** and then in the *Treasuries* of the shrine, where the superb faience snake-goddess was found. To the west of the lobby are two rooms with square pillars in their centre, with the double axe carved on them. These are the *Pillar Crypts* **20**, which are believed to have been of a sacred nature.

To the north of the first Crypt is the *Channel Room,* where the blood of sacrifices was collected. From the Lobby, a double door opened on to a number of store-rooms. The three last store-rooms to the south belong to the Old Palace.

From here, a narrow staircase leads up to an open area — the only part of the Palace to have been used in subsequent centuries, as the Greek temple which stood here testifies.

In the southwest corner of the Central Court, where the processional corridor ends, is a copy of the famous relief fresco called *The Prince with the Lilies* **21** in its original position. The fresco shows an idealised Minoan royal figure.

From the *South Entrance,* beneath which in Early Minoan times was an underground guard room hewn out of the rock, a corridor led eastwards to the small *Shrine of the Double Axes* **22**. This is an austere little building dating from the Late Minoan period. To the south of it there was a lustral area, together with the remains of a staircase and a light-shaft. From here, the *Corridor of the Sword Tablets* led north to the Queen's apartments; the corridor took its name from the clay tablets discovered there. Beneath the southeastern corner of the Palace are the ruins of houses from the Middle Minoan period. In the *House of the Chancel Screen,* which borders on the other two, there was a raised seat of

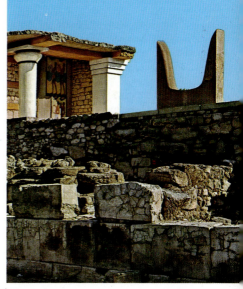

The "ox-horns", a sacred symbol for the Minoans

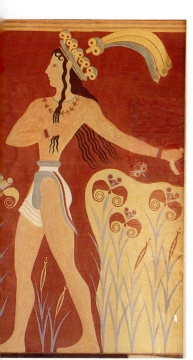

honour. A narrow corridor may have led to a staircase to the Central Court. From here, one can reach the *Southeast House* **23**, with its pillar crypt, a kiln and an altar for sacrifices.

The east wing of the Palace stood on a hill, and at some points it must have been five floors in height. This wing is dominated by the *Great Staircase* **24**, with its broad, low steps, one of the greatest works of ancient architecture. It begins about halfway along the eastern side of the Central Court and divides the east wing into its northern section, where the Palace's store-rooms and workshops were located, and its southeastern section, where the royal apartments were.

'The Prince of the Lilies'

We climb the Great Staircase, with its light-shaft and the columns which lined it, an outstanding example of Minoan engineering. On the east wall of the veranda on the first floor of the *Upper Portico* has been placed a copy of the *Fresco of the Octagonal Shields* **25**.

On the ground floor was the main *Hall of the Colonnades.* The shaft here supplied the rooms with light and fresh air. Though a door in the north east side of the Hall of the Colonnades we enter a corridor and turn right, coming to the *Hall of the Double Axes* **26**, so-called because of the frequency with which this motif is repeated on the walls. To the left is the *Outer Chamber of the Double Axes,* where a wooden throne now occupies the place of the original. To

the east and south of this hall there were colonnades and light-shafts.

We leave the inner hall through a doorway to the south, and after passing along a curving corridor reach the *Queen's Megaron* **27**. Over the entrance is the imposing *Dolphin Fresco.* On the north west side of this hall is a small room with a bath and a banded column, the *Queen's Bathroom* **28**. To the south west is the *Corridor of the Painted Pithos,* which ends at a *Toilet* **29**. Light comes from an open area called the *Court of the Distaffs* because of the symbols carved on to its flagstones. On the wall in a corner of the Toilet and above a stone step can be seen the holes used for the plumbing installation; in the eastern wall is the toilet itself, connected to an advanced

The grand staircase in the eastern wing

The dolphin mural from the queen's apartments

drainage network, details of which can be seen in the dark corridor which follows.

After this corridor, on the right, is another dark room: the *Dungeon,* which may have been a treasury. This room produced a large clay tablet with lists of names, next to each of which was pictogram showing whether they were men or women.

We continue along the corridor, coming to a staircase, on the left, to the upper floors. Under this stair was found the ivory *Bull-leaper* statuette. The corridor brings us back to the Hall of the Colonnades; from here, we continue through the Hall of the Double Axes to come out into the *East Portico* of the Palace.

Behind this is a hall with a square hypostyle, the *Stonemasons' Workshop* **30**, where pieces of Spartan basalt in the process of being worked on were found.

Then comes the *School of Pottery,* with benches and pits. To the north of this is the open-air *Court of the Stone Spout* **31**, which took its name from the spout which led off the rainwater from the roof of the *Great East Hall.*

To the east is the *East Bastion* **32** with the interesting *East Entrance,* where there is a complex system for impeding the force of the rainwater as it runs down. The flat space between here and the East Entrance and the stream may have been used as the *Bullring,* where, according to the myths, the Athenian youths and girls fought the Minotaur.

Further to the north of the Court of the Stone Spout are the *Magazines of the Giant Pithoi* **33**, remnants of the Old Palace. We continue along the paved *Corridor of the Draught-board* **34** where an inlaid gaming-board was found. Under the railing can be seen the clay pipes from the aqueduct of the Old Palace. To the west of this corridor is the *North West Hall* and to the north east are the *Royal Pottery Workshops* **35**, where the wonderfully delicate 'egg-shell' ware of the Middle Minoan period was found. To the south east of the Corridor of the Draught-board there is an open court with the upper part of the drain which ended in the Court of the Stone Spout. From here a doorway to the west leads to the *Corridor of the Bays* **36**whose

The reconstructed western colonn

A jar
symbol bearing the sacred double-axe

massive pillars show that there must have been a large hall on the upper floor. We continue, reaching the *Upper Portico* and, on the left, the *Upper Hall of the Double Axes.* The door to the south west leads to the *Upper Queen's Megaron.* The floor-plan here is exactly the same as on the ground floor. To the south, a narrow corridor —where the vases with the lilies were found— leads to two rooms which to-day have been covered. Behind these rooms, the *Corridor of the Sword Tablets* leads off to the little *Shrine of the Double Axes.*

We return to the Central Court and head north, going into the *North Entrance Corridor.* To the east of this were store-rooms, while to the west are the foundations of the oldest part

the north entrance corridor. In the background, the north tank

of the Palace, the so-called *Old Cells* **37**. When the New Palace was built, these rooms were buried beneath its floor. It was above this area that the *Saffrongatherer* and the *Miniature Frescoes* were found. The corridor ends in a hypostyle chamber, the socalled *Customs Post* **38**, to the east of which is the *North East Entrance Corridor*.

Initially, the North Entrance was the same width as the Customs Post, but in later times the fear of invasion caused the Minoans to narrow it to the width of this corridor and build bastions on either side. Above the bastions are porticoes with friezes in relief. The western portico, which has been restored, was chosen as the site for the modern copy of the wonderfully lifelike fresco of the *Charging Bull* **39** shown against the background of an olive grove. To the west of these porticos is the *North West Proportico* **40**, followed by an *Antechamber* and the *Lustral Area* **41**, where those entering the Palace from this side could be purified.

As we leave the Palace to the northwest, we come to the *Theatral Area* **42**. This flat paved area has tiers of seats on its eastern and southern sides, while in the southeast corner is a raised platform which, it is believed, was the 'royal box'.

To the west of the Theatre a road heading north for the *Little Palace*. From the Little Palace, continuing north, we can visit the *Royal Villa* which lies to the north east in the valley behind Knossos.

ROUTE 1

Herakleio - Ayia Varvara
Zaros - Phaistos
Matala - Kali Limenes
Lentas - Gortyn

The Prefecture of Herakleio is the part of the island with the greatest archaeological interest, without being in any way less attractive than the rest of Crete in terms of beautiful beaches and areas of more modern historical interest.

This first route is a fascinating combination of all those elements.

The road we shall be following crosses Crete's largest plain, the fertile Messara plain, with its picturesque little villages and historic monasteries. It takes us to archaeological sites of great importance, such as Phaistos, Ayia Triada, Lentas, Gortyn and others. Deviations from the route will lead us to fine beaches, such as those at Matala and Kali Limenes.

Since this route is quite a long one it can be followed in sections, and visitors have a wide choice as to where to focus their attention.

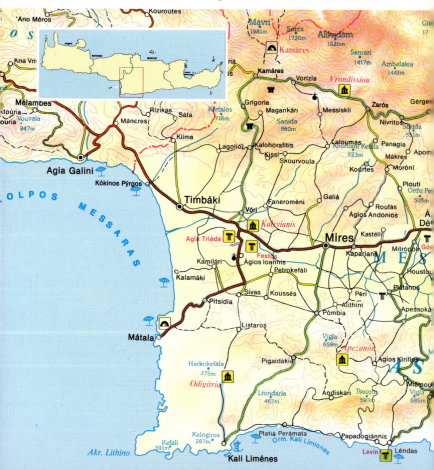

The Messara road starts in Herakleio and leads south, crossing the fertile plain of Finikia. After the picturesque chapel of **Christ Crucified**, 4 km. out from Herakleio, we can continue for Ayi(Varvara, through Ayios Myronas, by turning right (35 km) or by heading straight along the main Messara road (30 km).

If we choose to turn right, we will come in 16 km to **Ayios Myronas**. The road climbs across the most productive sultana vineyards in Crete. The village stands on a hill at an alitude of 400 metres.

Ayios Myronas is the chief town of the Eparchy of Malevizi and is one of the most important grape and wine producing centres in Crete. It takes its name from St Myron, who was born at ancient Raucos, nearby. His relics are kept in the village church, which bears his name and dates from the 11th century.

Our road continues, passing through the village of **Pyrgou** before coming to the pretty mountain villages of **Kato** and **Pano Asites**, in the eastern foothills of Mt Ida, 22 km from Herakleio.

It then runs though an upland plain, before coming after 30 km. to the picturesque mountain village of **Prinias**. To the north east, on a steep summit, is *'Patela tou Prinia'*, which stands on the site of ancient Rizenia. The city was important in antiquity because of its strategic position between Knossos and Gortyn.

Our attractive run through dense greenery continues to **Ayia Varvara**, 35 km. from Herakleio.

If we take the main Messara road, a turning to the left after 12 km will bring us in 6 km to the village of **Dafnes**, which is known for its excellent wine.

The main road continues, and at the 18th km comes to the village of **Siva**. After this, at 20 km, is the village of **Neo Venerato**. A turning to the right leads to the village of **Venerato**, from which a track runs on to the **Paliani Nunnery**, one of the oldest foundations on Crete. Beside the three-aisled church is an ancient myrtle tree, at the roots of which an icon of Our Lady was found. Since then, it has been treated as a holy tree.

We return to Neo Venerato, from which we continue to climb until reaching **Ayia Varvara** at 30 km.

The village stands on a site with a panoramic view towards Malevizi. The area around it is green and fertile, and is an important road junction. It takes its name from the church of St Barbara, a 13th century building which stands in the centre of the village. On a rock at the entrance to the village stands the **Church of the Prophet Elijah**, which is popularly said to be the centre of Crete.

As we leave the village, we leave behind the main road across the plain, by which we shall be returning, and take the right-hand fork and run downhill across a slope densely planted with fruit trees into the midst of a verdant valley with numerous streams.

We soon come to **Panasos**, a very old settlement with a number of early churches which has kept its pre-Hellenic name.

The road climbs once more, up the steep sides of Mt Ida, to the thickly-vegetated village of **Gergeri**, which may owe its name to the tumbling noise ('gargara') made by its many streams. This village is a centre for stockbreeding and handicrafts. A very poor road leads off to the left to the **Rouva forest**, at an altitude of 1300 m., surrounded by the highest peaks of Mt Psiloritis.

From Gergeri the road continues through the village of **Nivrytos**. We then come to **Apano Zaros**, (16 km from Ayia Varvara), set amid scenery where streams and dense vegetation dominate. It is in the foothills of Psiloritis. Nearby is the Votamos spring, where there are stone fountains and shady plane trees; perhaps of more interest to the hungry traveller, there are two trout farms, whose products can be sampled.

We leave the village and soon come to a turning (right), to the **Vrontisiou Monastery** (1 km.). The monastery stands clinging to the steep slopes of Mt Ida under huge plane trees. It has a panoramic view over the fertile Mesara plain.

The three-aisled church of St Fanurius, t... have survived

Its double-aisled church, which is dedicated to St Antony and St Thomas, contains some 14th century wall-paintings.

In a corner outside the church, on a stone plaque, is a sun-dial with Roman numerals. The belfry stands, characteristically, at some distance from the church, and has arches in the Western style. *Near the monastery entrance is a marvellously-crafted 15th century fountain. The relief in the centre of this shows Adam and Eve in Eden, God, and four figures at their feet to symbolise the four rivers of Eden. From the mouths of these figures runs the fountains' refreshing water.*

The Vrontisiou Monastery was one of the most important monastic centres in Crete during the final cen-

t of the Varsamoneri Monastery to

tury of Venetian rule. It also became a major centre of learning, where painting and the arts were taught. There is a tradition that the great Cretan painter Michail Damaskinos was a monk here and worked in the monastery, and that the walls of his cell were covered with paintings.

We return to the main road. As we cross a verdant stream-bed shortly before enteribg the village of **Voriza**, we see the **Varsamonero Monastery** to our left. This used to be an important foundation, with the Vrontisiou Monastery as one of its dependencies. Today it is ruined, and only the triple-aisled church of St Fanourios has survived intact. This church is of architectural interest; two of its aisles run in one direction while the third, built at a different time, intersects them at right angles. The wall-paintings in the church and its portable icons (many of which have been transferred to the St Catherine Monastery in Herakleio) are of considerable importance for the study of icon-painting in Crete.

From the village of Voriza, the fine Vorizanos gorge leads up to the Idaean Cave (p. 164).

We bypass Voriza and, at 26 km. from Herakleio, come to the pretty village of **Kamares**, which stands at an altitude of 600 m. It is a major centre for the production of folk art items and handicrafts. Above Kamares to the north west is the famous **Kamares Cave** or Black Cave, where Minoan pottery dating back to 2000 BC was found; this pottery has become known as 'Kamares ware'. The pottery is in the Early Palace style, with a black background and bright red and white decoration. It has been concluded from the style of this pottery and the fact that it was found in the cave that the inhabitants of Phaistos used to leave offerings to the deity which was worshipped there.

We leave behind the main road, which continues to the west and follows the line of the impressive mountain massif, joining the Amari road after the village of **Platanos**.

We take the road south from Kamares, running downhill. We pass through **Magarikari** and cross a fertile plain before coming in 20 km to the village of **Voroi**, which until 1912 was the chief town of the Eparchy of Pyrgiotissa. The village may have gained its name from the fact that it lies to the north ('voria') of Phaistos; there were certainly people living here in Minoan times.

To the south of the village we rejoin the main road at 60 km from Hera-

kleio, which is part of the Greek 'national' road. This would be the road to take from Herakleio for a direct visit to Phaistos.

On joining the main road, we turn right, and soon (in 5 km) reach the village of **Tymbaki**, chief town of the Eparchy of Pyrgiotissa since 1912. Today, the area's wonderful climate and the intensive cultivation of early vegetables in greenhouses have helped to turn Tymbaki into an important agricultural centre. The patron saint of the village is St Titus, whose church stands on the foundations of an ancient temple. On 25 August each year, the Pyrgotioi Games are held here, and are followed by feasting and dancing.

Close to Tymbaki (3 km) to the west is **Kokkinos Pyrgos**, an ideal bathing beach on the Libyan Sea. The village, stands on the shores of the Gulf of Messara and has a little jetty for fishing boats and yachts.

From here, the road runs on to Ayia Galini (see Rethymno, route 2, p. 155).

The western aspect of the Phaistos palace, and part of the west court. Behind, the Asterousia mountains

We return to the point where we joined the 'national' road outside Voroi and turn east. Before long there is a further turning to the right; a fine surfaced road leads us in 2 km to the famous archaeological site of **Phaistos** (63 km from Herakleio).

The territory controlled by Phaistos ran from Cape Lithino to Psychio (Melissa) and included the Paximadia islets. Thus it dominated the plain of Messara and its ports were Kommos and Matala. According to the myths, the dynasty which ruled Phaistos was founded by Rhadamanthus, son of Zeus, who was the brother of Minos and sat in judgement in the Underworld. During the Archaic, Classical and Hellenistic periods Phaistos retained its independence, but as a poor shadow of its status in Minoan times, when it was an important religious, administrative and economic centre. It participated in the Achaean campaign against Troy, sending troops along with the other Cretan cities. It minted its own coins, some of which showed Heracles and others the hero Talos. A further category had Europa on one side and the words ΦΑΙΣΤΙΩΝ ΤΟ ΦΑΙ-ΜΑ on the other. The city was forever at war with Gortyn, which it eventually managed to destroy in about 200 BC.

Archaeological investigation of the site has revealed two successive phases of palace-building; the Early Palace period (1900-1700 BC), after which the buildings were destroyed by earthquake, and the New Palace period (1650-1400 BC). Most of the ruins which can be seen today are from the second of these periods. The archaeological site of Phaistos is the island's second most important, after Knossos. In some ways, it could be said that its palace is in better condition than that at Knossos, since the archaeologists working here used different principles and avoided reconstruction altogether. The Minoan Palace stands on a hill 100 m high, with a panoramic view in all directions.

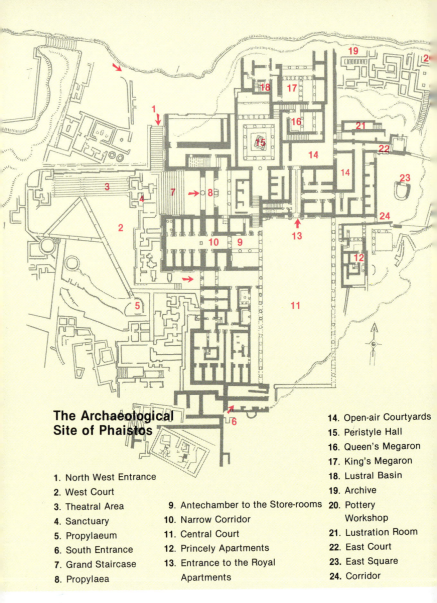

The Archaeological Site of Phaistos

1. North West Entrance
2. West Court
3. Theatral Area
4. Sanctuary
5. Propylaeum
6. South Entrance
7. Grand Staircase
8. Propylaea
9. Antechamber to the Store-rooms
10. Narrow Corridor
11. Central Court
12. Princely Apartments
13. Entrance to the Royal Apartments
14. Open-air Courtyards
15. Peristyle Hall
16. Queen's Megaron
17. King's Megaron
18. Lustral Basin
19. Archive
20. Pottery Workshop
21. Lustration Room
22. East Court
23. East Square
24. Corridor

Below, the fertile plain of Messara stretches away to the sea in the distance. To the south, the Asperoudia Mountains can be seen, while to the north towers the imposing massif of Mt Ida.

The excavations which brought this marvellous palace to life were conducted by Italian archaeologists, of whom the first was Federico Halbnerr, in 1900. A brief tour of the palace will take at least two hours.

The archaeological site: the numbering of the site will help visitors find their way around, and the numbers correspond to those on the diagram.

We start from the tourist pavilion at the upper end of the wall and enter the site by the *North West Entrance* **1**. Here is the paved *North West Court*, where the foundations of buildings from Greek and Roman times can be seen over the remains of the Old Palace, which at Phaistos are much more numerous than at other sites. The Court is crossed by a raised *processional ramp*, which had also been part of the first palace. To the north east of the North West Court, a staircase leads to the larger, paved, *West Court* **2**, which lies at a level six metres lower. On the north side of the Court are eight rows of seats, which together with the Court itself form the *'theatral area* **3'** for ceremonies and performances.

To the east of the theatre there was a room for religious purposes, the *Sanctuary* **4**, with offering altars carved with representations of animals. To the south of the sanctuary were other small rooms (storehouses, kitchens, etc.). These areas were flattened in the destruction of the palace. When the New Palace was built, the whole West Court, including this part, was raised, involving the covering over of four rows of seats in the theatre, and the new building went up seven metres to the east of the old one.

The processional way from the North West Court continues past the seats in the theatre and, in the middle of the West Court, forks: one branch leads west to the *deep pits*, similar to the rubbish pits at Knossos, and ends on the south side. Here there was an imposing *Propylaeum* **5** to a staircase which led to a corridor into the Central Court. To

the south of this Propylaeum were the storerooms of the Old Palace, where multi-coloured Middle Minoan pottery came to light, together with the head of a clay statuette which gives a clear idea of the Minoan concept of the human form.

A corridor starting from the Propylaeum separates the western part of the palace into two sections. To the south was the main *sanctuary*, with its altar and a series of interconnecting chambers with benches and posts. To the south of the sanctuary and outside the palace are the foundations of a building with a peculiar shape: this was the much later *Temple of Rhea*, the mother of Zeus. To the east is the *South Entrance* **6**, which in Phaistos was not as important as in other palaces. Here the West Entrance was the most important one.

On the eastern side of the West Court, opposite the theatral area, is the *Grand Staircase* **7**, a marvellous example of Minoan architecture; its 12 steps are slightly convex so as to stop the rainwater from gathering in puddles on them.

This staircase leads to the impressive *Propylaea* **8** of the New Palace, consisting of a colonnade with a paved floor. The colonnade was supported by a single column in the centre, the base of which can still be seen today. Beneath here we can see the store-rooms of the Old Palace, where painted storage jars were found. On the north side of the colonnade, another imposing staircase with large windows on the east and north sides of its landing led up to the royal apartments.

Behind the colonnade to the east was a lightshaft with three columns, and next to it an open-air courtyard. Another narrow staircase, to the south, led to the paved *antechamber to the store-rooms* **9**, which, to the east, communicated with the Central Court, while a *narrow corridor* **10** began on its western side. The storerooms lay to the left and right of this corridor. In the last store-room to the north there are still jars which were used to preserve various products and which are decorated with horizontal bands in relief. A receptacle sunk into the sloping floor was used to catch any liquids (wine or oil) which might spill from the jars.

From the antechamber to the storerooms we emerge into the paved *Central Court* **11**. To the east and west of the Court, pillars and columns formed a colonnade to separate it from the various wings of the Palace. This would have been the very centre of life in Phaistos: here the meetings, ceremonies, athletic contests and other events would have taken place, and this was the point where the four sides of the Palace met: there are processional corridors leading here from each of them. The south eastern side of the Court, where there may have been other apartments, has disappeared altogether. On the south west side, where the *South Entrance* **6** is, there are two rooms which may have been used as resting-quarters. On the eastern side of the Central Court there is a group of rooms. Three steps lead to an open-air hall where there was an antechamber with a lustral basin, and archaeologists believe that these were the apartments of officials, priests or perhaps members of the aristocracy or *Princely apartments* **12**.

On the north side of the Central Court, the pillars which can still be seen today testify to the existence of a colonnade. The two recesses to the right and left of the entrance were probably guard posts, for this was the *Entrance to the royal apartments* **13**. The impos-

ing painted door in the colonnade led into a paved corridor which ended in two *Open-air Courtyards* **14**, both of which belonged to the Old Palace. On the left of this corridor was a staircase. Along this north western side, the Palace had three storeys. On the first was an antechamber which led into a imposing hall, a wonderful example of Minoan architecture. On the second floor, the staircase brings us out at the famous *Peristyle Hall* **15**, a square room with four columns along each side, which communicates via six doors with another spacious loggia-like hall. This was probably the *Queen's Megaron* **16**; it had a floor paved with alabaster, benches and a light shaft. To the north is the *King's Megaron* **17**, whose walls were decorated with paintings and which also had a floor paved with alabaster. The western extremity of this complex of rooms contains an elegant *Lustral basin* **18** — or perhaps it was a bath-tub.

To the north east extends the complex of buildings comprising the Old Palace. In one of its halls, brick partitions create seven smaller rooms, and it is believed that this was the *Archive* **19**. In one of the rooms, *the famous Phaistos Disc* was found; although its hieroglyphic script has not been deciphered even today, we can admire it in the Herakleio Archaeological Museum. The disc bears symbols on both sides, written from the outside towards the centre in spiral fashion. The characters were stamped on the disc using moulds and that is why the disc is sometimes described as the oldest piece of printing to have survived. The text is believed to be a hymn to the goddess Rhea. The same room in the Palace also yielded an engraved plaque, bearing a legend in Linear A script.

The Phaistos disc, whose sacred symbols have still not yielded their secret

In the last hall to the east in this complex of buildings, archaeologists discovered a large number of unused pots arranged in rows, which suggests that it was a ˆ *ottery workshop* **20**. To the east of the workshop there are remains of the paved road which led down into the plain to the east of the Palace. To the south of the buildings of the Old Palace there were water tanks in which the palace's supply was stored; the water would also have been used for the lustration or purification of those entering the palace from the east. For this purpose, there was a *Lustration Room* **21** here. To the south of the lustration room, a *Formal Passage* linked the two open-air courts (where the main entrance corridor from the Central Court ended) with the *East Court*

22. The structure to the east of this passage is believed to have been a guard-post to protect the entrance. To the south east of the lustration room is the *East Square* **23**, in the middle of which a semi-circular kiln stands on the paved surface. Two pottery wheels were also found here. To the south west of the square is the starting-point of the *Corridor* **24** which links it to the Central Court.

To the west of Phaistos, at a distance of 3 km., are the remains of the royal palace of **Ayia Triada**. In Minoan times, a paved road ran directly from Ayia Triada to Phaistos, and traces of it can still be seen, with its asymmetrical stone slabs.

The village of Ayia Triada stands on the banks of the Yeropotamos river, at an altitude of 100 m. A medieval village, it took its name from the church of the Holy Trinity (Ayia Triada) which stood there. The village was inhabited until 1897, in which year it was looted by the Turks and abandoned. Among the ruins, the only building to survive is the single-aisled church of St George 'Galatas', which has a tiled roof and wall-paintings dating back to the 14th century. The archaeological site was uncovered very close to the village on the east. The royal palace of Ayia Triada may have been the summer residence of the kings of Phaistos. The hill on which it stands was inhabited as far back as the Stone Age, but the palace itself dates from about 1600 BC, when Phaistos and Knossos were at the height of their prosperity. The floor-plan of the palace is simpler than that of the other Minoan buildings, and is L-shaped. The characteristic central court is missing, as are the lustral water-tanks. However, the palace must have been luxurious and continues to be imposing. Historically, it had the same fate as Phaistos and Knossos, being destroyed around 1400 BC. At some later date, another grand building, rectangular in shape and with a colonnade, was erected on the site. By the Geometrical period the palace was no longer inhabited, but it continued to be a place of worship, as can be seen from the clay statuettes which have been found there. In the Hellenistic period, a small sanctuary to Zeus occupied the site.

Close at hand, on the spot known as 'Kamilari', a Middle Minoan tomb has come to light. The walls of the vault still stand about 2 m. high. Behind the vaulted area were a number of square and rectangular chambers. Numerous successive burials were carried out in these huge rooms, and so it seems more than likely that the tomb was in communal or family use. In one of the rooms, the famous stone Sarcophagus

The Harvester vase

of Ayia Triada was found; decorated with religious and cult scenes, it can be seen in Herakleio Archaeological Museum today (see photo. p. 29). The same museum also contains many other finds from Ayia Triada: fine steatite vases with scenes of harvesting, athletic contests, etc. in relief, frescoes showing lilies and wild-cats or motifs inspired by the sea, such as fish, octupuses, etc.

We return to the Phaistos-Matala road and turn south west. We soon come to the pretty village of **Pitsidia**, to the west of which, by the shore, is the archaeological site of **Kommos**. This was an ancient settlement, the first harbour which Phaistos possessed, and it has been revealed by archaeological investigations. The settlement is believed to date from the late Bronze Age. According to the myths, Kommos was where King Menelaus of Sparta's ships sank as he sailed home from Troy.

The road ends on the western coast of Messara, at **Matala** 9 km from Phaistos. Matala is the natural outlet of Phaistos on the sea, and in the Minoan period it was the palace's second harbour. After the destruction of Phaistos in 220 BC, its ownership passed to Gortyn.

There is a semi-circular sandy beach 300 metres in length, at either end of which are the cliffs which make the cove a rather private place. These cliffs are riddled with man-made caves hacked out of the rock. Once the famous caves of Matala were the homes of the fisherfolk who lived here, but during the 1970s they became one of the centres of the international hippy movement. Today, the caves have been fenced off by the Archaeological Service and it is forbidden to stay or spend the night in them.

Tombs from Greek, Roman and Early Christian times have been found in the caves, and it is believed that they were first inhabited —by the living— in the pre-historic period. There are also underwater caves, which can be visited by boat. Shipwrecks have been identified on the sea-bed, and archaeological finds, particularly from Roman times, are very common in the area.

The columns of an ancient temple have been found to the south east of the modern village, and a large marble larnax was discovered a little further along the coast. To the west of the village, on a rise, can be seen the remains of a fortified wall, inside which, on top of the hill, are the ruins of a beacon.

There is also an old church to Our Lady, hewn out of the rock. Inside this church are two marble altars

Matala: the cliff with the caves plunges into the azure waters of the bay

carved with Christian symbols. There are also column capitals from the early Byzantine period, which must be older than the church itself, and two very old icons of Our Lady.

Matala has a fine, mild climate, and this, together with its fine beach and sheltered bay, have made it an ideal place for bathing even in the winter months. In the summer, there is a daily caique service from Matala to Ayia Galini in the Prefecture of Rethymno.

We return to the main road from Herakleio to Rethymno via the Messara plain. To the left, at a short distance,

we can see among the trees which sur round it the **Monastery of Our Lady 'Kalyviani'**. The little church had fallen into disrepair and was no longer used when in 1873 a wonder-working icon of Our Lady was found there; today it is housed in the modern church. The church we see today is in the Byzantine style, with three aisles and a dome. In 1958, Bishop Timotheos (of Arkadia) began to use the revenues of the church to set up a number of foundations (a girl's orphanage, an old people's home, a school of domestic economy, etc.) which in 1961 were recognised as a

The sheltered beach at M.

monastic house. This new monastery has become very well-known, primarily thanks to its production of items of folk art and for the icons painted there: a combination of labour and religiosity. Many pilgrims come to the monastery on 15 August.

Close to the monastery is the village of **Kalyvia**.

We return to the main road and continue in a easterly direction. After 6 km we come to the village of **Mires**, which is 53 km from Herakleio. The village takes its name, derived from the Greek verb meaning 'to share', from the parcels of land which the Venetians granted to the refugees from the Peloponnese, who arrived when their native land was occupied by the Turks in 1453. Mires is the chief town of the Eparchy of Kainourgio, and has been a municipality since 1952. It has developed into a communications, commercial and argicultural town of major importance, and it is the seat of the Bishop of Gortyn and Arkadia. The large park just outside the town is well worth a visit; cobbled paths wind beneath huge trees, and the stone fountains provide a welcome cooling note.

...d the caves in the rock

A turning off the main road leads south, in 5 km., to the village of **Pompia**. To the east of the village can be seen traces of a Middle Minoan settlement, and it is believed that this was the site of ancient Boibe. In the village itself, there is a Venetian mansion known locally as the *'konaki'*, with carved window openings and impressive staircases.

We continue through the pretty village of **Pigaidakia** to **Kali Limenes** (24 km from Mires). There is an outstanding beach, 2 km in length, whose white sand provides a superb contrast with the blue of the water. The pretty little village with its harbour is ample compensation for the time and trouble it may take to reach this remote corner of southern Crete. The climate is warm even in winter — so warm that in this part of the island the swallows stay all winter.

Indeed, the very name of the place says something of its nature, for this is the 'Fair Havens' of St Paul.

St Paul landed here when on his way to Rome; this was where the teaching of Christianity in Crete began, and here St Titus was consecrated as the first bishop of Crete. Close to the village on the east and opposite the islet of Tafros, are the ruins of ancient Lasaia. There are the remains of buildings from the Roman period, an aqueduct and early Mycenean tholos tombs. The port for Gortyn was here in Roman times, when the area flourished. The town was independent and there were temples to Asklepios and the goddess Isis. Today there are installations for supplying ocean-going vessels.

From Kali Limenes a road leads north to the Hodeghetria Monastery.

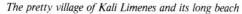

The pretty village of Kali Limenes and its long beach

The Hodeghtria Monastery

The **Hodeghetria Monastery**: The monastery is a stavropegic foundation dedicated to Our Lady 'the Guiding Force'. The church is twin-aisled, with fine portable icons and liturgical vestments of importance. In the past, the monastery was surrounded by a wall, some sections of which can still be seen today. The monastery gate bears the date 1568. To the right of the entrance the tower of Xopateras, one of the Cretan heroes who fought for liberty, still stands proudly (see Spanakis, CRETE, vol. A, p. 421).

In the vicinity of the monastery, the spades of the archaeologists brought to light, in 1981, a tomb complex of five chambers, an ossuary and a paved courtyard. In the tombs were found seals made of ivory, faience and steatite, bearing representations of animals and leaf and line motifs. Gold jewellery, copper utensils and ceramic and stone containers were also among the finds.

We return to Kali Limenes, from which we can travel by caique to Lentas or return by road to Mires.

From Mires we take the Messara-Herakleio road. After 2 km a surfaced road leads to **Zaros**. As we continue, shortly before Ayii Deka we turn right for **Mitropoli**, which soon appears from the olive groves. It takes its name from the founding here, during the early Byzantine period, of the island's first bishopric ('mitropoli'). The village stands on the site of ancient Gortyn. An early Christian basilica with a multicoloured mosaic floor was recently discovered here.

A further 4 km brings us to the upland villages of **Houstouliana** and **Yeropotamos**, while another kilometre separates us from **Platanos**. Near the village have been discovered two of the largest tombs of the Proto-Mycenean period: they contained seals, tools and gold jewellery which can now be admired in Herakleio Museum. To the south of Platanos (3 km) is **Plora**, which is believed to be identical with ancient Pyloros and where a marble Roman bust of Dionysus has been discovered. From Plora, a turning to the right leads in 10 km through the village of **Ayios Kyrillos** to the **Apezanon Monastery**. This foundation, which is also a parish church, stands among dense greenery at a height of 440 metres on the slopes of the Asterousia Mountains. The monastery is surrounded by a wall whose entry is on the north side. It is dedicate to St Antony 'Ayiofarangitis' and was founded in the 15th century. According to local tradition, it originally stood at Ayiofarango, which is to the west of Kali Limenes, and now belongs to the Hodeghetria Monastery. The initial site was abandoned by the monks because of the incessant raids of pirates; carrying their icons and sacred vessels, they headed for the hills and, at the point where, in the Cretan dialect 'epezepsan ta zoa' (which means where they unloaded their beasts of burden) they built their new monastery, which thus acquired its name. Under the Turks, the Monastery was a centre for Christian learning and had an excellent library with a fine collection of Byzantine music in manuscript. It was destroyed twice, in 1821 and 1866. Today, it has quite a number of monks and its treasures include many priceless ecclesiastical objects.

We return to Plora; 2 km after the village, we reach **Apesokari**, which is a road junction. If we take the turning to the right, we will climb up to the farming community of **Miamou**, at an altitude of 500 m., where a little cave used in Neolithic times has been discovered. From Miamou we descend towards the sea at Lendas.

The little fishing village of **Lendas** lies on the south coast of Crete, on a promontory in the shape of a crouching lion which runs down to a white strip of fine sand 300 metres in length before merging into the azure of the Libyan Sea. According to the myths, one of the lions which pulled the goddess Rhea's chariot was turned into stone here, thus giving the area its name.

Today, Lendas is an ideal holiday resort, which attracts large numbers of visitors drawn by the natural beauties of the spot and by its medicinal spring, whose waters are reputed to be efficacious in the treatment of disorders of the stomach and the blood. The spring was known in ancient times, and because of it there was a sanctuary to Asklepios, the god of healing. Ancient **Leben** was the port for Gortyn, and it had trading

The pretty fishing village of Lendas

links with Egypt. In Classical and Roman times, when it was at the peak of its prosperity, it was a sacred city. The divinities of Asklepios and Hygeia were worshipped here, and the Askleipeion, or sanctuary of Asklepios, attracted visitors from all over Crete and from Libya as well. The *Treasury* is the oldest of all the monuments which have survived on the site. This is a square well, constisting of seven rows of ashlar masonry. The floor of the Treasury is a fine mosaic with black and red tesserae. The mouth was circular and was covered which a slab which could only be opened with a special key. The famous Asklepeio had a fine temple with a superb mosaic; the altar to the god stood in the innermost recesses of the temple. The most important part of the Asklepeio was the Abaton or Adyton, which could be entered only by the priests and the pilgrims who came to the sanctuary as patients; after their sojourn in the Abaton they emerged cured. There was accommodation for the priests and for the pilgrims. In addition, there were lustral facilities for the patients, and it was at this time that the medicinal spring came to light.

Archaeologists have discovered here a number of large Early Minoan tholos tombs, which yielded jewellery and other objects which accompanied the dead on their last journey.

From Lendas, there are plenty of things to see and longer or shorter trips can be made. A caique can be taken to the **Koudoumas Monastery** and to Kali Limenes.

We return to main road after Mitropoli and turn right. Shortly before Ayii Deka we come to **ancient Gortyn**, the archaeological site of which straddles the road to north and south. The ruins cover an enormous area, from the villages of Houstouliana and Mitropoli to the west as far as Ayii Deka to the east. In other words, they are located on both banks of the Letheaios river, now known as the Mitropolianos. Gortyn is one of the most ancient cities on Crete and it dominated the Mesara plain from pre-historic times into the Classical period.

The site was inhabited by the Minoans, but it did not develop into a city until after the Dorian invasion. Plato describes it as one of the richest cities of Crete. The law-abiding nature of the Gortynians is demonstrated by the large slabs bearing the city's laws which were built into the Odeum. This is the famous *Code* or *Law of Gortyns*, on whose principles many of the provisions of modern criminal law are still based. The text is in the Doric dialect and is written boustrophedon — that is, the first line is read from right to left and the next from left to right, as though one were ploughing a field. It dates from the late 6th or early 5th century BC. The provisions include rules of civil procedure and the fundamentals of civil, family, agrarian and commercial law. No barbarous punishments for offenders were laid down and the death penalty was not provided for; on the other hand, it was essential that the objective guilt or innocence of the person charged be proved.

The Gortynians had friendly relations with the Achaeans and later with the Ptolemies of Egypt. They took the side of the Romans at a time when Knossos was opposed to the new power, with the ultimate aim of securing the domination of Crete. Thus Gortyn escaped the destruction by the Romans which was the fate of other Cretan cities. When the Romans joined Crete and Cyrenacia as an administrative unit, Gortyn became its capital and continued to be the chief city of Crete even in later times. It was also the first city in Crete to feel the influence of Christianity and the first Christian churches were built there.

The oldest and most important of these buildings is the metropolitan basilica of *St Titus*, dating from the 6th century, the ruins of which can still be seen today. The city continued to flourish until 828, when the Arabs took Crete and razed it.

Archaeological investigations have brought to light only a part of the ancient city. Among the most interesting features are the *acropolis*, on its hilltop, and the *area of the theatre* below it. To the south of the Herakleio-Phaistos road lies the *Praetorium*, which was the seat of the Roman commander. To the west of this is the *temple of Apollo Pythius,* dating from the 7th century. To the south of the Temple is a *theatre* and to the north lies the *Temple of Isis and Serapis*. Further south are the *amphitheatre, the baths* and the 2nd century *stadium.*

On the north side of the road are the ruins of the *Agora,* with its *temple of Asklepios* and the *Odeum* into whose rear wall the plaques with the laws were built.

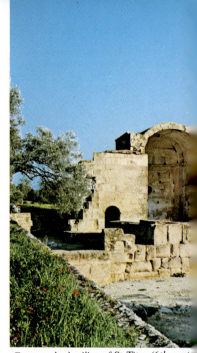

Gortyn: the basilica of St Titus (6th cent.

The C

We leave Gortyn, and after 1 km, come to **Ayii Deka**. The village stands on a wooded hill and has a wonderful view over the ruins of ancient Gortyn across the olive groves of the northern end of the Messara plain. It is believed that its site was the cemetery of the ancient city. Many of the houses were built using stone from ancient structures. There is a small museum with finds from the area.

The village takes its name (which means 'ten saints') from the ten Cretan Christians who were martyred here in the reign of the Roman Emperor Decius, in 250 AD. A Byzantine church stands on the spot where they met their end, and a display-case contains the stone on which they knelt to be beheaded.

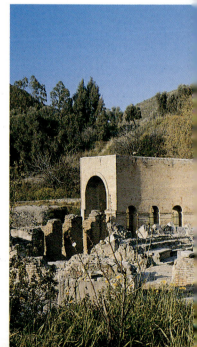

We leave the village; to the east is the island's main road south, which runs through Viannos before ending at Ierapetra.

From Ayii Deka we take the road north, which twists upwards on our return route to Herakleio. The highest point on the itinerary, shortly before the village of Ayia Varvara, is a good place to stop and admire the surrounding landscape. To the south, there is a fine views of the plain of Messara, the bread-basket of Crete, with its tiny white villages. To the east, the Lasithiotika mountains can be dimly discerned, and to the west the azure embrace of the Gulf of Messara can be seen. The road runs down to **Ayia Varvara** after this viewpoint, after which we take the main road across the plain of Messara and return to Herakleio, which we enter by the Chania Gate.

re the inscribed laws of Gortyn were found

A Roman statue from Gortyn

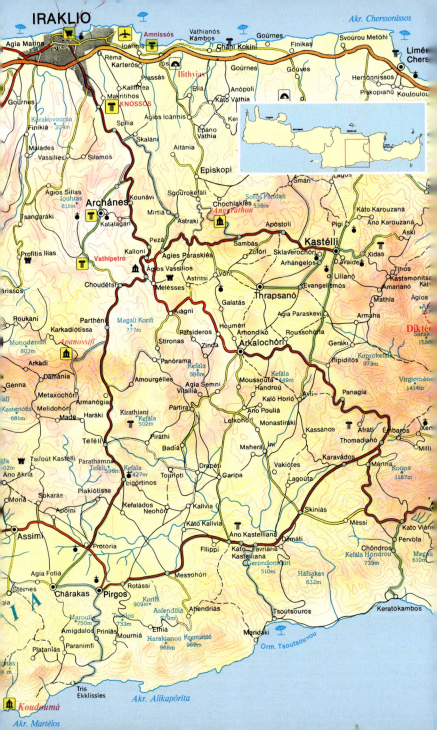

ROUTE 2

Herakleio - Archanes
Apanosifi Monastery
Viannos - Kasteli

This second route which we have selected is not among the classic itineraries which more or less all the tourist guides to the island propose. However, bearing in mind the fact that the Prefecture of Herakleio is the most difficult around which to guide visitors because of the wealth of its archaeological sites, its many modern points of interest and its abundance of fine beaches, we have attempted to produce a circular route which will provide visitors with an acquaintance with the central area of the prefecture and contain something of interest for all. So this route includes archaeological sites, historic monasteries and traditional mountain hamlets and also beaches for bathing.

From the city of Herakleio (Eleftherias Square) we exit through the New Gate ('Kainourgia Porta'). We take the good surfaced road for Knossos, which we pass on our left 5 km out of the town.

At 8 km we pass **Spilia** and on our right we can see a structure with arches. This is the superb aqueduct which was built during the Egyptian occupation of Crete (1830-1840). The water of the Fountana spring flows through tunnels from here to the Morosini Aqueduct in Herakleio. The landscape is peaceful, and the green of vineyards and olive groves is the dominant colour. A turning to the left leads to Skalani, Varvari and the Kazantzakis Museum (see return route).

After 10 km a turning to the right leads in 6 km to the little town of **Archanes**, which stands on the slopes of a low hill; the surrounding countryside contains numerous vineyards and there are streams everywhere. This area produces the best Cretan table grapes (known as 'rozakia') and the famous Archanes wine is made. The little town of Archanes consists of picturesque narrow lanes and neo-Classical houses whose balconies and courtyards are like a permanent floral exhibition.

Nearby, traces have been found of a Minoan house which dates from approximately 1450 BC. To the north west of Archanes, at the spot known as **Fourni**, archaeological investigations in the late 1960s brought to light the largest necropolis ever found in Crete. It consists of tholos tombs with chambers hewn out of the rock, as well as groups of shaft graves. The cemetery was used between the Early Minoan and Mycenean periods.

These tombs contained larnaces, copper and stone vessels, seals, statuettes, gold jewellery and other items, and, of course, hundreds of human skeletons. At Anemospilia, 4 km from Archanes on the northwestern slopes of Mt Youchtas, the only known Minoan temple was found. The temple, which was destroyed by an earthquake in about 1700 BC, contained an altar and there is evidence that human sacrifice was carried out there — perhaps in an effort to appease the gods and stave off the impending catastrophe.

The Venetian period, too, has left its mark on this area. There are also two Byzantine churches, that of the Holy Trinity and that of St Paraskevi, which have fine wall-paintings. To the south (1 km), amongst vineyards in the deserted settlement of Asomatos, is the church of the Archangel Michael, with wall-paintings dating from 1315.

Archanes stands on a site which faces the sacred mountain of Youchtas. According to the myths, the summit of Youchtas was the spot where Zeus chose to die. The shape of the mountain —it resembles the head of an old man lying on his back— was perhaps the source of this tradition about the tomb of Zeus.

The chapel which stands on the peak is dedicated to the Transfiguration of the Saviour, and is the scene of a feast on 6 August each year. However, the view over the island from this point will be ample compensation for the effort involved in getting here.

From Archanes we turn south and, after 2 km, reach **Vathypetro**, a small settlement which is uninhabited today. At the spot known as Piso Livadia, on a fine site with a good view of the valley and slightly off the road, is a Minoan house. This was in fact a farmhouse, the only one of its type discovered to date, as demonstrated by the looms, pottery workshop, olive press and grape press (for wine) found inside it. It will be remembered that even today the best varieties of grape come from around here.

We return to the main road, 10 km from Herakleio, and continue south. To our left, we have a panoramic view of almost the whole of the Eparchy of Pediada. At 15 km we come to the upland village of **Kounavi**. The village has a triple-aisled church dedicated to Christ the Lord, St Nicholas and St Demetrius. Archaeological finds have come to light in the area, including a plaque inscribed with 'boustrophedon' script and dating from the time of the Gortyn inscription.

At a distance of 17 km from Herakleio we pass the village of **Peza**, where since 1933 a Union of Agricultural Co-operatives has been responsible for collecting and marketing all the area's agricultural produce. To the south of the village and to the north west of Kalloni, is the vine-covered hill of Kastelos, to which access can be gained only from its south eastern side. Here there is a chapel to Our Lady and there are grape-presses dug out of the rock (probably dating from Venetian times). On the top of the hill are the remains of a medieval fortress.

We continue, bearing right, for **Kalloni**, (20 km). This is a very old village, which kept its ancient name of Skyllous until recently, when it was renamed. It is pretty and set amid a verdant landscape which produces grapes that are made into currants and wine as well as being served as table grapes.

At 21 km we come to **Ayios Vasileios**, which has a panoramic view over the plain and a church of St John with excellent wall-paintings. As we drive on, we see on our right the Monastery of Our Lady 'Spiliotissa', a foundation which is a dependency of the Monastery of St Catherine on Mt Sinai. The monastery is shaded by large planetrees.

We continue to climb and by 23 km from Herakleio have reached an altitude of 440 m. Here we encounter the village of **Houdetsi** and about 5 km

further on, a turning to the right leads up to a pretty hill on which, amid the plane-trees and the gurgling of streams, is the **Monastery of St George 'Apanosifis'**. This is one of Crete's most important monasteries, and it also owns large areas of land. It was built about the year 1600. The monastery became very riche and, by providing shelter for freedom fighters, played an important part in the island's struggle for self-determination. It was also a major centre of learning where numerous Cretan priests were trained.

Back on the main road, we continue to run south through a number of upland villages: **Armanogeia** at 33 km and **Tefeli** at 38 km At 40 km we come to **Ligortyno**, from which the fertile Messara plain stretches out to the west. We travel downhill, and just after we cross the Anapodaris river, in the middle of the plain 45 km from Herakleio, we see the village of **Praitoria**. Here there is a junction with the main south road, which joins the 'national' road through the Messara plain some 20 km away, to the west of the village of Ayii Deka.

An attractive road runs south under the trees from Praitoria, across the plain. After approximately 5 km it leads to **Harakas**, a village which stands on the foothills of the Asterousia Mountains. Its site is on a hilltop, and it used to be known as Ayios Ioannis from the 3rd century church of St John which stood there. On the top of the hill are the remains of a fortress.

From Harakas, we head Pyrgos on a passable road 3 km in length, or turning at the crossroads at Praitoria.

Pyrgos stands in the northern foothills of the Asterousia Mountains and apart from being an agricultural centre is also the chief village of the Monofatsi eparchy. It has churches of St Gerasimos and St Constantine, with wall-paintings.

Koudoumas Monastery, in its isolated position facing out over the Libyan Sea

To the south of Pyrgos, a road 12 km in length crosses the Asterousia Mountains and leads to the coast of the Libyan Sea, at **Treis Ekklisies**. The village took its name from its three Byzantine churches, of the Transfiguration, St Antony and the Annunciation. The little houses of the village stand in semi-circular arrangement at the foot of the wild Ambas gorge, with a view over the fine beach and out to the azure sea. All around are steep cliffs, which mean that this little cove is protected from the wind.

From Treis Ekklisies we can visit the isolated **Koudoumas Monastery**. A fishing-boat will take us in approximately one hour to the beach of Koudoumas Bay where, on the shore under the pine-trees and with Mt Kofina in the Asterousia Mountains as backdrop, is the monastery, set against the bare grey mountain rock.

It was initially founded somewhere between the 10th and the 12th century, but pirate raids destroyed this building.

In 1873, it was reconstructed. The monastery (a male foundation) is dedicated to the Dormition of the Virgin.

We return to Pyrgos and continue along the main south road, heading east. The road passes through a number of little farming settlements such as **Mesochori** and **Kasteliana**, from which a road to the left leads to Arkalochori and another to the right, in about 10 km, to the beach of **Tsoutsouros**.

This was the site of ancient Itanos, where the goddess Eileithyia was worshipped, if we are to judge from the cult objects of the Geometrical period which have been found there in a cave. We continue for **Demati** and **Skinia**.

Ano Viannos clings to the sides of Mt Dikte

From Skinia there is a main road to Arkalochori. We continue to the east and reach the village of **Martha** (the distance from Pyrgos to Martha is 30 km). The road forks here: if we take the southeast road, we will reach **Kato Viannos** after a total of 63 km from Herakleio, and **Ano Viannos** after 65 km.

The latter of these villages, built in a semicircle on the slope forming the foothills of Mt Dikte, has a fine view over the most fertile olive groves in the Viannos Eparchy, of which it is the chief town. The modern settlement stands on the site of the ancient city of Biannos, which was independent and issued its own coins, showing the head of a woman on one side and a flower on the other.

In Venetian times Viannos was a large and prosperous village, but under the Turks it was destroyed twice, in 1822 and in 1866.

Today, it is a verdant settlement with numerous streams of fresh water and a mild climate. Steep and narrow lanes lined with houses in the traditional architectural style lead up to pretty little squares with stone-built fountains from which cool water flows. The site of the village is dominated by plane trees, birches and myrtles, and the little cafés under the shade of their branches add another cooling note. The village is known for its olive-oil, its carobs and its dairy products.

It is also an important communications junction, as it stands on the Herakleio-Ierapetra road and is the starting-point for access to the sandy beaches of **Keratokambos**, and **Psari Forada** on the Libyan Sea.

Viannos was the birthplace of Yannis Kondylakis, one of the most important modern Greek prose writers and journalists. Among other sights in the village is the church of St Pelagia, with wall-paintings of 1360.

We leave Ano Viannos and head east. After 6 km we come to the village of **Amira**. Here we fork south and cross a plain with banana trees before running downhill to the beautiful beach of the village of **Arvi**. The white sandy beach and the almost tropical climate make this an ideal bathing-place, even in the winter. The imposing gorge known as 'Axio Theas' is nearby, while the yellow and green of the banana plantations are the dominant colours. To the east of the gorge is a monastery of St Antony. The village preserves the name of the Helleno-Roman settlement on the same site.

We return to Amira, where the eastern fork in the road passes through the village of **Pefko** before eventually leading to Ierapetra.

We head west along the road, back to the crossroads after the village of Martha. Here we leave behind the main south road and turn to the right, travelling north and climbing. At a distance of 52 km from Herakleio we come to the village of **Thomadiano** and at 51 to **Embaros**. This village stands on the site of the ancient city of Archadia or Archades, which was said to have been built by Arcadian settlers from the Peloponnese. The area has yielded tholos tombs, a Hellenistic acropolis and other finds. Its modern name comes from the Arabic word for a valley and it is known for its fine wines, as demonstrated by the following folk saying:

From Embaros wine
From Viannos olive oil
From Mylopotamos
Olives and paximadi (= a kind of rusk or dried bread)

The village is also worth visiting for its church, which has wall-paintings by Emmanouil Fokas.

We continue to climb and, at 43 km from Herakleio, pass the village of **Panayia**. At 39 km we come to a cross-

roads. The road to the left (north west) leads through Arkalochori to the city of Herakleio. That to the right (north) also returns us to Herakleio, but via Kasteli.

We take the left-hand fork for a short way, coming after 6 km to **Arkalochori**, which is 33 km from Herakleio. This is an important commercial and administrative centre. The principal sight in the village is its Byzantine church of the Archangel Michael, which has wall-paintings. Near Arkalochori, at the spot known as Profitis Ilias, a cave has been found which, to judge from the finds of double axes (some of them gold), bronze swords and knives discovered there, must have been a shrine where some military deity was worshipped.

We return to the crossroads. Taking the right-hand fork and heading north, we come in approximately 8 km to the town of **Kasteli** (36 km from Herakleio), chief town of the Pediada Eparchy. The town stands on the eastern edge of a small plain known by the same name, a fertile area densely planted with vines and olives. Near the entrance to the village a Roman cemetery has been discovered. On the site of the secondary school was a Venetian castle which was also called Kasteli. This is a pretty and lively village, and it acts as the commercial and administrative centre for the whole surrounding area.

6 kilometres to the east of Kasteli, near the village of **Xidas**, are the remains of the ancient city of **Lyttos** or **Lyctos**. This city one of the oldest and most important cities in Doric Crete, and rivalled Knossos. It occupied a semi-circular site on the foothills of the sacred mountain Dikte —which gave it its alternative name of Diktaia— in a high and easily fortified position. Its exits to the sea were at Chersonisos and Milatos, on the northern shore of the bay of Mallia. As a Doric colony, it took part in the Trojan War.

In its heyday, which occurred in historical times, it dominated the whole of eastern Crete. It was often at war with Knossos, which eventually destroyed it in 219 BC. It was rebuilt at a later date, but never regained its former glory.

In the Roman period, Lyttos flourished once again. Various types of coin minted by it have been found, as well as coins from the Roman period. The site has not been excavated systematically, but such investigations as have been made have brought to light the remains of a Roman acropolis and an aqueduct. Some Roman statues have also been found and are in Herakleio Museum.

We return to Kasteli and take the surfaced road north, which soon brings us to the densely-wooded village of **Bit-zariano** (recently renamed **Pighi**). Near the village, in an ideal situation where there is a gushing spring and where the sunlight on the leaves of the trees plays through all the colours from the lightest to the darkest green, stands the triple-aisled church of St Pantaleimon.

The surfaced road continues to a junction 29 km from Herakleio, where it joins the road to the Lasithi plateau. Straight ahead (north), the road goes on to end at Limenas Chersonisou.

If we leave Kasteli in a westerly direction, we shall soon come to a fork. The road to the left leads in approximately 7 km to **Thrapsano**. This village is a major centre for the making of pottery and it is worth visiting to see (and perhaps purchase something from) the workshops which supply the whole of Crete.

Kastelli Pediadas spreads across one of the most fertile parts of Crete

The Kazantzakis Museum at Myrtia

We return to the main road and head west. At 32 km from Herakleio we pass the village of **Apostoli** and at 30 km draw level with the village of **Sambas**. From here, a minor road to the right leads to the historic **Angarathou Monastery**. The foundation is situated in an outstanding position with a boundless view over the Cretan Sea and the plain backing Herakleio. The monastery is dedicated to the Dormition of the Virgin (feast day 15 August) and takes its name from the 'agkarathia' ('bush') under which the very old icon of Our Lady still on display today was found. The door of the abbot's quarters bears the date 1551. In Venetian times, it was an important centre of education.

We return to the main road. At approximately 22 km from Herakleio, just before the village of Ayies Paraskeves, the road turns to the right (north).

Ayies Paraskeves stands on a hilltop and has a panoramic view over the verdant plain of Peza. The top of the hill is dominated by the old church of St George, while the church of the Holy Girdle (Ayia Zoni), with wall-paintings, stands in the main square of the village. A tholos tomb from the Geometric period has been discovered in the vineyards below the village.

We continue north, and after a further 5 km come to the village of **Varvari**, recently renamed **Myrtia**, birthplace of the father of Nikos Kazantzakis. In the square of the village, a restored house serves as the **Nikos Kazantzakis Museum**, with a collection of personal effects, manuscripts, first editions and photographs of Crete's most important writer.

The road runs downhill after leaving Myrtia and soon comes to the attractive village of **Skalani**, which has a fine view. The village is entered along a cobbled road with steps, which accounts for its name (from 'skala', a step).

After Skalani we turn left and soon come to the Knossos road, which brings us back to Herakleio.

227

ROUTE 3

Herakleio - Krousonas
Arolithos - Tylisos - Fodele
Ayia Pelagia - Rogdia
Savvathianon Convent

In this third route we shall be touring the north western side of the Prefecture of Herakleio. By sticking to the old 'national road' from Herakleio to Chania for most of the way, we shall be able to enjoy a very pretty run, crossing fertile plains where oranges and lemons are the most frequent crop; their delicate scent fills the air in spring, while in the background the vineyards and olive groves rest the eye with their various shades of green.

After some diversions to visit the large upland village of Krousonas, the ruins of ancient Tylisos, and Arolithos, the unique modern village which has neen constructed entirely along traditional lines so as to act as a living museum of the way life has been lived in Crete for centuries, we shall come to the wonderful beaches of Fodele and Ayia Pelagia.

We leave the city of Herakleio along the old 'national road' for Chania. The road is surfaced but winding. After 6 km we come to the village of **Gazi**, on the banks of the river Galanos.

After we leave the village, a turning to the left leads in 14 km to the attractive village of **Krousonas**. The road to it leads a cross the most fertile vineyards of the Malevizi Eparchy. Krousonas is one of the largest villages on Crete; standing on the eastern slopes of Mt Ida, it is a centre for stockbreeding. Its name comes from the word 'krousos' and 'koursos' and means that it was built by the Corsairs, or, more likely, destroyed by them. It was first built in the 10th century. The remains of castles and other fortifications from that period can still be seen today. Near the village, at an altitude of 700 metres, is the **Convent of St Irene**. The surrounding countryside has numerous chapels.

We continue along the old 'national road' and at about 10 km from Herakleio come to the traditional village of **Arolithos**.

Traditions are kept up at Arolithos

From Fodele north after 3 km, we take the new 'national road' for a while, in an easterly direction. After some eight kilometres we turn off this road and head down to the left, towards the coastal village of **Ayia Pelagia**, a modern tourist village which stretches along the shores of an attractive sheltered bay where the northerly winds of summer do not penetrate. A long beach with enticing yellow sand —which becomes coarser and white in some places— and little white pebbles accounts for the area's importance as a resort.

Agia Pelagia and the little cove of **Lygaria** which lies about one kilometre away constitute a most attractive unit.

Ayia Pelagia takes its name from the church of St Pelagia which stood about 1 km to the west of the bay and was a dependency of the Savvathianon Convent. On the northern shore of the bay is a cave known as 'Evresi' ('finding-place'), and it is said that an icon of the saint was discovered there.

This, according to the archaeologists, was the site of ancient Apollonia. At the spot known as Kladotos, recent digs have yielded both Minoan and Hellenistic finds. Chamber tombs of the Late Minoan period, hewn out of the rock, have also come to light. However, the main find was the Prytaneion, headquarters of the elders of the town, which was built in the 4th century BC and destroyed in the 2nd century. Houses have also been disovered, together with a pottery workshop.

The resort of Ayia Pelagia, where development has been taking place

We return to the main road and head in the direction of Herakleio. After 7 km, on the right, there is a turning for the village of Rogdia. The road passes across the Almyros lake, though fine scenery.

After 5 km, we come to **Rogdia**. The view around us is superb; to the east lies the city of Herakleio, with the glittering sea behind. This village, too, stands among dense greenery in a well watered landscape. In the village are the ruins of the 15th century mansion of Modinos, a feudal overlord. Next to the mansion is the church of Our Lady 'Kera Rodia'.

Close to Rogdia to the north west is the **Savvathianon Convent**. This foundation stands in a pretty valley, among dense natural vegetation and cultivated orchards. The valley is sealed off from the outer world by steep, high cliffs, which give the landscape an imposing air and yet suit it for the monastic life.

The convent is dedicated to the Nativity of Our Lady, but the nuns have added an aisle dedicated to St Savvas, from whose name that of the convent is belived to derive. The church door bears the date 1635, but the foundation is referred to as the Savvathianon Monastery in documents from as early as 1549.

A seasonal river runs down the centre of the valley, and over it is a stone bridge in the 16th century —more specifically, in 1535, as can be seen from the key-stone of the arch.

About two hundred metres to the west of the convent, on the other side of the valley, is a 15th century church of St Antony, hewn out of the rock.

The Savvathianon foundation was originally a male monastery, and its monks included the icon-painter Ioannis Kornaros. Today it is a coenobitic female convent and has quite a number of nuns.

We return to the crossroads. To the left, is the coastal village of **Linoperamata**.

We take the old national road to the right, and after passing through the seaside tourist resort of **Ammoudara**, reach Herakleio.

The long beach of Ammoudara. To the west, the road which climbs the hillside and heads towards Rethymno. To the east, the bustling city of Herakleio

ROUTE 4

**Herakleio - Amnisos
Eileithyia Cave
Limani Chersonisou
Seli Ambelou
Mochos - Stalida - Mallia**

This fourth route completes our tour of the Prefecture of Herakleio. It takes us through some of the loveliest countryside on the whole island, and since most of it lies along the coast there will be no shortage of opportunities for a swim. Nor is there any lack of archaeological sites (Amnisos, Mallia etc.), and in the realm of impressive mountain scenery we shall be climbing to the Seli Ambelou Pass (at a height of 900 metres), near the magnificent Lasithi Plateau, which forms the natural boundary between the Prefectures of Herakleio and Lasithi. One additional source of interest on this route is the large number of stone-built windmills which we shall be passing, at Seli and at Mallia. Near the end of the route, we pass through the imposing gorge of Ayiou Yeorgiou 'Selinari' before reaching Ayios Nikolaos.

We leave Herakleio from Eleftherias Square, and head east. We shall be taking the old 'national road'. At 3 km from the centre of town we come to the coastal suburb of **Nea Alikarnassos**, which was founded in 1925 by refugees from the town by the same name (ancient Halicarnassus) in Asia Minor. This is the site of Herakleio International Airport. We continue across the fertile plain of Karteros, which was once known as the Omphalio plain. According to the myths, when the Kouretes were bringing Zeus from the Diktaean Cave where he was born to Mt Ida, in order to hide him, his umbilical cord ('omphalos') fell here. At 6 km from Herakleio, on our right in a cave, is the little church of St John the Baptist. At 7 km we come to the beautiful beach of **Karteros**, while on our right are the ruins of ancient **Amnisos**, which surround the hill known today as **Palaiochora**. The ruins on the top of the hill belong to the 16th century Venetian castle of Mesovouni.

Amnisos was the port of Knossos and Minos was said to have his shipyard at the Karteros river. It was at Amnisos, according to the myths, that Theseus disembarked when he came to Crete to slay the Minotaur, and it was from here that Idomeneus, grandson of Minos, set out with 80 ships to help Agamemnon in the campaign against Troy. Odysseus, too, called here when wandering the Mediterranean on his tortuous way home to Ithaca.

Archaeological investigations have revealed a Middle Minoan III villa with wonderful wall-paintings, including the lily frescoes to be seen in Herakleio Museum.

The beach at Amnisos rivals the archaeological site as an attraction

In 846, the Byzantine General Karteros landed at Amnisos to fight the Saracens, and in the end gave his name to the whole area.

From the top of the hill there is a wonderful view of the long beach with the white-topped waves of the Cretan Sea which sweep it, while in the distance we can see the islet of **Dias**. According to the myth, this islet (whose name is the modern Greek form of 'Zeus') was the first place that Zeus reached after kidnapping Europa, princess of Sidon in Phoenicia (Lebanon, today), who became the mother of Minos, subsequently king of Knossos. In order to honour Europa, the whole continent was given her name. Today, the islet is uninhabited, and its sole use is as a habitat for the Cretan wild goat. Underwater investigations by Jacques Cousteau have revealed traces of a Minoan settlement.

On the slopes of the hill, above the road, is the famous **Eileithyia Cave** or cave of the fairies. This was one of the earliest centres of worship on Crete, and it was dedicated to Eileithyia, daughter of Hera and protector of women in childbirth (the name comes from the participle meaning 'she who comes to render aid'). The worship of the goddess, naturally enough, was the responsibility of women; before giving birth —and also after the child was born— they would make her offerings of garments and veils, and they would crown her statue with dittany, a herb associated with childbirth.

The cave is very beautiful, with stalactites, pillars of rock and little lakes. Approximately in the centre of the cave is a rectangular altar built around two cylindrical stalagmites which rather resemble the figures of a man and a woman. So many votive offerings were found around this altar that some people have claimed they must have been produced in the cave.

We return to the main road, still heading east. We cross the fertile Vatheianos plain, with its large area of fields. At 13 km we come to the excellent beach of **Kokkini Chani**, which has fine white sand. The whole of this area is subject to strong north westerly winds and is good for wind-surfing. To our right is the archaeological site of **Niros**. Excavations here have revealed a well-preserved Minoan building dating from about the time of the second palaces of Knossos and Phaistos. The walls have survived up to a height of about one metre, and there was a paved court in front of the building's eastern entrance. In the interior of the building, which consisted of 40 rooms, were found many items related to the worship of the gods, which led the archaeologists to call it the 'the high priest's house'.

The settlement has a little harbour with a jetty, at the spot called **Ayii Theodori**, which according to the archaeologist Spyros Marinatos is the oldest harbour in the Mediterranean. Today, there are the ruins of the church to the Sts Theodore which gave the spot its name and the remains of the Minoan settlement can be discerned.

At 15 km from Herakleio, we pass the attractive beach of **Gournes**. The village of the same name stands on our right, on the left-hand bank of a seasonal river. There are remains of Minoan buildings, and Late Minoan shaft tombs wit = ceramics, pottery, amphorae and ivory and steatite sealstones have come to light.

We continue, and at a distance of 20 km from Herakleio come to the sandy beach of **Kato Gouves** or **Finikas**. A side-road to the right leads to the village of **Gouves**. After the village, a further side-road to the right takes us to the **Skoteinou Cave**. This natural feature is well worth a visit. It was one of the most important religious centres on Crete. It has a depth of 160 metres and consists of four different levels and a number of galleries, with fine stalagmites. In a layer of ash, archaeologists have found potsherds and bronze statuettes in positions of worship, among other finds. The cave continued to be used for religious purposes into the Christian era, as we can see from the remains of a chapel on the western side of its entrance. A more recent church, dedicated to St Paraskevi, was built above the cave in Venetian times.

We return to the main road at 20 km from Herakleio and join the new high-speed highway. At 23 km there is a turning to the right which leads up to the Lasithi plateau. This is the road which will be taken by those whose trip began in western Crete and who wish to visit the plateau; it is the classic itinerary. We describe the route as far as the plateau, since the tour of it forms part of Route 2 in the Prefecture of Lasithi (p. 270).

We take the plateau road for a short way as it crosses the fertile plain of Langada. After 7 km a further turning to the right leads to Kasteli in the Eparchy of Pediada (see Route 2, p. 226). At 11 km, among dense orange and olive groves and clumps of plane-trees, we come to the pretty village of **Potamies**. To the left, before we enter the village, is the church of Our Lady, inside which there are well-preserved 14th century wall-paintings. This church is all that has survived of the very old **Monastery of Our Lady 'Governiotissa'**, which was cruciform in shape and dedicated to the Dormition of the Virgin.

Appreciating the peace on the beach of Kokkini Chani

Striking a traditional note at Seli, Ambelou

We continue uphill through the verdant valley, passing **Sfendyli** at 17 km, to **Avdou** among its olive groves and orchards. This is a traditional village with numerous little Byzantine churches. At the spot known as Kondaria the ruins of a church to St Avdios have been discovered, and this presumably gave its name to the village. The villagers played an important part in all of Crete's struggles for freedom.

Outside the village to the west, at an altitude of about 1,000 metres, are the caves of Faneromeni, which has produced quite a number of ancient finds, and Ayia Foteini, which has a chapel.

We continue up the valley and at 18 km come to the densely-vegetated village of **Gonies**. This is where the real climb on to the Lasithi Plateau begins. We can see the surfaced road winding up ahead of us, running through the attractive Ambelos gorge

alongside the Aposelemi river before arriving up on the plateau. At 21 km from Herakleio a side-road (left) leads to Mochos (see below).

We continue to climb, and after a further 3 km the verdant village of **Krasi** emerges from among the tall trees which surround it.

We are now at an altitude of 600 metres. The village has abundant springs, and next to the fountain with its rushing water is an enormous old plane tree. In Minoan Crete, plane trees were sacred, since it was under a plane tree in Gortyn that Zeus and Europa coupled, Minos being the fruit of their union.

The road continues upwards, across the steep slopes of the mountain. After 3 km more amid plane trees and walnuts we see the **Kera Kardiotissa Monastery**.

At an altitude of 630 metres, this foundation stands amid dense vegetation in a spot with a wonderful view. It is dedicated to the Nativity of Our Lady, and was once a dependency of the Angarathou Monastery. In 1720 it became stavropegic (i.e. under the protection of the Patriarchate in Constantinople) and acquired great wealth, much of it in votive offerings.

Our road continues upward, and after passing the village of **Apano Kera** or **Minitis**, at a height of 680 metres, we reach the pass of **Seli Ambelou**, 3 km further on.

Now we have ascended to an altitude of 900 metres and we are on the border between the Prefectures of Herakleio and Lasithi. The view is striking. At our feet lies one of the most fertile parts of the Prefecture of Herakleio, surrounded by the azure waters of the Cretan Sea, while on clear days the view extends as far as Santorini.

To the right and left of the road are strong stone-built windmills, which were used for grinding wheat. In front

The busy beach at Chersonisos

of us, to the south, the towering peaks of Mt Dikte can be seen in the background, all around the magnificent and famous plain of Lasithi. The road continues through a number of picturesque villages before ending on the plateau (see Lasithi, Route 2, p. 270). At this point we could perhaps rest and take some refreshment before returning the way we came.

We return to the main road, at a distance of 23 km. Now we head east, and at 26 km. arrive at **Limani Chersonisou**, which stands on the western edge of the Bay of Mallia. It takes its name from the peninsula ('chersonisos') on which it stands and which creates two sheltered little bays with fine sandy beaches. Today, the village has developed into a well-organised tourist resort with all the necessary installations and a lively night-life. To the south of the harbour, not far away, is the village of

Chersonisos in a verdant setting. The village remains the picturesque traditional setlement it has always been, indifferent to the hum and bustle of the harbour.

To the west of the village stood the ancient city of Chersonesos, which was the port of ancient Lyttos. It was inhabited in prehistoric times, as can be seen from the traces of a Minoan settlement; it was autonomous, and minted its own coins, which showed the head of Artemis on one side and Apollo with a lyre on the other. It is believed that the first settlers were refugees from tyranny who brought with them the cult statue of Britomartis, 'the sweet virgin', a Minoan deity who was one of the most important figures in the Minoan pantheon. Later she became identified with Artemis. At the famous shrine in Chersonesos, Britomartis was worshipped because of her success in evading the clutches of Minos. After

The beach and little harbour of Chersonisos

he had laid siege to her for months, she threw herself into the sea. The shrine, which has not survived, was Minoan, while the scanty remains to be seen today date from Roman times. There are the ruins of an acropolis, an amphitheatre and a theatre, an old harbour and a fountain with mosaics showing fishermen. The foundations of two Early Christian basilicas have also come to light, with mosaic floors whose tesserae are arranged in geometric shapes.

In the bay of Chersonisos there is a isolated rock whose shape is reminiscent of a female body upright out of the sea and holding a basin on its head. The locals call the rock 'the girl', and if asked have numerous tales to tell about it.

The road continues along the coast, to the pretty cove of **Stalida**, 32 km. from Herakleio. This is an attractive tourist resort with abundant greenery and market gardens. There is an excellent beach with fine, white sand.

From Stalida, a side-road to the right climbs up through dense olive groves to **Mochos** (9 km). This village stands at an altitude of 400 metres and has a panoramic view over Mallia Bay. Picturesque alleys lead to fine houses with courtyards crammed with flowers, and in the centre of the village there is a large square with a dance floor. On 15 August each year, the Herakleio Travel Club organises a festival of folk dance and song.

After a further 3 km we join the road to the plateau; which we have described.

The pretty bay of Stalida

From Stalida, we take the national road east.

The scenery is wonderful, with the deep blue sea on our left and the green of the plain, with its oranges, lemons, bananas and olives, on our right, and the Lasithiotika mountains in the background. At 34 km from Herakleio, we enter the attractive town of Mallia, which straddles the road.

Mallia is a modern town, in a fertile area well supplied with water and noted for its market produce and windmills. It has its own beach, with fine, white sand; one of Crete's finest. Its archaeological site lies approximately 3 km to the east of the town.

This was the site of an important Minoan town whose ancient name is unknown to us. The contemporary name comes from the word 'omalia' ('flat'), thus indicating the lie of the terrain.

Archaeological finds have shown that the ancient city prospered between the Early and Late Minoan periods. Here the ruling dynasty was that of Sarpedon, brother of Minos and Rhadamanthus. The city issued its own coinage, which had a head of Athena on one side and two dolphins on the other. At the spot known as Chrysolakkos, a Minoan cemetery has been found and yielded gold funeral offerings. Among them was the fine piece of jewellery with two bees which can be seen today in Herakleio Museum.

Apart from the archaeological interest, Mallia also has an excellent bathing beach

The long beach at Mallia

But the most important discovery of all was the city palace, which occupied an area of 8,800 square metres and dates from the same time as the palace of Knossos. It is also laid out to the same plan as Knossos. One of the four largest Minoan palaces found so far, it is situated in a valley, at some distance from the sea. Although it does not possess the majesty of Knossos or Phaistos, and has neither their wall-paintings nor their theatres, it is nonetheless imposing and fascinating. Like all the other Minoan palaces, it was destroyed by earthquake around 1700 BC and later rebuilt in the form we see today. It, too, has a long and narrow central court, surrounded by four wings with five entrances. The western side of the palace is the most important and impressive.

245

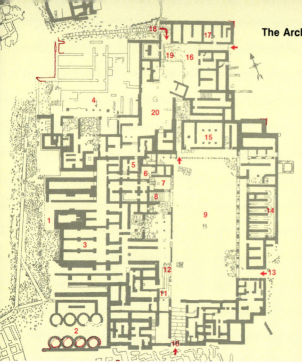

The Archaeological Site of Malia

1. West Court
2. Circular Store-rooms
3. Store-rooms
4. Polythyro
5. Workshops
6. Room of the Weapons
7. Loggia
8. Great Staircase
9. Central Court
10. South Entrance
11. Kernos
12. Broad Staircase
13. South East Entrance
14. Storerooms
15. Hall with
    6 Columns
16. North Court
17. Storerooms
18. North Entrance
19. Olive press
20. Court of the Tower

The archaeological site: the numbering of the site will visitors find their way around, and the numbers correspond to those on the diagram.

We begin our tour in the *West Court* **1** of the palace, which was paved. A road, also paved and one metre wide, ran along the western wall of the palace, oriented north-south. Where this ends, there is a fork; one branch leads to 8 *circular store-rooms* **2**. The *West Entrance* had guard-posts (bastions) to the right and left of it, while to the south of the entrance corridor there were *store-rooms* **3**. To the north was an official apartment, possibly that of the queen, whose architecture, as manifested in the colonnade, the light-shaft and the bathroom, is similar to that of Phaistos and Knossos. On the north side was the *Polythyro* **4**, a large hall with a portico. The most important objects found here were 2 long swords with gold-studded hilts.

The entrance corridor now encounters another corridor running at right angles to it, from north to south, which divided the palace into two wings at this point. On the north eastern side of the corridor were the principal royal apartments, with *workshops* **5** for bronze and ivory separating them from the 'queen's apartments'. The main palace block consists of a number of rooms, such as store-rooms, an armoury, a lustration room, etc. In the *Room of the Weapons* **6** was found the fine royal sceptre with the head of a leopard and a double axe. The palace communicated with the Central Court through the *Loggia* **7**, a large open-air hall with four steps into the court. A door with two steps in the southern wall led to the landing on the *Great Staircase* **8** to the upper floor. This is the only Minoan staircase to be shut off with a door.

The *Central Court* **9** at Mallia was rectangular with an altar in the centre, just like those at Phaistos and Knossos, but even more impressive. Around it stood the various palace buildings. In its south western corner was the *South Entrance* **10**, to the left of which there was an open-air shrine.

Next to this was the *Kernos* **11**, the altar on which sacrifices were placed, which is hewn from tough limestone. The Kernos was circular and around its edge are small recesses in which were placed the seeds of the fruit offered to the gods, while in the centre was a larger recess for the candle with the sacred flame.

Beyond the Kernos was the *Broad Staircase* **12**, the finest in the palace, some of whose 13 cm steps have survived. Between the Broad Staircase and the Great Staircase was the most important hall in the palace, beautifully constructed and with a handsome facade on to the Central Court. To the right of the South Entrance was a labyrinthine group of buildings, which, however, has been completely destroyed.

After the store-rooms comes the *South East Entrance* **13** to the palace. A large piece of sandstone marks its exact position, while the recesses with their marks of wear show that must have been a double door here.

From the Southeast Entrance, on the eastern side of the Central Court, begins the marvellous Portico, 34 metres in length, with alternating rectangular and circular columns. The portico was separated from the Court by a railing, its floor was paved, and there were doors at both the north and the south ends.

Behind the portico to the east was a series of *storerooms* **14** ,whose func-

tion is demonstrated by the large numbers of jars and pithoi found there.

On the north side of the Central Court was another paved *Portico* which was supported on round columns, thirteen of the bases of which have survived. The bases of the railing which separated the court from the portico can also be seen. From this portico, a wooden door led into the antechamber of *a hall with six columns* **15** in two lines. This hall is in many ways similar to corresponding buildings found in Egypt. Next to the hall was a staircase which led to the upper storey. To the left was a door opening on to a paved corridor which led to the North Court of the palace.

The *North Court* **16** had paved porticoes with pillars on its north, east and south sides and ended with a *group of six rooms* with three exits to the corridor and the court. The finds indicate that these rooms were *store-rooms* **17**. Next to these rooms, on the left, is a paved anteroom from which a paved corridor runs to the *North Entrance* **18** to the palace. Just next to the anteroom is the *olive press* **19**. To the south of this complex of rooms is the *court of the tower* **20**, as the archaeologists have named it.

Between the Court of the Tower and the North Court there is a building on a different alignment to that of the rest of the palace. Its more advanced construction, with smoothed stone, indicates that it was added at a more recent period, and it has much in common with the 'megaron' type of building described by Homer.

From Mallia the road continues to the south east into the hinterland, and after passing through the impressive gorge of Ayios Yeorgios 'Selinaris' arrives at Ayios Nikolaos.

Its monuments and picturesque features have m

...rsonisos one of the island's most cosmopolitan resorts

THE PREFECTURE OF LASITHI

The Prefecture of Lasithi occupies the easternmost part of Crete and has an area of 1,818 km². Its population totals approximately 70,000 and the principal occupations are farming and stock-breeding. The main products of the Prefecture are cereals, olive oil, olives, carobs and currants. Thanks to the warm —almost African— climate of the southern provinces of the Prefecture, there is considerable production of early vegetables and bananas. The Iera-petra and Gra Lygia areas, in particular, which have the highest number of hours of sunshine and the lowest rainfall, have developed into important centres for the production of early vegetables, and especially tomatoes. The Lasithi plateau is among the most fertile parts of the province; it produces large quantities of potatoes and very high-quality apples.

There are two theories as to the origin of the name 'lasithi': the first relates it to the ancient Greek word 'lasios', which means fertile area —and indeed Lasithi has been verdant since

ancient times— while the second, attributed to Paul Favre, relates the name to Siteia, which the Venetians rendered 'La Sitti'.

The capital of the Prefecture is Ayios Nikolaos, an attractive little harbour standing on a deep bay. Ayios Nikolaos and nearby Elounda have developed into tourist resorts of major importance, with many large hotel complexes. However, quiet beaches, isolated cafes and striking interchanges of landscape can still be found throughout the Prefecture — the famous palm forest at Vai, for example, or the forest of pines and wild cypresses at Selekano. There are important archaeological and historical sites, too, such as the palace of Zakros, and the admirable historical monastery of Toplou.

Communications by sea between the Prefecture and Piraeus are conducted through Herakleio. There are also sailings for Piraeus from Ayios Nikolaos and Siteia, via the Cyclades. Buses meet the flights into Herakleio airport. Siteia airport has flights for Rhodes, Carpathos and Kasos. Inside the Prefecture itself, the villages are served by the town and long-distance KTEL buses.

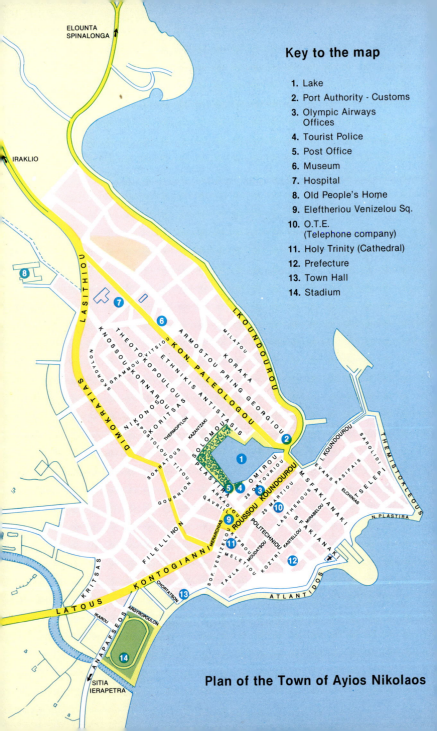

Key to the map

1. Lake
2. Port Authority - Customs
3. Olympic Airways Offices
4. Tourist Police
5. Post Office
6. Museum
7. Hospital
8. Old People's Home
9. Eleftheriou Venizelou Sq.
10. O.T.E. (Telephone company)
11. Holy Trinity (Cathedral)
12. Prefecture
13. Town Hall
14. Stadium

Plan of the Town of Ayios Nikolaos

The Town of Ayios Nikolaos

Ayios Nikolaos has been the capital of the Prefecture of Lasithi since 1904. It stands at the north western extremity of the calm bay of Mirabelo, in a situation protected by mountains. It is an attractive modern town of some 8,000 inhabitants which, thanks to its exceptionally mild climate, verdant setting and calm sea, has become an international tourist resort. Its wind-free harbour is a meeting-place for countless pleasure craft, as well as the fishing-boats which are based there. .

The harbour area, with its numerous restaurants and picturesque cafes, pulses with life and movement and is cosmopolitan in atmosphere. The town has retained a personality of its own, particularly in the centre, where the houses are built in the traditional style, the alleyways are paved and there are flights of brick steps. A road runs to the right from the harbour to the paved seaside square with the fish restaurants.

The little circular lake called *Voulismeni* in the centre of town is an undoubted attraction. A small zoo has been set up on the south-west side of the pretty lake. According to a myth, the goddess Athena used to come here to bathe. The lake, which must have been the result of volcanic action —though according to others it is the outlet of an underground river— has a depth of 64 metres. In olden days, it was believed to be bottomless and to be the haunt of spirit. Since 1870 a channel, along which fishing-boats moor, has linked it to the sea. In the summer there is an arts festival here.

Ayios Nikolaos

The picturesque appearance of the town is set off byu the two islets at the mouth of the quiet bay. The larger is called *Ayion Panton;* it has a church of the same name ('All Saints') and a lighthouse, and it is used as a breeding-ground for the Cretan ibex.

In antiquity, the site of Ayios Nikolaos was occupied by the port of Lato to Kamara, which served the Doric city of Lato Hetera. In the 3rd century BC this was a flourishing commercial port and an autonomous city which minted its own coins.

After this, it disappears from history and is not mentioned again until the 13th century. In 1206 the Genoans built the fortress of Mirabelo on Kefali hill, where the Prefecture now stands, and it gave its name to the town and the whole bay. The fortress was flattened by earthquake and later completely demolished by the Turks; today, no trace of it has survived.

In the 16th century, the Venetians gave the town its current name, which it took from the chapel of St Nicholas on the small promontary.

A view of Ayios Nikolaos from the south

The town reflected in the calm waters of the seafront

This chapel is very old; it is a single-aisled structure with a dome, and inside there are important wall-paintings in two layers. The first layer dates from the 9th century, during the iconoclastic controversy, as a result of which it contains only geometrical and floral motifs.

Under the Turks, the town of Ayios Nikolaos was uninhabited, and only the harbour —known then as Mandraki— was used for exporting agricultural produce. After 1870, people from Sfakia and Kritsi settled here to escape from T%kish persecution. Their little hamlet grew slowly, but it was not until recent years, with the rapid expansion in tourism, that it became famous.

As a modern town, Ayios Nikolaos has no sights of historical interest. However, it does have an **Archaeological Museum**, founded in 1970 and located in a building at *68 Palaiologou St.* The collection contains recent finds, most of them from eastern Crete.

Gallery I contains Early Minoan finds from Myrtos, figurines and pottery, and stone vessels from Mochlos. In *Gallery II* there are Protopalatial vessels from Zakros. *Gallery III* has Late Minoan finds from Kritsa and Myrsini (Siteia). *Gallery IV* contains pottery and figurines from the Early Geometrical period. *Gallery V* has exhibits from the Greek and Classical periods, mostly from Elounda (figurines and other objects). *Gallery VI* houses a collection of figurines, reliefs and funerary inscriptions from the Hellenistic and Roman periods.

The town has its *Koundoureios Municipal Library*, which contains 10,000 volumes.

The tourist season in Ayios Nikolaos begins in April. Ultra-modern tourist accommodation and hotel units in the style of traditional Cretan villages have sprung up in the outskirts of the town and along its fine beaches, offering all the amenities for a pleasant stay, a variety of entertainment, sea sports and a lively night-life.

257

Kritsa - Lato Hetera (12 km)

We shall take Ayios Nikolaos as our starting-point for a tour of the Prefecture of Lasithi, beginning with a visit to the traditional village of **Kritsas**, with its unique church of Our Lady 'Kera', and the archaeological site of **Lato Hetera**.

The picturesque traditional village of Kritsa, with its Byzantine church of Kera Panayia lies 11 km south west of Ayios Nikolaos. Its murals, which are in a good state of preservation, are some of the best in Crete and are considered to be the level of those of Mystras, the Macedonian School and Mt Athos. They are typical examples of the painting and style of the 14th and 15th centuries. North of the village are the remains of Lato Hetera, one of the oldest and most important cities of the island.

We leave Ayios Nikolaos in a southerly direction, taking the Siteia road. At 1.5 km we turn right, following a good surfaced road. We pass on our right a turning for Lakonia and the Lasithi Plateau.

The road crosses a verdant plain with olive and almond trees; at 7 km it passes the little village of **Mardati**. A little before it reaches the village, at the spot known as **'Logari'**, 100 metres to the right of the road, we can see the gleaming white church of *Kera Panayia. This is a three-aisled building, dedicated to the Dormition of the Virgin, St Anne and St Antony. It is rectangular and domed and was built in three stages, between the 13th and mid 14th centuries.*

*The Pantokrator in the niche of
St Antony (north aisle)*

The interior is decorated with fine murals: the *Pantocrator,* near the entrance, four *Angels,* many saints, the *Birth of Christ, St Anne,* the *Virgin*, the *Ascension, Paradise* and the *Punishment of the Damned* - an artistic treasure of the 14th and 15th century, a period when the Venetians ruled Crete, but allowed the islanders to build and decorate their churches as they wished.

At 11 km the road enters the large village of **Kritsa**. This is an attractive place, built in ampitheatre style on the foothills of the Kastellos mountain, with wonderful views of the plain of olives and almonds which stretches out below it and the tranquil gulf of Mirabelo.

This is a village which has retained its traditional Cretan colour, both in its whitewashed two-storey houses, with the elaborate ironwork of their balconies and the picturesque alleyways, and in the age-old occupations of the residents —particularly those of the women, who work at the loom— as well as the strict observance of the local customs. Its textiles, embroidery anz knitting are renowned for their design and colours.

There has been a village here since Roman times. It was destroyed by the Arabs, but rebuilt in the 10th century.

Under the Venetians it was the biggest village in Crete, and continued to be so until recently. Because of its involvement in all the uprisings of the Cretans, it was repeatedly damaged in reprisals.

Kritsa has a number of decorated Byzantine churches. Of these, after Our Lady Kera, the three-aisled church of St John the Divine, built in the Late Byzantine period and constituting a dependency of the Toplou Monastery, is the most important.

Kritsa was chosen by the French director Jules Dassen for the filming of his masterpiece *Celui qui faut mourir,* based on the novel by Kazantzakis *Greek Passion*. It was here also that another of Kazantzakis' novels —*Christ Re-crucified*— was filmed.

From Kritsa a narrow road leads to the **Katharo plateau**, an area with ample greenery whose villages are inhabited only in summer, when their houses serve as holiday homes.

An earth track leaves Kritsa in a northerly direction and after approximately 3 kilometres reaches the ruins of the ancient city of **Lato**.

These imposing archaic remains form an amphitheatre in a valley between two mountain peaks. Great simplicity and peace reign here, while the view, from the sea to the mountains of Lasithi is captivating.

The city was built in the 7th century BC by the Dorians and took its name from Leto, the mother of Apollo and Artemis ('Lato' being the Doric form of 'Leto'). It was called 'Hetera' (= 'other') Lato to distinguish it from the Lato near Kamara which is the present-day Ayios Nikolaos. It was reputed to be one of the strongest cities on the island, fortified with towers and with two acropolises. Its port was Lato near Kamara, with which in effect it constituted a single city, since they had the same admistration, the same representatives and worshipped the same divinity, Eileithyia, goddess of childbirth. Their common coinage shows the heads of Athena, Artemis or Eileithyia on the one side and Hermes and the words 'Hetera of the Latians' on the other.

The archaeological site is entered from the west, through the gate of the city from which a stepped road leads uphill. On the right were workshops and shops, which were protected on the south side by a wall. On the left, the road leads to an impressive entrance formed by two towers of the wall, giving access to the main part of the city. At the top of the road uphill, between two hills, is the agora, which is pentagonal and served not only as a centre for trade, but also for politics and culture. The remains of an arcade, a temple, a water tank and a banqueting hall with benches and a staircase are to be found here. The steps are similar to those in Minoan theatres. The Prytaneum (administative headquarters) is behind this theatre area.

The walls and buildings which we can see today belong chiefly to the 5th and 4th centuries BC.

The imposing position of the Doric city of Lato Hetera

ROUTE 1

Ayios Nikolaos - Elounda
Spinalonga - Plaka
Milatos - Selinaris

Our first route will be an exploration of the areas which lie to the north west of the town of Ayios Nikolaos. We shall visit Elounda, one of the island's most important resort areas, with its luxury hotels and we shall be able to admire the Venetian fortress on the islet of Spinalonga. We shall enjoy the enchanting beaches at Milatos and Sisi, and see something of the history of these places through their antiquities. Then we shall return to Ayios Nikolaos, traversing the Vrachasi gorge and stopping for a moment at the church of St George 'Selinaris', admire the superb scenery.

We start from Ayios Nikolaos, taking the coast road north.

As the road climbs, with the tourist complexes in the traditional island style and the hotels, large and small, on either side, the eye is caught by the wonderful indented coastline below.

At 6 km from Ayios Nikolaos the road broadens into a parking-place, which affords an opportunity to stop and admire the fine retrospective view of the Gulf of Mirabelo with the islets of Ayii Pantes and Mikronisi and the town of Ayios Nikolaos standing in the background.

Now the road runs downhill once more and the scenery occupies our attention.

At our feet is the sheltered bay formed by the Spinalonga peninsula and the eastern shore of Elounda.

Today, the peninsula is joined to the main body of the island by an isthmus cut by French sailors in the late 19th century and known as Poros. A narrow bridge crosses from the island to Spinalonga, next to a windmill which has been converted into a picturesque café.

This was the site of ancient Olous, near to the city of Naxos, the whole of which sank into the sea, as proved by the ruins which can be seen on the sea-bed when the weather is calm. Zeus Tallaios, Artemis Britomartis and Ares were worshipped here, and these gods were shown on the city's coinage. In ancient times, the city was known principally for its shrine of Britomartis; it was said that the wooden cult idol of the goddess was made by Daedalus, King Minos' head craftsman and technician. The importance of the city is proved by an inscription dating from the 3rd century BC, which refers to a pact of friendship between Olous, Lato and Knossos. The finds in the area include rock tombs with funerary offerings and other objects, which are on display in Ayios Nikolaos Museum.

To the east of this area, near the isthmus and next to the little white chapel which can be seen today, are the ruins of a basilica; it has a mosaic floor incorporating designs with fish and plants. Part of an inscription in the Doric dialect recording the end of the alliance between Olous and Rhodes was found build into the wall of the church.

To the south of Elounda are the remains of a rectangular building of the Geometric period. From the finds made on the site, the archaeologists have concluded that this must have been a temple to the immortal lovers, Aphrodite and Ares.

Elounda bay

Elounda today consists of seven different sections, of which **Schisma**, by the sea, is the most lively in the summer. The whole area is an enormous tourist resort, with the most modern facilities, and it attracts visitors from all over the world.

Before this, however, Elounda was also world-famous for its whetstones; the surrounding hills have deposits of a particularly fine-grained emery, unique in Greece, which was mined to make grinding tools.

From Elounda there are boat-trips to the rocky islet of **Spinalonga**.

The islet, which in 1954 was renamed **Kalydonia**, lies off the northern tip of the peninsula. On it there have been fortifications since antiquity, to protect the harbour of Olous from pirates. The Venetian answer to the threat posed by the Turks was to construct strong castles all over Crete during the 16th century.

Spinalonga island with its impregnable castle

Rethymno, Chania and Herakleio were all protected with formidable fortifications, and castles were also built to guard points of strategic importance such as Souda Bay. In 1579, the Venetians built a seemingly impregnable castle on the rock of Spinalonga, whose dimensions are only 200×400 m. The castle was designed to protect Elounda Bay and the whole of Mirabelo as well. Throughout the Turkish-Venetian war, which lasted 24 whole years, the castle, with its enormous cannon, resisted every attempt to capture it. And when the Turks finally took the rest of Crete, in 1699, Spinalonga remained in Venetian hands along with Gramvousa and Souda in western Crete. It was not until 1715, by a special treaty between the two warring states, that it passed into Turkish hands.

We enter the fortress between two strong battlements and beneath the Mocenigo battlement, on which most of the cannon were placed. The main line of defence, with double battlements, faced east. After the rise in the ground was a further line of defence. The San Michele bastion protected the northern shore, while the rest of the castle buildings were on the western side, which was safe from attack.

The name Spinalonga is a corruption of the Greek phrase 'stin Elounda', 'at Elounda'; from this corruption, the Venetians and Greeks managed to produce the name Macracantha: spina = acantha (thorn) and longa = makra (long). However, whatever name was used later came to be synonymous with human misery, for in 1903 the castle was turned into a leper colony by decision of the Cretan State. The lepers of Crete lived here until the colony was closed in 1957.

Plaka, on Elounda bay

From Elounda we continue north, and having passed the pretty spot of **Tsifliki Eloundas** at 12 km from Ayios Nikolaos, we come to **Plaka** (15 km). This is an attractive fishing village with a picturesque harbour and a beach with fine white pebbles and clear blue water.

We return to Elounda and the main road, which now turns to the left and heads west, towards the hinterland of the Prefecture. After approximately 10 km we enter the attractive and fertile village of **Fourni**, whose name comes, as it appears, from the French verb 'fournir', meaning to produce or supply — in other words, a fertile place.

After Fourni, a poor road leads to the **Areti Monastery** (8 km) close to the village of **Karydi**.

The **Areti Monastery** stands at an altitude of 530 metres amid woods of cypresses, almonds and olives. It was founded at some point during the 16th century and is dedicated to the Holy Trinity. It soon amassed a considerable fortune in property and became a major factor in local economic life, lending large sums of money even to Venetian nobles.

The road now runs downhill. We pass, on our left, the pretty village of **Nikithiano**, with its picturesque windmills. To the right is the hill of Ayios Antonios which has a chapel to St Antony on its summit. Here, on the ridge, are the remains of ancient **Dreros**, a rival of Lyttos. The ruins of the Agora, of a public building and a Delphinium (a temple to Apollo) can be seen. The temple is thought to be one of the most ancient Greek temples on Crete, dating back to about 1000 BC. Inside it was an altar on which the wild goats of the island were sacrificed. In this room were found bronze statuettes of Apollo and of two female forms —one with a serious and one with a happy expression— which may be representations of Leto and her twin sister Artemis. The statuettes are on display in Herakleio Museum. Among other finds was a plaque recording the oath sworn by the ephebes (the youths of the city); it is written in the Doric dialect and states their solemn devotion to Knossos and their hate for Lyttos. Today, the plaque is in Istanbul Museum. In 220 AD a civil war broke out among the inhabitants of Dreros; this weakened their position and eventually led to the destruction of their city.

After Nikithiano, we join the old national road, which passes through Neapoli. joining the old 'national road' which we shall be following for most of this itinerary. At 18 km from Ayios Nikolaos we come to the village of **Latsida**, which has two churches of the 14th-15th centuries, to St Paraskevi and Our Lady, with wall-paintings.

After Latsida we turn right (north) for **Milatos**. Minoan Milatos stood between the modern village and the fine sandy beach which is 1 km away. In the myths, Milatos was a boy who, like Romulus and Remus, was brought up in the forest by a she-wolf. When he grew up, he killed the tyrant of the city and escaped to Asia Minor, where he was said to have founded the famous city of Miletus (Milatos being a Doric form of Miletus), where the revolt of the Greek cities against the Persians began in 499 BC. In the 3rd century BC Milatos was destroyed by Lyttos.

Near the village, in a deep gorge, is the historic **Milatos cave**. It has eight entrances spaced out over 40 metres of the cliff-face and on three different levels, and it has a total area of 2,100 square metres. There are no particularly interesting geological phenomena in the cave, but it is famous for its historical connections. Here, in 1823, a large number of women and children took shelter from the Turks, who surrounded the cave and cut off the escape of its occupants. When the Greeks were forced to surrender, 15 days later, Husein Bey, who was in charge of the Turkish forces, slaughtered all the old men and the few fighting troops and sold the women and children into slavery in Egypt.

The sheltered little harbour at Sisi

From Milato a road leads in 5 km (west) to **Epano Sisi**. Near the village is the coastal settlement of **Sisi**, with a fine beach and a sheltered harbour.

At Sisi we join the old national road, which runs through the Vrachasi Gorge at this point. On the right-hand side of this beautiful cleft in Mt Selena is the little chapel of **St George 'Selinaris'**, where miracles are said to occur. It is the custom for passing travellers to stop to light a candle to the Saint, and also to admire the imposing grandeur of the surrounding scenery. In front of us are the steep slopes of Mt Anavlochos, in the vicinity of which some Cyclopean walls have survived. Today they support the terraces on which there are dense almond groves. Many archaeological finds have come to light in the area.

The **Monastery of St George 'Seli-naris'** was founded in 1961 on the remains of a 10th century foundation which was laid waste by pirates. It is a male foundation. The old people's home also stands on the ruins of old monastic cells.

The road continues to climb and after approximately 3.5 km reaches the pretty little town of **Vrachasi**. This stands on an amphitheatrical site on the southern slopes of Mt Anavlochos and it has a superb view. All around are the imposing mountains of the Selena and Stavros ranges, while at our feet is the valley of *Skafi Mirabelou*, densely planted with almond trees.

After passing through the attractive village of **Limnes**, with its abundant running streams, its picturesque windmills and its verdant orchards, we take the new or the old national road and head back to Ayios Nikolaos.

Ayios Nikolaos - Neapoli Lasithi Plateau

This second route takes us up to the Lasithi Plateau and the famous Diktaean Cave. Here, of course, we shall be far from the sea and beaches. Suitable clothing and footwear will be necessary, for some walking is anticipated and we shall be descending into the Diktaean Cave.

After visiting the pretty town of **Neapoli**, we begin to climb towards the plateau, which lies high in the Mt Dikte range, at a height of 817-850 metres. The plateau, which occupies an area of 2,500 hectares, is surrounded by the high peaks of the range. Thanks to the geological composition of the ground, the plateau retains the rainfall and some 10,000 windmills raise the water from wells to irrigate the plain; apart from being picturesque, they also make the plain among the most fertile parts of Crete.

Archaeological investigation has shown that the Lasithi Plateau was occupied as early as Neolithic times (Trapeza Cave, Diktaean Cave). Settlements have been found at Karfi and Plati. In historical times, the area was part of the territory of the city-state of Lyttos. Under Byzantium, there was a large town at Avgoustis. In 1263, however, the Venetians drove out all the inhabitants of the plateau, which had become a centre of resistance to their rule. They forbade any cultivation of the fields, on pain of death. And so for two whole centuries the plain lay fallow, its villages deserted and its fields waterlogged in winter. But when the Venetians had to deal with a shortage of wheat, they were compelled to allow the plateau to be farmed and inhabited again. They also helped to drain the area, digging the ditches which can still be seen today. Nonetheless, the plateau continued to be a centre of revolt and a hiding-place for fugitives all through the period of Turkish rule.

Today, the plateau is in the Eparchy of Lasithi; it has a total of 21 villages organised into 12 communes (administrative units).

Thanks to its healthy climate, the fame of the Diktaean Cave and the spontaneous and unselfish hospitality of its people, it has become a major tourist attraction.

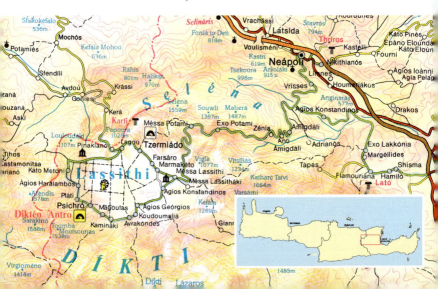

We take the old 'national road' out of Ayios Nikolaos, crossing the fertile and verdant plain of Mirabelo. At 15 km from our starting-point, in the middle of the plain, we come to the attractive upland town **Neapoli**.

In Venetian times this was a little village named Kares. It was later destroyed and rebuilt with the name Kainourgio Chorio or Neochori (both of which mean 'new village'), which it kept throughout the Turkish period. In 1768, Adosidis Costis Pasha developed it into a town, building parks, the courtrooms, the high school (the only one in the Prefecture until 1823) and the Seragaki (the pasha's residence, now a boys' orphanage). He also changed the name to Neapoli, moving here the administrative services of the Prefecture together with the Bishopric of Petra, which had formerly been based at Areti and Fourni. Neapoli continued to be the capital of the Prefecture until 1904, when it was moved to Ayios Nikolaos.

Today, Neapoli is an attractive commercial centre, laid out on a national town plan. It has fine modern buildings and the installations of a School of Domestic Science.

The church of Our Lady 'Megali Panayia' is imposing, and stands in a fine square with a garden, looking over the valley of Mirabelo. The church has three dedicatees: the Dormition of the Virgin, the Ten Saints and the Holy Trinity.

To the south west of Neapoli, at a distance of 1.5 km, is the 16th century **Kremasta Monastery**, which is dedicated to the Archangel Michael and also fuctions as a parish church.

We leave Neapoli and take the left fork, heading south. The road passes through the pretty village of **Vryses** and enters the verdant valley of Drasi.

Now we begin to climb, with bend after bend, and we pass the villages of **Apano** and **Kato Amygdali** and **Zenia**. We continue to climb through wonderful scenery, watching as the landscape changes and becomes wilder and more grand. At 20 km from Neapoli and an altitude of 850 m., we pass the village of **Exo Potami**. A further three kilometres through a green valley where the vegetation is dominated by ilexes brings us to **Mesa Potami**, a picturesque village standing at 880 metres above sea level. The road continues to wind upwards, and at the spot known as *'tou Patera ta Sellia'*, reaches its highest point, at an altitude of 1100 metres. The view all around is superb, with the wild beauty of the gorge behind us and the plateau, with its white windmills breaking the otherwise static landscape, stretching out in front.

The road now runs downhill into the plateau. At 30 km we come to the first village on the plateau, **Mesa Lasithi**, which stands at an altitude of 870 m. From here a side-road to the right leads to the **Kroustallenias Monastery**. This foundation, with its wonderful view, stands nestling against a rock covered with ancient maples and oaks and clad in ivy which winds itself round the trunks and branches of the trees.

The monastery was founded around 1540 and is dedicated to the Dormition of the Virgin. It takes its name, which means 'of crystal', from an icon of Our Lady which was found here, painted on crystal. The monastery played an important part in the struggle for Greek liberation, which is why the Turks destroyed it twice, and in the field of learning: it housed what was until 1870 the only primary school in Lasithi.

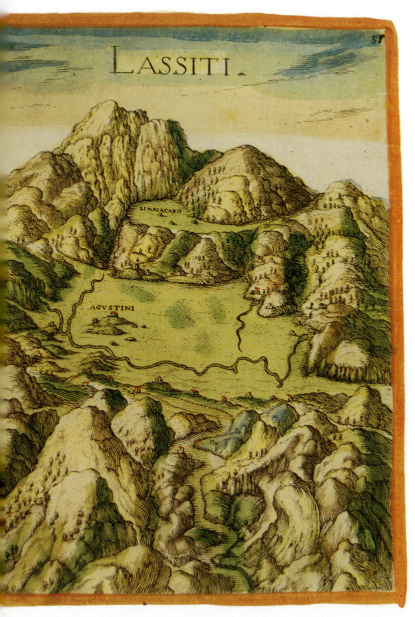

The Lasithi plateau, in an engraving by M. Boschini (1651)

After the monastery, we can drive in a circle round the plateau, initially heading north west. The circuit is about 23 km in length. We pass through the villages of **Marmaketo** and **Farsaro** before coming to **Tzermiado**, the principal town of the Eparchy of Lasithi. This village, on the southern slopes of Mt Selena, has the excellent climate of all the plateau and was first founded in the 15th century. Archaeological finds from the Middle Minoan period have come to light in the area.

To the east of Tzermiado is the **Trapeza cave**, which is thought to be the earliest centre of cult worship on the plateau and is of great archaeological interest. It was first used as a dwelling-place, and later, when the habitations moved to the Kastelos hill to the east of Tzermiado, it became a burial-place and shrine. Systematic archaeological investigation has brought to light finds from all the periods between the Neolithic and the Byzantine, which means that it continued to be used even after its position as a centre of worship had been usurped by the Diktaean Cave.

On the hill-top known as **Karfi**, above Tzermiado to the north at a height of 1100 metres, was a large Late Minoan settlement whose remains can be reached on foot or by donkey. The settlement was inhabited by Eteocretans during the time of the Dorian invasion of Crete, and the inaccessibility of the site helped them remain free from 1150 BC to about 1000. These tough descendants of the Minoans, living high above the plain, built their city in the old Minoan style they remembered, in the hope that one day they would return to their former homes.

The fertile plateau provides work for its inhabitants all the year round

On the highest peak they erected a shrine with an altar, and many votive offerings were discovered there together with statuettes in a stance of prayer and the arms raised. Below the cliff they built tholos tombs for their dead.

The city itself had no town plan, since they believed it would only be a temporary settlement. Yet for a century and a half they kept alive a Minoan way of life which had died out in the lower parts of the island.

There is another reason, too, for ascending to Karfi: the view over the landscape, which is truly magnificent. Below us to the north is the charming eparchy of Pediada, while further out one's eye can scan the Cretan Sea and even pick out the Cyclades when the weather is clear. To the south east is the flat and peaceful Lasithi Plateau. The magical calm of the landscape is peacefully disturbed by the white circular motion of the thousands of windmills, which rise proudly out of the natural panorama.

From Tzermiado the road continues and, after passing through the villages of **Lagou** and **Pinakiano**, joins the road which climbs up to the plateau from Herakleio at Seli Ambelou (see p. 240).

After the crossroads with the entrance to the plateau in the direction of Herakleio, we continue our circular route.

On the western extremity of the plateau, is the deserted monastery of **Our Lady 'Zoodochos Pighi' or 'Vidiani'**, nestling amid a verdant landscape. The foundation dates from 1854 and there was a little village, ruins of which can still be seen, at its entrance.

We continue through the unspoiled villages of **Kato Metochi** and **Ayios Haralambos** to reach **Plati**. This village, built in a fertile landscape where fruit trees flourish on the lower slopes of Mt Afentis Christos, is of considerable archaeological interest.

The Diktaean Cave

We leave Plati and shortly before entering Psychro encounter the NTOG pavilion. From here it is a 15-minute walk (donkeys are also available) to the magnificent entry to the Diktaean Cave.

The **Diktaean Cave** stands at an altitude of 1025 metres on the northern slopes of Mt Dikte. This, according to the myths, was the place where Zeus, the father of gods and men, was born.

Wonder and awe overcome one at the sight of the enormous entrance to the cave, crowned by trees and bushes and surrounded by wild flowers whose aroma fills the air. As one begins the descent into the cave, the atmosphere changes and becomes more solemn and suggestive, redolent of religious significance. The light of one's candle or torch is one's only companion.

Huge stalactites hang from the ceiling, like giants whose backs have for countless centuries been supporting the roof of the cave. The damp atmosphere and the deathly silence are broken only by the fluttering of the occasional wild dove; birds still nest in the cave. And in the half-dark the stalactites glimmer: the forms of Zeus, of Hera, of Artemis and of Athena can be seen. At the back of the cave, above the pure water of a little lake, a forest of stalactites known as *"the cloak of Zeus"* is reflected in the water like a gigantic candelabrum. (see photo p. 9).

In here, in this magnificent cave, that Rhea took refuge and, with the help of her mother Gaea, gave birth to Zeus, the divine infant. The cave extended its generous protection to the baby and managed to save it from the murderous plans of its father Kronos. It could be said that the Diktaean Cave stands to pagan religion as Bethlehem stands to Christianity.

The birth of Zeus, from a hand-drawn map of 1554 (Paris, National Library)

It was only natural that this enormous cave, with its wealth of stalactites, its dark and menacing atmosphere and also its ease of access to man should develop into a shrine and supplant the Trapeza cave in terms of religious significance. And it was also natural that together with the deities worshipped here the stalactites should also become the objects of devotion, as can be seen from the votive offerings found among their folds. The finds which archaeologists have discovered in the Diktaean Cave are more ancient than those in the Idaean Cave, which justifies the point of view that Zeus was born in the Diktaean Cave but brought up in the Idaean Cave (see p. 164).

(see p. 164)

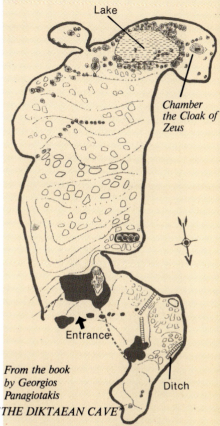

Chamber the Cloak of Zeus

Lake

Entrance

Ditch

A bronze chariot: a votive offering from the Diktaean Cave

From the book
by Georgios
Panagiotakis
"THE DIKTAEAN CAVE"

The Diktaean Cave consists of two parts. The first or northerly part, the antechamber, is flat and has a total length of 42 m., a width of 19 m. and a height of 6.5 m. Here an altar had been built and around it were tables for offerings, statuettes in stances of devotion, Kamares ware pottery and other items. The second part, which runs from north to south, is the main cave and slopes downward. Its total length is 85 m., its width is 38 m. and its height is between 5 and 14 m. At the back on the left is a further small chamber, and tradition has it that a hidden recess in it is where Zeus was born. On the right is the lake, whose dimensions are 16×8.5 metres.

Stalagmites in the Diktaean Cave (or Psychro Cave)

We return to the tourist pavilion, where refreshments will give us an opportunity to think back over what we have just seen and contemplate the myths connected with this place.

We continue, and enter **Psychro** (at an altitude of 840 m.), also first built in the 15th century. The village owes its name (which means 'cold') to the fact that the weather is often cold.

The road continues through the attractive villages of **Kaminaki** and **Avrakones** before coming to the large village of **Ayios Yeorgios**.

Here we should stop to visit the **Folklore Museum of Crete**. In a lovely house dating from 1800, a strict example of the local style of architecture, and in an adjacent more modern building restored to the style of a middle-class residence of the early 20th century, are the Museum's collections. These are arranged in harmonious order and in a functional form so as to provide a picture of traditional life in the home and in the fields; there are complete sets of equipment for iron-working, cheese-making, basket-weaving, a host of domestic utensils, a traditional fireplace, looms, an oven, a plough, a boiler for distilling raki, and much, much more. One room is devoted to the folk painters and wood-carvers of Crete.

A reconstructed store-room in the Folk Museum

Also on show are delicately-woven textiles in traditional patterns, finely-worked wooden furniture, hanging lamps, a wealth of photographs and other documentary evidence and even weapons.

From Ayios Yeorgios it is possible to climb up to *Spathi*, which, at 2,148 metres is the highest peak of Mt Dikte.

We continue, and after passing through the village of **Ayios Konstantinos**, we complete our circuit round the Lasithi plateau.

Now we return to Drasi, where we leave on our left the turning back to Neapoli and continue to the right, for Ayios Nikolaos.

We run through the verdant Drasi valley and pass pretty villages such as **Exo Lakonia**, **Fioretzides** and **Flamouriana** before reaching Ayios Nikolaos.

The Lasithi Plateau

ROUTE 3

Ayios Nikolaos - Pacheia Ammos - Ierapetra Makriyialos - Kapsa Monastery - Myrtos Anatoli

In this route, we shall first acquaint ourselves with the coastal villages along the Gulf of Merabelo, to the south of Ayios Nikolaos and crossing the narrowest part of Crete will suddenly find ourselves on the shores of the Libyan Sea. Of course, there will also be some archaeological sites to see on the way down to Ierapetra. Once there, we shall be able to enjoy the fine beaches to the east and west of the town. Among other possibilities are short boat trips to the islets of Chrysi and Koufonisi. We shall return to the Gulf of Mirabelo by a different route through upland country.

We leave the town of Ayios Nikolaos along the coast road for Ierapetra and Siteia, heading initially south. At 4-6 km from the town we pass an attractive resort area where the hotels and the other buildings are in the harmonious style of the Aegean islands. We cross the Istronas river and at 11 km from Ayios Nikolaos pass on our right a road to Kalo Chorio (see the return route). We continue with Istros beach on the left.

Shortly before we reach Gournia there is a crossroads from which a passable unsurfaced road leads in approximately 6 km to the **Faneromeni Monastery**. This foundation stands in an isolated site high up in the mountains, amid fine scenery. Its twin-aisled little church stands inside a cave, where an icon of Our Lady was revealed ('fanerothike', hence the name) to the faithful. On 15 August there is a major religious and secular feast here.

At 19 km along the main road, on the right, there is a large Minoan settlement at the spot known as **Gournia**. The ancient name of this site remains unknown to us, while the modern name is derived from the small ancient cisterns ('gournes') discovered here before the main excavations took place. According to the archaeologists, the settlement was built around 1600 BC, on a low, flat-topped hill, and it occupied an area of more than 15,000 square metres. Around 1450 BC —that is, only 150 years later— it was destroyed in the same catastrophe which struck the other large Minoan palaces. It was never rebuilt.

The lay-out of the city is somewhat irregular, and as was also the case elsewhere in Crete, there were no city walls. On the top of the hill was the palace, and a small shrine with votive offerings has also been discovered here. This site has been described by the

The beach at Istros

archaeologists as the remains of a primarily commercial city; many tools came to light here (saws, lathes, needles, hooks, etc.).

It was not rich, and the king lived close to his subjects, as can be seen from the houses clustered around his palace. However, the site is of great archaeological value for the light it sheds on the ordinary everyday life of the Minoans and their daily occupations.

We continue along the main road, and at 21 km from Ayios Nikolaos come to **Pacheia Ammos**. As the name suggests (it means 'thick sand'), there is a fine sandy beach here. The surrounding area is also attractive, with dense olive groves and hothouses. One kilometre further along we come to a crossroads, where we leave behind the road to Siteia and head south for Ierapetra. This part of the island, from Pacheia Ammos to Ierapetra, is the narrowest area of Crete, being only 12 km broad. After about 3 km a side-road to the right leads to the village of **Vasiliki**, whose archaeological sites were explored by Richard Seager. Its importance lies in the fact that some of the island's few surviving Early Palace period buildings (2600-2000 BC) were found here. The sophisticated houses (and in particular the 'House on the Hill') were the forerunners of the magnificent palaces built later on. The 'House on the Hill' was a little palace in its own right, with a paved court on the western side and impressively large rectangular rooms where traces of red plaster can still be seen on the walls.

In the periods during which Knossos did not dominate eastern Crete, Vasiliki developed into a cultural centre of some importance. Near the ruins were found some superb vases with long necks which swivel at the end. These vases, which are rather like teapots, were hand-thrown and painted in various shades of red and black. Since they are of a pattern unknown elsewhere, they have come to be called Vasiliki ware.

At 28 km from Ayios Nikolaos we come to **Episkopi**, the highest point on our route. The view all around is marvellous. Here we leave behind us the Cretan Sea and soon we can see the vast expanse of the Libyan Sea stretching out before us.

On the eastern side of the main square in Episkopi is a little Venetian church with a coat-of-arms. At one time this building was in parallel use by the Catholics and the Orthodox congregation of the village, each of which had half of it. The Orthodox influence is plain in the Byzantine dome. To the north of the village are a number of ancient tombs which produced the larnaces on show in Ierapetra Museum.

At 29 km we pass the pretty village of **Kato Chorio** with its abundant streams and thick vegetation, and we soon come to **Ierapetra** (33 km), the most southerly town in all Greece.

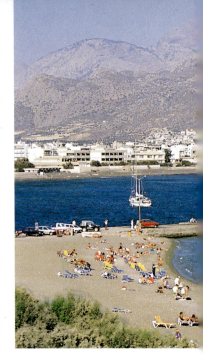

The site of the modern town was occupied by one of the most important cities in ancient Crete. It was initially called Cyrbas, from the name of its founder; Later it was called Kamiros, Pytna, Ierapytna and eventually Ierapetra.

It reached the height of its prosperity in the 2nd century BC, when it dominated Praisos and almost the whole of the Siteia area. It also managed to subdue another powerful city in the vicinity, Larisa, today called Kalamafka, and to populate it with colonists of its own.

As an independent and autonomous city, it minted its own coins, which showed tripods and wreaths or the head of Zeus and a palm-tree. It resisted the Romans bravely, and was the last Cretan city to be conquered and destroyed by them, in 66 BC. However, it was soon rebuilt and regained its former eminence.

The sandy beach at Ierapetra, with the town in the background

Up to the 10th century there were two theatres, numerous places of worship, an amphitheatre, an aqueduct and statuary which demonstrated its prosperity. In 824 it was laid waste by the Saracens, and in 1508 it was flattened by an earthquake. In Venetian times, Morosini built a fortress here on the site of an earlier castle; his rectangular building had towers at all four corners, an inner courtyard and a water tank. Remains of this building can still be seen today (called the 'Gule'). In 1647 the town was taken by the Turks, who renovated the fortress and added new buildings to it. Remnants of the presence of the Turks can still be seen today in the old town, with its pretty alleys and low houses. In 1798, it is said that Napoleon spent the night in the town on the way to Egypt, and the house in which he stayed can still be seen.

The little **Archaeological Museum** of Ierapetra contains exhibits dating from between Early Minoan and Roman times, including inscriptions and statues, mostly from Vasiliki and Gournia. The most interesting exhibits are the striking though rather crude larnaces from Episkopi, fashioned from clay and decorated with pictures of animals in lively colours. There is also a fine Roman statue discovered in Ierapetra; it stands 1.5 metres high and shows the goddess Demeter (Ceres) holding a bunch of wheat. There are two little snakes entwined in her hair.

The town also has a number of interesting churches dating from more modern times, with carved wooden screens and important icons.

Today, Ierapetra is an attractive modern town; the indented coastline has some superb sandy beaches. Thanks to its mild climate and

285

generally good weather, it has the most sunshine and the least rainfall of anywhere else in Crete, making it an ideal spot for holidays summer and winter. It is also one of the most important fruit and vegetable-growing centres in Greece, since the climatic conditions are favourable to early crops. Something of an industrial centre, it is particularly noted for the manufacture of knives.

From Ierapetra there are beaches to visit both east and west of the town and on the islet of Chrysi.

Chrysi lies about 15 km off the coast to the south of Ierapetra. As the name indicates (it means 'the golden one'), the islet's beaches have fine golden sand running down into greenish-blue water. The harmony of the landscape is supplemented by a forest of ceder trees.

The Venetian fortress of Ierapetra

The resort of Makriyalos, on the beautiful bay of Kala Nera

The Kapsas Monastery, beside the Perivolakia ravine

We leave Ierapetra and head east, taking the surfaced coast road. We pass through the coastal areas of **Ayii Saranta** and **Ferma**, with plantations of pine trees, before reaching **Ayia Fotia**, 12 km. This village, concealed by tall pines, stands in an idyllic spot and has a fine sandy beach.

We continue through the coastal villages of **Galini, Achlia, Mavro Kalympo, Ayios Pantaleimon** and **Koutsouras**. At 24 km from Ierapetra we come to the pretty seaside village of **Makriyialos**, on the attractive bay of Kala Nera.

This village has developed into an important tourist resort thanks to its long beach, with white sand and clear blue waters. Next to the modern village church, archaeological investigations have revealed a Minoan villa. A villa dating from Roman times in the same area has also been explored.

The road continues along the coast pretty village of **Analipsi** (27 km), after which it heads for Siteia.

After Analipsi, a passable unsurfaced road along the coast leads in about 5 km to the **Kapsa Monastery**, which stands near the shore, on a steep-sided rock close to the fine Perivolakia Gorge. The monastery is believed to have been founded in the 15th century, though in 1471 it was laid waste by pirates and abandoned. In 1841 it was renovated by Yerontoyannis, a reformed robber who lived there as a hermit. He built the church, dedicated to John the Baptist, and added new cells. Today the monastery is run by Toplou Monastery. Its feast day is on 29 August, when there is a large secular festival.

The track continues along the coast to **Goudoura**, five miles south of which is the islet of **Koufonisi** or **Lefki**, which forms part of a group of islets. These islets were once used for the cultivation of wheat. On Koufonisi there was an ancient settlement with a theatre and a temple, but it was destroyed in the 4th century BC.

We return to Ierapetra and head west, along the main coast road. At approximately 5 km from the town we come to the seaside village of **Gra-Lygia**. The village runs down to a long beach with coarse sand. Gra-Lygia was the first village to introduce the growing of early vegetables in hothouses, a practice which later extended to all the villages in the area.

The road continues in the direction of Myrtos. At about 10 km from Ierapetra, on a hill to the right of the road at the spot known as 'Fournou i Koryfi', a Minoan settlement has been discovered. This Early Minoan town produced finds of large numbers of Vasiliki ware vases which are on show at Ayios Nikolaos Museum, seal-stones, tools and other items.

Shortly before we enter Myrtos, a path to the right of the road leads to a low hill, on which, at the spot known as 'Pyrgos', a second Minoan settlement has come to light. On the top of this hill, the spades of the archaeologists revealed a large villa which must have stood two or three storeys in height. It belonged to the Late Palace period. To the west of the village the remains can be seen of a Roman settlement.

Myrtos, 16 km from Ierapetra, is an attractive village with extensive groves of banana and orange trees. It stands on the banks of the Kryos river and has an attractive beach with fine sand and pebbles, running down to clear waters.

From Myrtos our road continues to the north west for Viannos and Herakleio.

Myrtos, on the banks of the river Kryos

The mountains of Lasithi from the Selekano valley

We return to the crossroads outside Gra-Lygia. After about 12 km, the road to the left takes us up to a height of some 600 metres, where the village of **Anatoli** is situated. The view over the Libyan Sea from here is superb. The village has a number of 13-14th century churches with wall-paintings.

In Anatoli there is a fork. If we turn left (north west), the road will take us in about 7 km to the **Xakousti Convent**, which is dedicated to the Nativity of Our Lady.

A further 3 km brings us to what in Venetian times was the largest village in the Ierapetra area, **Malles**. There is a fine church of 1431 in the village, dedicated to Our Lady. Between Malles and Christos, 2 km to the west, was ancient city of Malla, an independent city-state which issued its own coins. They showed the head of Zeus on one side and on the other an eagle and the letters 'MAL'. Pottery and other items from Roman times have come to light in the area.

Today, Malles and Christos are pleasant upland villages (at an altitude of 600 metres) on the slopes of Mt Dikte, in the centre of the wooded Selekano district, among dense pines and cypresses.

We return to the fork in Anatoli. Now we take the right-hand turning, to the north west, and pass through the picturesque villages of **Kalamafka** and **Prina**, 12 km from the turning. Shortly after Prina, (2 km) a side-road to the right leads to the village of **Meseleri**, which stands on the site of ancient Oleres.

From Prina the road continues for another 4 km before reaching **Kalo Chorio**, a village situated in a pretty valley with abundant streams and dense vegetation.

Shortly after the village, a road leads left to Ayios Nikolaos.

ROUTE 4

Ayios Nikolaos - Siteia Toplou Monastery - Vai Palaikastro - Zakros

This route covers the very pretty town of Siteia, the historic Toplou Monastery and the exotic and magical spot called Vai. We shall also be visiting the archaeological sites at Itanos, Palaikastro, Zakros and Praisos. It is a combination of knowledge and entertainment in which the old interchanges with the modern and yesterday is bound up with today.

With this last route, we conclude our tour of the Prefecture of Lasithi and also our extensive acquaintance with the hinterland of Crete. It would be inaccurate, of course, to claim that we have provided visitors with an exhaustive description of the island, for that would require much greater length on our part and much more time on the part of the visitors. However, the first acquaintance has been made, and we would like to think that it will stimulate visitors to come back to this beautiful island again and again.

Ródos - Kárpathos

N. PAXIMADA

N. DRAGONADA

N. GIANISSADA

Akr. Sideros

Akr. Moúros

195m
Moúros
Itanos

Orm. Grandes
Erimoúpoli

Váï   Finikódassos

SITIAS

Toploú

N. GRANTES

Palékastro
Mertidia   Angathia
Lídia
Fotiá   Modi
539m   Ágios Nikólaos
Ekklissia

Akr. Plá

Petsofas
215m

Xirolimni
Krionéri   Mitáto
ónos   Vrissidi
Karidi   Kellária
Adravásti

Langáda

Orm. Kouroules

Chochlakiés

Azokéramos
Traóstalos
515m

Klissidi

anos   Zákros

Vigla Zákrou
711m

Káto Zákros

Akr. Avláki

Chamétoulo

aló Chorió
Agridomoúri
628m

Xerokambos

Agía Iríni   N. KAVALI

We leave Ayios Nikolaos along the coast road for Siteia, as we did in Route 3 when heading for Pacheia Ammos.

We pass the turning for Ierapetra and at 26 km from Ayios Nikolaos we reach the village of **Kavousi**, which stands in a fertile valley full of olive trees and crossed by a seasonal river.

Kavousi Bay is at the end of the Gulf of Mirabelo, on the edge of one of the largest plantations of olive trees on Crete. There is a spring with cool water and plane trees, an ideal spot for a drink and to look at the view.

In the village, there is a little medieval church of St George, above the central square. It was built in the time of the Venetian occupation but in the Byzantine style.

Ancient Cavousi, which stood on the slopes of the hill above the modern village, was the first archaeological site in Crete to be investigated by American scholars.

From Kavousi it is possible to ascend the steep sides of Mt Kapsas. The Gulf of Mirabelo ends here.

The road begins to climb, crossing the picturesque valley of Lastros, where the village of the same name lies between two hilltops, and at 42 km comes to the village of **Sfaka**. From here, a track (6 km) runs down to the seaside and leads to the attractive fishing-village of **Mochlos**. From its attractive cafés there is a unique view along the steep rocky coastline.

From Mochlos there are boat trips to the islets of Ayios Nikolaos and Pseira.

The coast at Mochlos, and the islet of Ayios Nikolaos

Ayios Nikolaos lies directly off Mochlos. There is a chapel to St Nicholas on it. In antiquity, the island formed a peninsula jutting out from the mainland, with bays on its eastern and western sides. In the Early Minoan period there was a prosperous settlement in the area, since this was the first port at which ships sailing to Crete from the Middle East and Egypt called. Interesting tombs, which are rather reminiscent of houses, have been found on the western slopes of the rock. The 'treasure of Mochlos', which is today in the Museums of Herakleio and Ayios Nikolaos, consists largely of gold jewellery; it includes a superb diadem decorated with animal motifs. Also in the treasure were bronze tools and weapons which must have been made from bronze imported from Cyprus, Minoan double axes, and fine stone vases in decorating which the skilled artisans had made use of the natural grain of the stone. From these finds it would appear that the islet was a centre for prehistoric shipping.

To the west of Mochlos is the barren little island of **Pseira**, which is uninhabited today. In Minoan times, it had an important settlement by the natural harbour on the east side of the island, which is suitable for small vessels. When excavating here, Seager discovered a number of stone-built houses in an amphitheatrical layout. Three of the rooms of one of the houses were filled with stones, presumably for use as missiles. Another house contained an excellent Minoan wall-painting of two bare-breasted ladies, dressed in blue, sitting on a rock. The Romans built a military camp on the highest point of the island.

We return to Sfaka. The road continues to climb, and comes to the village of **Tourloti**, which stands on top of a hill called Kastri. There are remains of an ancient city in the vicinity, and statuettes and pottery have been found.

After Tourloti we come, on our left, to **Myrsini** (46 km), where shaft graves containing sacrophagi, clay pottery tools and other utensils have been investigated.

At 51 km is the village of **Mesa Mouliana**, which stands on an amphitheatrical site in an area heavily planted with vines. The famous Mouliana wine is made here. In the village itself, two tholos tombs have been found; they were used during the Early Geometric period, at which time the dead were cremated, and during Mycenean times, when they were entombed. A vase decorated with a representation of a mounted warrior —the only one of its kind discovered in Crete— was also found here.

We continue, passing at 53 km through the village of **Exo Mouliana**, which has a church of St George with wall-paintings. At 59 km we come to **Hamezi**, an attractive upland village. To the south of the village is the famous 'Oval House', a fortress-like building of the Middle Minoan period. The village Folklore Museum is worth a visit; it has interesting collections of all kinds of folklore items. In late September every year, the village is the scene of the 'Kazanemata', the festival to mark the traditional distilling of tsikoudia, the national drink of Crete, which is followed by general jollification.

After Hamezi the road begins to run downhill, passing through the village of **Skopi** before arriving in the attractive town of Siteia, 70 km.

Siteia, which is the capital of the Eparchy by the same name, stands at the head of Siteia Bay, which is the most easterly of the large inlets on the north side of the island. Its amphitheatrical site occupies the sides of a low hill. This pleasant coastal town continues today to have much of the calm and charm of bygone days. The landscape here is not so wild as elsewhere on Crete, and the mountain ranges on the horizon are much gentler: none of them exceeds 800 metres in height. The surrounding countryside is green and fertile. The beach, with its fine, white sand, running down to clear blue waters, is a constant invitation to bathe. The local residents, too, are lovers of peace and quiet; cheerful and hospitable, they are known for their pleasure in music and feasting.

The modern city stands on the site of ancient **Eteia**, which was the port of Praisos. The surrounding area, and particularly that of the district known as Petra to the east of the modern town, has been inhabited since the Bronze Age. This is the area where the Eteocretans lived: they were the indigenous islanders who retreated to isolated areas when the Dorian invasion occurred so as to avoid intermingling with the interlopers. Eteia was the home of Myson, numbered among the Seven Sages of ancient Greece. The port gained in strength after 146 BC, when the people of Praisos settled there on the destruction of their own city by Ierapetra. At this time, the city minted its own coinage. Eteia continued to flourish throughout the Roman, Byzantine (when it was the seat of a bishopric, later moved to the village of Episkopi) and Venetian periods.

In 1508, the town was destoyed by an earthquake and in 1538 it was sacked by pirates. After this it went into decline, and in 1651 it was abandoned by its inhabitants, who moved to the district of Liopetro.

At about this time, the Venetians themselves ruined their own castle to prevent it falling into the hands of the Turks. These ruins can still be seen today, to the east of the town. Only a tower with three floors has survived, together with some other buildings protected by a polygonal defensive wall with battlements. This section of wall crowned the eastern wing of the castle. Before the Venetians, the Genoese had build a fortress in Siteia in 1204, on the foundations of earlier Byzantine buildings. Some remains of

Roman fishing installations can be seen near the Customs House. On the northern side of the fortress, there was under the Venetians the **Santa Maria Monastery**, which was demolished by the Turks. On its ruins was built a little chapel, and since then the area has been used as a cemetery. The town itself was rebuilt in 1870 to plans by the progressive Turk Avni Pasha.

Siteia was the birthplace of the famous Cretan poet Vincenzo Kornaros, writer of *Erotokritos* (see 'Yesterday and Today', p. 63).

Examples of the prosperity and culture of the ancient city can be admired in the **Archaeological Museum**, which has been housed in a modern building since 1984 and is the third-largest in Crete. On display are finds from the wider area around Siteia and from the palace at Zakros; they are arranged in such a way as to provide visitors with a most informative tour. The town also has a **Folklore Museum**, with collections of textiles, embroidery, local costumes, traditional furniture and domestic utensils which give visitors a full picture of what life used to be like in these parts.

At the theatre, which is against the renovated part of the city wall, there are interesting cultural events each summer.

There are ferry sailings from Siteia to the Dodecanese, the Aegean Islands and Kavala in northern Greece. Since 1984 there has also been an airport, which is only 10 minutes from the centre of town.

Siteia will be our starting point for visits to the archaeological sites of Palaikastro, Zakros and Praisos. We shall also be making the acquaintance of the historic Toplou Monastery and going to Vai for a swim in wonderful natural surroundings.

Morning on the beach, and evening on the seafront at Siteia

Siteia

We leave Siteia and head east. At 5 km from the town we come to **Ayia Fotia**, a pretty little seaside village with a fine beach. The houses date from Venetian times and have recently been renovated. Near the village, Greek archaeologists have discovered the largest Early Minoan cemetery ever found, with 250 tombs of all sizes. Among the finds which they discovered are vases and clay and stone objects which can be seen today in the museums of Ayios Nikolaos and Siteia.

Our road continues, and at 12 km from Siteia comes to a crossroads. The road to the right leads to Palaikastro and Zakro. We take the turning to the left and after 5 km come to the historic **Toplou Monastery**.

The monastery rises fortress-like out of an arid landscape. It is also known as Our Lady 'of the Cape' ('Akrotiriani') because of its proximity to Cape Sidero. It acquired the name of Toplou in Turkish times because it had had a cannon ('top') since Venetian days to protect itself from pirates. In its current form, it dates from the 17th century, but the wall-paintings in the church make it plain that the original buildings go back to the 14th century. It is believed that the foundation was built over the ruins of an earlier monastery dedicated to St Isidore.

The Monastery is square, with the ground-plan of a fortress and a total area of 800 square metres. There are three storeys, and the whole structure is surrounded by a wall. Among the principal features is the belfry, which stands to a height of 33 metres; it has crowns in relief and bears the date

The fortress-like Toplou Monastery

Part of the portable icon 'Great art Thou, O Lord', which includes 61 scenes

1558. In the little inner courtyard is a well which never runs dry and which supplies the monastery's water. Opposite the well is the twin-aisled basilica which is the main monastery church, dedicated to the Nativity of Our Lady and to St John the Divine. To the left, before we enter the church, is an important 2nd century BC inscription referring to an alliance between the cities of Itanos and Ierapytna.

Among the important portable icons in the church is one by Ioannis Kornaros known as 'Great Art Thou, O Lord', dating from 1770. The paintings in the north aisle are from the 14th century. The icon of Our Lady was found in a cave where there is a spring; its water is regarded as holy.

In 1662, the monastery collapsed during an earthquake but was soon rebuilt. In 1821 it suffered further severe damage. It has been stavropegic (under the protection of the Patriarchate of Constantinople) since 1704, and this helped it to survive despite the inevitable depredations of the Turks. Before Crete was free, it was a centre for revolutionary meetings and provided shelter for freedom fighters on the run from the authorities. A secret school operated there throughout the period of Turkish rule.

During the German occupation, the Toplou Monastery had a secret wireless post.

It was also one of the richest monasteries on Crete, and even today large tracts of land round about belong to it. At the height of its prosperity, it had 150 monks.

Its feast day is on 26 September, when there is a great festival which attracts large numbers of pilgrims.

The tropical beach at Vai

From the Toplou Monastery, the good, surfaced road continues north east for Vai. At 25 km. from Siteia there is a turning (right) for Palaikastro. We continue north, and after a further 2 km. a road to the right takes us down to the beach through the famous palm forest of **Vai**.

The 5,000 palm trees stand in an attractive valley between two hills, arranged amphitheatrically and overlooking the golden beach. Here the landscape has changed once more: now it is tropical and idyllic.

According to the myths, the existence of the palm trees was attributed to the Phoenicians, who called here and threw away the stones of the dates they were eating. The trees, 'vayia' in the local dialect, have given Vai its name.

Today the whole area and all routes of access to the beach are carefully fenced off and camping is strictly forbidden. The main entrance is open from sunrise to sunset, and so the calm and beauty of the landscape can still be enjoyed while sipping a cool drink in one of the pretty little cafés.

We return to the side-road for the beach and turn north.

After about 3 km. the road ends at a quiet sandy bay, **Erimoupoli**. This is the site of one of the most important cities of eastern Crete, ancient **Itanos**. The name comes from Itanos, one of the Kouretes who brought up Zeus. According to the myths, the Argonauts built a temple to Athena here.

As archaeological finds have shown, Itanos was occupied between Minoan times and the Christian era. There are remains of a large Byzantine basilica.

We head back the way we came, passing the turning for the beach, and at 27 km from Siteia take the road left for **Palaikastro**. Two kilometres away is its beach, with a fine expanse of sand and a natural harbour looking out to the islet of Grandes. Near the village important Minoan remains have come to light. At the spot known as Rousolakkos, the spades of the archaeologists have uncovered a Middle Minoan settlement. The main road running through the centre of the town was intersected by smaller streets at right angles to it, separating off the different neighbourhoods with their impressive house facades. The settlement had a sophisticated sewage disposal system. Although it has not been proved, the archaeologists assume that this must have been ancient Dragmos.

In the same area is the wonderful *Shrine of Zeus Diktaios*. Among the ruins and the other important finds was an inscription recording the hymn to Cretan Zeus which youths sang in the temple, while dancing the dance of the Kouretes.

To the south of Palaikastro is the steep hill of **Petsofas**. On the summit, an open-air shrine of the Middle Minoan period has been excavated and has produced important finds, including a number of fine statuettes, 10-17 cm. in height, representing people in attitudes of prayer. The male statuettes are austerely dressed, but the female figures provide a marvellously vigorous picture of the female dress of the period.

From Palaikastro we take the difficult uphill road to Zakros. At 17 km from Siteia we reach the village of **Epano Zakros**, which stands on two hills covered with fruit trees and olives. Cobbled lanes lead between the whitewashed houses with their charming courtyards. From the village square a surfaced road leads to an attractive sheltered bay where the village of **Kato Zakros** stands. Here recent investigation has revealed a large Minoan palace, the fourth-largest in Crete and the only one to have escaped robbery. It was built around 1600 BC, covered an area of 8,000 square metres and had 180 rooms.

The first archaeologist to investigate the site, D.G. Hogarth, dug up some buildings near the palace, but it was Professor Platon who uncovered the palace itself. Although smaller than Knossos or Phaistos, it was laid out along the same lines. There was a central paved court with three entrances to the west and an altar in front of the main entrance. On the western side were the official apartments. On the north side were light shafts, kitchens, a dining-room and large basins which must have been used in cult worship. In the Treasury a number of superb vases were found. The eastern side contained the principal living apartments, while the south side of the court consisted mostly of workshops.

Mystery still shrouds the purpose of the four channels next to the modern entrance to the site. Among the most interesting finds from the site are vases decorated with olives which look as if they have just been harvested, long swords encrusted with sheets of gold, bronze decorative objects from Cyprus and an amphora showing a hill-top shrine and wild goats. Many of the pots found at Zakros were smashed, possibly during the course of the destruction of the palace by earthquake.

The site of the palace is of great importance, since standing as it does on the east coast of Crete it would be in an ideal position to import goods from the East and sell them to the other palaces. Thus its harbour developed into a major commercial port and the whole Minoan 'thalassocracy' relied heavily upon it.

The archaeological site of Kato Zakros

The imposing **'gorge of the dead'** ('Farangi ton Nekron'),begins in the vicinity of Epano Zakros and ends at Kato Zakros. The remains of a Minoan mansion have been discovered next to the gorge, which took its name from the presence here of the graveyard of the surrounding settlements. The tombs have been excavated.

Apart from the value of its archaeological site, Kato Zakros is also a wonderful place, with a fine sandy beach and clear blue waters: an invitation for a swim.

We return to Palaikastro and take the left turning, north west, coming after 6 km to the main road from Siteia to the Toplou Monastery.

We now leave Siteia along the road heading south for Lithines. After about 2.5 km we come to the village of **Manares**, where a Minoan villa of the Late Palace period has been discovered. A little further along, a side road some 5 km in length leads to another Minoan villa near the village of **Zou**, from whose springs the water supply of Siteia is run.

The road continues and after 4 km comes to the pretty village of **Piskokefalo**, which stands near the old village of Kato Episkopi on the hill of Kefali from which it takes its name. Under the Venetians, this area belonged to the feudal estate of the Kornaros family. There is a fine old church of St George, dating from the 15th century. Professor Platon, the archaeologist, concluded from the archaeological finds on the site, and particularly from the statuettes of men and women in attitudes of prayer, that there must have been a shrine here rather like that of Petsofas.

However, the statuettes yielded by this site are of a more sophisticated technique; the female figurines have cunning hair-styles, hats and rich clothing. They are of exceptional importance for the study of ancient clothing and hair-dressing in Crete.

The 'kazanemata': the traditional manner of distilling raki

Piskokefalo is another village where the *'Kazanemata'*, the traditional late-September feast to celebrate the making of the 'tsikoudia' is held. There are large-scale festivities with much consumption of the local delicacies.

The road continues, passing at 9 km the village of **Maronia** and at 10 km that of **Epano Episkopi**, which in the 16th century was the seat of the Bishop of Siteia. Here the road forks. To the right (south west), the road leads to Lithines and then on to Ierapetra. We take the left-hand turning, which heads south east and after crossing a fertile valley comes to **Nea Praisos** at 15 km Arrows point the way to the site of ancient **Praisos**, which was an Eteocretan town. The oldest settlement was near the ruins we see today, and in the 12th century BC the Eteocretans and Dorians built a new city, spread over three hills and surrounded by walls, remains of which can be seen today. The city was autonomous. Overall, however, this site was occupied from the Stone Age to Venetian times. In 145 BC the city was destroyed by Ierapytna.

After 20 km, we pass **Handras**, leaving on our left a very fertile plateau with numerous windmills, like a miniature version of the Lasithi plateau. At 25 km we come to **Ziros**, where there is a church of **St Paraskevi**, with wall-paintings. From Chandras, a road leads left through Armeni to **Etia**, which was important town under the Venetians and has Byzantine churches. Afther a further 7 km we emerge on the Siteia-Ierapetra road.

This is the end of our tour of Crete. We would like to think that readers have gained a first acquaintance with a considerable proportion of this enormous island, and that we have stimulated their curiosity to come back again and again, discovering by themselves still more details of this place, so wonderful and unusual in its natural and human aspects.

A complete guide for drivers and travellers

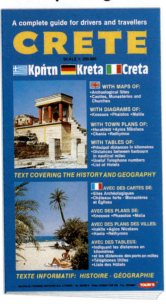

Crete

scale 1:200.000

WITH MAPS OF:
- archaeological sites
- castles, monasteries
  and churches

WITH DIAGRAMS OF:
- Knossos • Phaistos • Mallia

WITH TOWN PLANS OF:
- Herakleio • Chania
- Rethymno • Ayios Nikolaos

WITH TABLES OF:
- principal distances
  in kilometres
- distances between harbours
  in nautical miles
- useful telephone numbers
- list of hotels

**TEXT COVERING THE
HISTORY AND GEOGRAPHY**

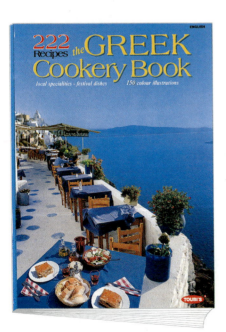

Available in 6 languages

222 Recipes *the* GREEK Cookery Book

- *Local Specialities*
- *Festival Dishes*
- *Homemade-style Sweets*

greek coffee · cheeses
wines · pickles · drinks
herbs · spices · aromas · herb teas

**With 150 colour illustrations
and CALORY count**